A Book of Russian Quotations

# Words of the Wise

PROGRESS PUBLISHERS
MOSCOW

# Мудрая мысль России

## Сборник высказываний

# Words of the Wise

## A Book of Russian Quotations

Compiled by V.V. Vorontsov

Translated from the Russian by *Vic Schneierson*
Designed by *G. A. Dauman*

МУДРАЯ МЫСЛЬ РОССИИ

*На английском языке*

© Издательство «Прогресс», 1979
English translation © Progress Publishers 1979

*Printed in the Union of Soviet Socialist Republics*

# CONTENTS

| | Page |
|---|---|
| PUBLISHER'S NOTE | 11 |
| OF MOTHERLAND, PATRIOTISM, AND INTERNATIONALISM | 13 |
|     Greatness of the Soviet People | 13 |
|     Internationalism | 16 |
|     Love of Country | 23 |
| OF POLITICS AND STATESMANSHIP | 36 |
|     Politics | 36 |
|     Role of the Masses | 39 |
|     Appeal to the People | 48 |
|     The Leader's Authority | 53 |
|     The Art of Leadership | 57 |
|     Chiefs and Subordinates | 61 |
|     Fame True and Untrue | 64 |
|     Red Tape and Bureaucracy | 66 |
| OF PEOPLE AND HISTORY | 70 |
|     History and Historians | 70 |
|     The Present and Future | 75 |
|     Historical Activity | 79 |
| OF PROBITY | 82 |
|     Basic Moral Principles | 82 |
|     The Collective and the Individual | 87 |
|     Man—Adornment of the World | 92 |
|     Personal Relations | 98 |

|  |  |
|---|---|
| Humanitarianism | 103 |
| Beauty of Body and Beauty of Soul | 107 |

OF MAN AND NATURE . . . . . . . . . . 110

OF THE PURPOSE OF LIFE, PURSUIT OF HAPPINESS, JOY, AND HOPE . . . . . . . . 120

|  |  |
|---|---|
| The Purpose of Life | 120 |
| Life and Time | 131 |
| The Pursuit of Happiness | 133 |
| Joy, Sadness, Grief, and Hope | 140 |

OF LABOUR . . . . . . . . . . . . . . 144

|  |  |
|---|---|
| Man's Main Condition | 144 |
| Socialism and Labour | 151 |
| Sense of Duty | 158 |
| Activeness | 160 |
| Man and Action | 164 |
| Work Is a Pleasure and a Joy | 168 |
| Work Lengthens Youth | 172 |

OF WAR AND PEACE . . . . . . . . . . 174

|  |  |
|---|---|
| The Peoples Want Peace | 174 |
| All People Must Safeguard Peace | 178 |
| The Causes and Nature of Modern Wars | 181 |

OF HEROISM, COURAGE, AND BRAVERY . . . 185

OF CONVICTIONS, CRITICISM, AND MISTAKES 196

|  |  |
|---|---|
| Convictions and Ideals | 196 |
| Aims and Purposes | 201 |
| Ardour, and Enthusiasm | 205 |
| Indifference | 207 |
| Criticism | 208 |
| Wrong Judgement and Slander | 216 |
| The Attitude to Errors | 219 |

OF KNOWLEDGE, UPBRINGING, AND EDUCATION . . . . . . . . . . . . . . . . . . . 223
    Knowledge . . . . . . . . . . . . . . 223
    Moral and Intellectual Development . . . . 228
    School, Teacher, and Learner . . . . . . 235
    Self-Improvement . . . . . . . . . . . 249
    Ignorance . . . . . . . . . . . . . . 255
    The Uselessness of Too Much Knowledge . 256

OF WISDOM, INTELLIGENCE, AND STUPIDITY . 259
    Wisdom and Reason . . . . . . . . . . 259
    Intelligence . . . . . . . . . . . . . . 263
    Humour . . . . . . . . . . . . . . . 265
    Stupidity . . . . . . . . . . . . . . . 271

OF THE CONTINUITY OF CULTURE . . . . . 275

OF APHORISMS . . . . . . . . . . . . . . 279

OF ART AND LIFE . . . . . . . . . . . . . 282
    The Significance and Purpose of Art . . . 282
    Art's Allegiance to the People and Its Ideological Commitment . . . . . . . . . 296
    Truth and Fiction . . . . . . . . . . . 306
    Harmony of Content and Form . . . . . 317

OF INSPIRATION AND TORMENT OF CREATION 330

OF THE WRITER AND ARTIST . . . . . . . 338

OF MUSIC, POETRY, ARCHITECTURE, ART, AND THEATRE . . . . . . . . . . . . . . . . 349
    Music . . . . . . . . . . . . . . . . 349
    Poetry . . . . . . . . . . . . . . . . 353
    Architecture . . . . . . . . . . . . . . 357
    Painting . . . . . . . . . . . . . . . 358
    Theatre . . . . . . . . . . . . . . . . 360

| | |
|---|---|
| OF SATIRE | 362 |
| OF LITERARY CRITICISM | 368 |
| OF TRASH AND HACKS | 372 |
| OF LANGUAGE AND WORDS | 375 |
|     The Basic Medium | 375 |
|     The Russian Language | 381 |
|     Power of Words | 392 |
|     Eloquence | 396 |
|     Dispute | 403 |
| OF BOOKS AND READING | 409 |
|     In Praise of Books | 409 |
|     Choice of Books | 423 |
|     Reading | 428 |
| OF RELIGION AND SUPERSTITIONS | 434 |
|     Origin and Harm of Religion | 435 |
|     Superstitions | 437 |
|     Religion—Enemy of Reason | 439 |
|     Religion and Morality | 442 |
| OF CIVILISATION, SCIENCE, AND SCIENTISTS | 448 |
|     Progress and Science | 448 |
|     Imagination, Hypothesis, and Daring | 459 |
|     Importance of Experience and Experiment | 472 |
|     Understanding the Truth | 475 |
|     The Scientist's Responsibility | 485 |
| OF LAW AND FREEDOM | 496 |
|     Freedom and Discipline | 497 |
|     Wrongdoings and Crimes | 499 |
| OF HUMAN VIRTUES | 501 |
|     Courage, Genuineness, and Modesty | 501 |
|     Fairness and Honesty | 504 |

| | |
|---|---|
| Truthfulness and Sincerity . . . . . . . | 506 |
| Diffidence, Conscience, and Honour . . . | 510 |
| OF FRIENDSHIP . . . . . . . . . . . . . | 515 |
| A Great Blessing . . . . . . . . . . | 515 |
| The Pillars of Friendship . . . . . . . | 516 |
| False Friends . . . . . . . . . . . | 520 |
| OF LOVE . . . . . . . . . . . . . . . | 522 |
| The Flower of Life . . . . . . . . . | 522 |
| Women and Men . . . . . . . . . . . | 527 |
| Facets of Love . . . . . . . . . . . | 532 |
| Love and Morality . . . . . . . . . . | 536 |
| Jealousy . . . . . . . . . . . . . | 541 |
| OF FAMILY, PARENTS, AND CHILDREN . . . | 543 |
| Family and Society . . . . . . . . . | 543 |
| Matrimony . . . . . . . . . . . . . | 545 |
| Family Upbringing of Children . . . . . | 552 |
| Parents' and Children's Mutual Respect . . | 565 |
| OF CHARACTER . . . . . . . . . . . . . | 571 |
| Strength of Character . . . . . . . . | 571 |
| Will and Fortitude . . . . . . . . . | 573 |
| Tests of Character . . . . . . . . . | 577 |
| Self-Control . . . . . . . . . . . | 580 |
| OF RULES OF BEHAVIOUR . . . . . . . . . | 582 |
| Acts and Actions . . . . . . . . . . | 582 |
| The Sense of Dignity . . . . . . . . | 585 |
| The Art of Conversation . . . . . . . | 587 |
| Of Courtesy, Rudeness, Appreciation, and Gratitude . . . . . . . . . . . . . | 589 |
| Mentorship, Advice, and Praise . . . . | 591 |
| OF FAULTS, WEAKNESSES, AND FAILINGS . . | 593 |
| Idleness . . . . . . . . . . . . . | 593 |

| | |
|---|---|
| Drunkenness | 596 |
| Selfishness | 605 |
| Envy and Greed | 607 |
| Cowardice and Faint-Heartedness | 609 |
| Vanity, Arrogance, and Bragging | 611 |
| Pride, Haughtiness, and Mendacity | 612 |
| Hypocrisy, Servility, and Time-Serving | 615 |
| Talkativeness | 617 |
| Meanness and Cruelty | 620 |
| Petulance, Unsociability, Contentiousness | 622 |
| OF GOOD HEALTH | 624 |
| The Greatest Boon | 624 |
| Physical Training | 626 |
| The Benefits of Moderation | 631 |
| Ailments, Medicine, and Medical Ethics | 632 |
| OF YOUTH, OLD AGE, AND IMMORTALITY | 636 |
| Youth | 636 |
| Old Age | 643 |
| Immortality | 645 |
| NAME INDEX | 652 |

## PUBLISHER'S NOTE

This book of quotations is a collection of aphorisms and phrases by statesmen, political and public leaders, writers, musicians, artists, and educators of by-gone and present times. In addition to Russian and Soviet sources, it covers the eastern lands, the Transcaucasus, and other territories now part of the Soviet Union. Also covered are antique thinkers who belong equally to the Soviet Central Asian republics and the countries of the Middle East.

The compiler, Vladimir Vorontsov, deliberately ignored proverbs and popular sayings, for the purpose of the book is to acquaint the reader with the development of the social outlook in our country, to show the continuity of the progressive traditions and the wide scope of interests that engaged the authors represented between these covers.

Vladimir Vorontsov was born into a peasant family in 1906. During the Second World War

---

English translation © Progress Publishers 1977.

## PUBLISHER'S NOTE

he was deputy chief of staff of the partisan movement in Stavropol territory. For over thirty years he has engaged widely in journalistic pursuits.

The Publisher hopes that *Words of the Wise* will help readers abroad gain a closer and better understanding of our country.

## OF MOTHERLAND, PATRIOTISM AND INTERNATIONALISM

### GREATNESS OF THE SOVIET PEOPLE

We are the people who have been able—not because of any special services or of historical predestination, but because of a definite conjunction of historical circumstances—to accept the honour of raising the banner of the international socialist revolution.

*V. I. Lenin*

\*

To the Russian workers fell the honour and the good fortune of being the *first* to start the revolution, the great, and only legitimate and just war of the oppressed against the oppressors.

*V. I. Lenin*

\*

In the space of a few days we destroyed one of the oldest, most powerful, barbarous, and brutal of monarchies.... We awakened the faith of the millions upon millions of workers of all countries in their own strength and kindled the fires of enthusiasm in them.

*V. I. Lenin*

\*

A socialist Soviet republic in Russia will stand as a living example to the peoples of all countries, and the propaganda and revolutionising effect of this example will be immense.

*V. I. Lenin*

\*

The Russian revolution has charted the road to socialism for the whole world and has shown the bourgeoisie that their triumph is coming to an end.

*V. I. Lenin*

\*

It is our task to build a new socialist state. We shall be working tirelessly towards that goal, and we shall be neither intimidated nor deterred by any obstacles.

*V. I. Lenin*

Our natural wealth, our manpower, and the splendid impetus which the great revolution has given to the creative powers of the people are ample material to build a truly mighty and abundant Russia.

*V. I. Lenin*

\*

The Soviet movement ... is the form which has been won in Russia, which is now spreading throughout the world and the very name of which gives the workers a complete programme.

*V. I. Lenin*

\*

I know the Russian people and am not inclined to exaggerate their virtues, but I am convinced they can contribute to the spiritual life of the whole world something of their own, something profound and important for all people.

*Maxim Gorky*

\*

A wonderland, a land of miracles! These words out of the fairy-stories of childhood are now applicable to our land, the Land of Soviets, where we go from miracle to miracle.

*Konstantin Fedin*

We are the Edisons of unheard-of flights, energies, and lights. But the main thing in us—and this nothing can obscure—is our Land of Soviets, our Soviet will, Soviet banner, Soviet sun.

*Vladimir Mayakovsky*

NTERNATIONALISM

To the old world, the world of national oppression, nation-bickering, and national isolation the workers counterpose a new world, a world of the unity of the working people of all nations, a world in which there is no place for any privileges or for the slightest degree of oppression of man by man.

*V. I. Lenin*

\*

Economic expediency and internationalist and democratic instinct and consciousness demand the earliest association of all nations and their merging in a socialist society.

*V. I. Lenin*

Marxism cannot be reconciled with nationalism, be it even of the "most just", "purest", most refined and civilised brand. In place of all forms of nationalism Marxism advances internationalism.

*V. I. Lenin*

※

One who has adopted the standpoint of nationalism naturally arrives at the desire to erect a Chinese Wall around his nationality, his national working-class movement; he is unembarrassed even by the fact that it would mean building separate walls in each city, in each little town and village, unembarrassed even by the fact that by his tactics of division and dismemberment *he is reducing to nil* the great call for the rallying and unity of the proletarians of all nations, all races and all languages.

*V. I. Lenin*

※

The interests of the working class and of its struggle against capitalism demand complete solidarity and the closest unity of the workers of all nations; they demand resistance to the nationalist policy of the bourgeoisie of every nationality.

*V. I. Lenin*

Capital is an international force. To vanquish it, an international workers' alliance, an international workers' brotherhood, is needed. We are opposed to national enmity, national strife, national exclusiveness. We are internationalists.

*V. I. Lenin*

\*

Only a socialist alliance of the working people of all countries can remove all grounds for national persecution and strife.

*V. I. Lenin*

\*

The unity of the workers of *all* nationalities coupled with the fullest equality for the nationalities and the most consistent democratic state system—that is our slogan.

*V. I. Lenin*

\*

We must always and unreservedly work for the *very closest* unity of the proletariat of all nationalities. . . .

*V. I. Lenin*

We want a *voluntary* union of nations—a union which precludes any coercion of one nation by another—a union founded on complete confidence, on a clear recognition of brotherly unity, on absolutely voluntary consent.

*V. I. Lenin*

\*

The unity and fraternal alliance of the workers of all countries are incompatible with the use of force, direct or indirect, against other nationalities.

*V. I. Lenin*

\*

To be an internationalist Social-Democrat one must *not* think only of one's nation, but place *above it* the interests of all nations, their common liberty and equality, fight *against* small-nation narrow-mindedness, seclusion and isolation, consider the whole and the general, subordinate the particular to the general interests.

*V. I. Lenin*

\*

Socialists cannot achieve their great aim without fighting against all oppression of nations.

*V. I. Lenin*

Only by casting off every savage and foolish national prejudice, only by uniting the workers of all nations into one association, can the working class become a force, offer resistance to capitalism, and achieve a serious improvement in its living conditions.

*V. I. Lenin*

\*

There is one, and only one, kind of real internationalism, and that is—working whole-heartedly for the development of the revolutionary movement and the revolutionary struggle in *one's own* country, and supporting (by propaganda, sympathy, and material aid) *this struggle,* this, *and only this,* line, in *every* country without exception.

*V. I. Lenin*

\*

Love of the socialist Motherland is a step to internationalism.

*A. N. Tolstoy*

\*

The patriotism of the best Russians has always blended with respect for the national honour and dignity of other nations, and with the wish that Russia and Russian culture should play a progressive part in the development of mankind.

*Alexander Fadeyev*

\*

Real patriotism transcends personal relationships and interests and is closely bound to love for all humanity.

*Nikolai Dobrolyubov*

\*

Vital and active patriotism excludes all international enmity. Its bearer is eager to do his best for all mankind if he can be useful.

*Nikolai Dobrolyubov*

\*

Love of one's Motherland must flow from love of humanity as does the particular from the general.

*Vissarion Belinsky*

\*

Legitimate national pride, the accessory of your love of country, must be clearly distinguishable from boastful self-adoration; one is a virtue, the other an evil that retards progress which, I am sure, requires that all nations should be equal.

*Dmitry Mendeleyev*

No people in history can be likened to an animal herd any more than a people can be called a select assembly.

*Alexander Herzen*

\*

Shun not your own, but, should it be worthwhile, learn also from what is not your own.

*Taras Shevchenko*

\*

Take with both hands all the good there is abroad.

*V. I. Lenin*

\*

We Russians are heirs to the whole world. We shall take as our own all that is exclusive in the life of every European nation. Take it we shall not as exclusive, but as an element added to our own life, the exclusive side of which must be versatility.

*Vissarion Belinsky*

## PATRIOTISM AND INTERNATIONALISM

OVE OF COUNTRY

Patriotism is one of the most deeply ingrained sentiments inculcated by the existence of separate fatherlands for hundreds and thousands of years.

*V. I. Lenin*

\*

Is a sense of national pride alien to us, Great-Russian class-conscious proletarians? Certainly not! We love our language and our country. We are full of national pride because the Great-Russian nation, *too*, has created a revolutionary class, because it, *too*, has proved capable of providing mankind with great models of the struggle for freedom and socialism.

*V. I. Lenin*

\*

The Fatherland, i.e., the given political, cultural, and social environment, is a most powerful factor in the class struggle of the proletariat. The proletariat cannot be indifferent to the political, social, and cultural conditions of its struggle; consequently, it cannot be indifferent to the destinies of its country.

*V. I. Lenin*

What is the Motherland? It is the whole people in historical motion in a given space. It is the past, present, and future of the people. It is the people's peculiar culture, language, and character. It is the purpose of their revolutions, their historical thrust, the twists of their history.

*A. N. Tolstoy*

\*

Soviet patriotism is the natural heir to the constructive achievements of our forebears, the movers of our people's progress.

*Mikhail Kalinin*

\*

We love our Motherland. It is the air we breathe.

*Alexander Fadeyev*

\*

Beloved and radiant Motherland! We give you our boundless filial love, with you we associate all our aspirations.

*Mikhail Sholokhov*

\*

Russia as represented by her enlightened men nurtures unconquerable anticipation of the greatness of her mission, the grandeur of her future.

*Vissarion Belinsky*

\*

For many centuries to come we are happily destined to improve ourselves and to make our life better and better.

*Nikolai Chernyshevsky*

\*

Be a son to your country, deeply feel your ties with the native land, treat it with filial love, and repay it a hundredfold for what you receive from it.

*Konstantin Ushinsky*

\*

Many are the countries of the world, yet every man has but one mother, and likewise but one Motherland.

*Konstantin Ushinsky*

\*

It is our sacred duty to love the country that raised us like a mother.

*Mikhail Sholokhov*

Every person of worth is deeply conscious of his kindred bonds with the Motherland.

*Vissarion Belinsky*

\*

I dearly love the Russian people and treasure the honour and glory of being its particle.

*Vissarion Belinsky*

\*

Any sensible Russian with a hot heart is unfailingly a patriot.

*Nikolai Chernyshevsky*

\*

*Many things there are
To love you for,
To cherish you for,
Mother Russia.*

*Ivan Nikitin*

\*

There can be no true personality without a sense of country, its every trifle unique, dear, and lovely. It is self-renouncing feeling, and it quickens our interest in everything.

*Konstantin Paustovsky*

## PATRIOTISM AND INTERNATIONALISM

Patriotism is not mere love of country. It is much more—an awareness of being inseverable from it and inescapably involved in its joys and sorrows.

*A. N. Tolstoy*

∗

He who shares not in the grief of his people is sure to feel an outcast when it celebrates its joy.

*Leonid Leonov*

∗

The individual is first of all a son of his country, a citizen of his Motherland, taking its interests close to heart.

*Vissarion Belinsky*

∗

A patriot spares neither his possessions nor his life for the glory of his country and love of his people; he will sacrifice himself for their wellbeing and freedom.

*Mirza-Fatali Akhundov*

∗

Patriotism's educational effect is tremendous; it is a school that elevates the individual to the idea of humanity.

*M. E. Saltykov-Shchedrin*

The idea of the Motherland is equally good for everyone. In the honest it nurtures a longing for great deeds and the dishonest it averts from many an infamy they would otherwise have doubtless committed.

*M. E. Saltykov-Shchedrin*

\*

The idea of the Motherland must be ingrained in its sons equally at times of celebration and in workaday surroundings, for only with this clear idea does the individual acquire title to being a citizen.

*M. E. Saltykov-Shchedrin*

\*

Patriotism consists not of florid orations and platitudes, but of ardent affection for the Motherland expressed without rhetoric and revealed not in rapturous praise, but also in jealous animosity towards the base that unavoidably exists in any land and consequently, in any Motherland.

*Vissarion Belinsky*

\*

Patriotism, anyone's patriotism, is proved not by word but by deed.

*Vissarion Belinsky*

The duty to the Motherland is sacrosanct.

*Vassily Sukhomlinsky*

\*

A Russian's mark in history is measured by his services to the Motherland, and his human dignity by the stoutness of his patriotism.

*Nikolai Chernyshevsky*

\*

Supreme patriotism is the ardent and uncontrollable wish that all should go well with one's Motherland.

*Nikolai Chernyshevsky*

\*

Love of country is no abstract concept but a real movement of the soul requiring organisation, development, and culture.

*A. N. Tolstoy*

\*

In any decent person patriotism is a craving to work for the wellbeing of his country, deriving from a craving to do good—as much as possible and as well as possible.

*Nikolai Dobrolyubov*

Our Russia bewitches us most of all with her great future, for which we want to work indefatigably, selflessly, and zealously.

*Nikolai Dobrolyubov*

\*

Love of the Motherland is most of all a deep, ardent and anything but abstract wish of success and enlightenment, a readiness to place one's possessions and very life in her service, a fervent sympathy for the good that she has and a proud anger against that which mars her perfection.

*Nikolai Nekrasov*

\*

A patriot is someone who serves his Motherland, which is first of all the people.

*Nikolai Chernyshevsky*

\*

Patriotism is the most diffident and delicate of feelings. Spare us the sacred words, shout not your love of country from every housetop. It is so much better to work unobtrusively for its prosperity and power.

*Vassily Sukhomlinsky*

## PATRIOTISM AND INTERNATIONALISM

In the recent past, patriotism amounted to extolling all the good there is in the Motherland; nowadays this is not enough to be a patriot. Apart from praise there must be pitiless censure of the bad we still have.

*Nikolai Dobrolyubov*

\*

All manner of means should be applied for the wellbeing of the people and every evil harming the Motherland must be torn out with the roots.

*Ivan Krylov*

\*

Patriotism must not blind us; love of the Motherland is a motion of the seeing mind, not a blind passion.

*Nikolai Karamzin*

\*

We love Russia and her people, but are not obsessed by patriotic adoration or frenetic Russophilia.

*Alexander Herzen*

\*

The intrinsic virtues of the Russian people are good cheer, courage, bravery, inventiveness, diligence, perspicacity, and heroism in battle against invaders.

*Vissarion Belinsky*

*

The fondest and most urgent undertaking takes a back seat in face of danger to the Motherland.

*Leonid Leonov*

*

Speaking of life's beauty, its supreme manifestation is dedicated struggle for the good of the Motherland.

*Mikhail Kalinin*

*

Russia can get along without any of us, but none of us can get along without Russia; woe to him who thinks differently, and more so to him who gets along without her.

*Ivan Turgenev*

*

There is no happiness away from the Motherland; sink your roots in native soil.

*Ivan Turgenev*

## PATRIOTISM AND INTERNATIONALISM

The more conscious you are of your ties with the Motherland, the more readily and realistically you conceive it as a living organism.

*Alexander Blok*

∗

Love, love, love your Motherland. That is still the main thing. For it gives you strength to accomplish all other things more easily.

*M. E. Saltykov-Shchedrin*

∗

I love Russia to the limit of pain and cannot conceive myself anywhere but in Russia.

*M. E. Saltykov-Shchedrin*

∗

None but the vacuous lacks the exquisite and exalted sense of country.

*Ivan Pavlov*

∗

*Those drained of love of country
Are wretches with a crippled heart.*

*Taras Shevchenko*

He who does not belong to his Fatherland, neither does he belong to humanity.

*Vissarion Belinsky*

\*

I cannot stand exalted patriots who make capital on interjections, but I do confess that cold-blooded and detached skeptics, those homeless vagabonds, are for me more wretched and detestable.

*Vissarion Belinsky*

\*

The power of patriotism is always proportional to what you put into it: vagabonds and idlers are inevitably devoid of a sense of country.

*Leonid Leonov*

\*

To renounce your Motherland is to renounce your conscience.

*Yaroslav Galan*

\*

To betray your Motherland you must have an unusually base soul.

*Nikolai Chernyshevsky*

## PATRIOTISM AND INTERNATIONALISM

A traitor cannot be compared to anything or anyone. And being compared to a traitor would, I think, insult even a typhus-bearing louse.

*Maxim Gorky*

## OF POLITICS AND STATESMANSHIP

POLITICS

Politics involves the actual fate of millions of people.

*V. I. Lenin*

\*

Politics is the most concentrated expression of economics.

*V. I. Lenin*

\*

Politics is a science and an art that does not fall from the skies or come gratis.

*V. I. Lenin*

\*

Politics needs a flexible mind, for it has no immutable or eternal rules. In politics immutable or eternal rules lead to inevitable and swift *defeat.*

*G. V. Plekhanov*

POLITICS AND STATESMANSHIP

Only he who does not evade conflict and directs his efforts in keeping with the course of society's development can be an effective leader.

*G. V. Plekhanov*

\*

Whatever field of human activity one may take, only those trends that are in harmony with the needs of society show rapid progress.

*Nikolai Chernyshevsky*

\*

A policy based on principles is the most practical policy. Such a policy alone can really win ... the lasting sympathy and confidence of the masses.

*V. I. Lenin*

\*

Revolutionaries and Communists must not deny the dangers and difficulties of the struggle.

*V. I. Lenin*

\*

The surest way of discrediting and damaging a new political (and not only political) idea is to reduce it to absurdity on the plea of defending it.

*V. I. Lenin*

\*

All extremes are bad. All that is good and useful, if carried to extremes, may become—and beyond a certain limit is bound to become—bad and injurious.

*V. I. Lenin*

\*

Face the truth squarely. In politics that is always the best and the only correct attitude.

*V. I. Lenin*

\*

False rhetoric and false boastfulness spell moral ruin and lead unfailingly to political extinction.

*V. I. Lenin*

\*

Honesty in politics is the result of strength; hypocrisy is the result of weakness.

*V. I. Lenin*

We must most resolutely condemn those who regard politics as a series of cheap tricks, frequently bordering on deception.

*V. I. Lenin*

※

The leaders of the working class are not angels, saints or heroes, but people like anyone else. They make mistakes. The Party puts them right.

*V. I. Lenin*

※

Sincerity in politics, that is, in that sphere of human relations which involves not individuals but the *millions, is a correspondence between word and deed* that lends itself to verification.

*V. I. Lenin*

# ROLE OF THE MASSES

Creative activity is the basic factor of the new public life. Socialism cannot be decreed from above. Its spirit rejects the mechanical bureaucratic approach; living, creative socialism is the product of the masses themselves.

*V. I. Lenin*

\*

History is now being independently made by millions and tens of millions of people.

*V. I. Lenin*

\*

Socialism cannot be implemented by a minority, by the Party. It can be implemented only by tens of millions when they have learned to do it themselves.

*V. I. Lenin*

\*

We must recruit our forces from the masses of the working people.

*V. I. Lenin*

\*

The Russian Communists, adherents of Marxism, *in their activities should ... never forget the enormous importance of democracy.*

*V. I. Lenin*

The greater the scope and extent of historical events, the greater is the number of people participating in them.

*V. I. Lenin*

*

As man's history-making activity grows broader and deeper, the size of that mass of the population which is the conscious maker of history is bound to increase.

*V. I. Lenin*

*

There can be no victorious socialism that does not practise full democracy.

*V. I. Lenin*

*

The proletariat cannot be victorious except through democracy, i.e., by giving full effect to democracy and by linking with each step of its struggle democratic demands formulated in the most resolute terms.

*V. I. Lenin*

*

Every citizen must be put in such conditions that he can participate in the discussion of state laws, in the choice of his representatives, and in the implementation of state laws.

*V. I. Lenin*

\*

Whoever fights for freedom for the people, but does not fight for the sovereignty of the people in the state, is either inconsistent or insincere.

*V. I. Lenin*

\*

Only those aspirations are strong and only those institutions endure that are supported by the mass of the people.

*Nikolai Chernyshevsky*

\*

The people is that sole and inexhaustible source of energy that can turn the possible into the necessary and dreams into reality.

*Maxim Gorky*

\*

Serious politics can only be promoted *by the masses.*

*V. I. Lenin*

Every mass of people is a source of wonder-working possibilities.

*Maxim Gorky*

\*

The people is the soil that conserves the lifeblood of progress.

*Vissarion Belinsky*

\*

In the final analysis, the reason our revolution has left all other revolutions far behind is that through the Soviet form of government it has aroused tens of millions of people formerly uninterested in state development, to take an active part in the work of building the state.

*V. I. Lenin*

\*

The socialist revolution can be made only with the active and direct participation of tens of millions in state administration.

*V. I. Lenin*

\*

The Soviets of Workers and Peasants are a new *type* of state, a new and higher *type* of democracy, a form of the proletarian dictatorship, a means of administering the state *without* the bourgeoisie and *against* the bourgeoisie.

*V. I. Lenin*

\*

Soviet power ... raises to a new democracy and to independent participation in the administration of the state tens upon tens of millions of working people.

*V. I. Lenin*

\*

Never yet has the world seen political power wielded by the *majority* of the population, power *actually* wielded by this majority, as it is in the case of Soviet rule.

*V. I. Lenin*

\*

Soviet, or proletarian, democracy has for the first time in the world created *democracy* for the masses, for the working people.

*V. I. Lenin*

\*

Compared with the bourgeois parliamentary system, the Soviets are an advance in democracy's development which is of worldwide, historic significance.

*V. I. Lenin*

＊

Soviets are something great, something new and unprecedented in the history of world revolution.

*V. I. Lenin*

＊

The Soviets have been created by the working people themselves, by their revolutionary energy and initiative, and that is the only guarantee of their working entirely to promote the interests of the masses.

*V. I. Lenin*

＊

We do not shut ourselves off from the revolutionary people, but submit to their judgement every step and every decision we take. We rely fully and solely on the free initiative of the working masses themselves.

*V. I. Lenin*

＊

We can administer only when we express correctly what the people are conscious of.

*V. I. Lenin*

Communism implies Soviet power as a political organ, enabling the mass of the oppressed to run all state affairs—without that, communism is unthinkable.

*V. I. Lenin*

\*

We do not claim that Marx knew or Marxists know the road to socialism down to the last detail. It would be nonsense to claim anything of the kind. What we know is the direction of this road, and the class forces that follow it; the specific, practical details will come to light only through the *experience of the millions* when they take things into their own hands.

*V. I. Lenin*

\*

I am strongly convinced that the people or society is the best and the most unerring critic.

*Vissarion Belinsky*

\*

We want the government to be always under the supervision of the public opinion of its country.

*V. I. Lenin*

POLITICS AND STATESMANSHIP

The masses must have the right to choose responsible leaders for themselves. They must have the right to replace them, the right to know and check each smallest step of their activity.

*V. I. Lenin*

\*

The people is always expressive of the truth. The life of a people cannot be a lie.

*Alexander Herzen*

\*

Individuals can deceive themselves, society cannot: if perchance society deceives itself, this will not be for long. The more ardent its obsession, the more merciless will be its revenge, and the louder its brief applause, the more scornful will be its derision.

*Vissarion Belinsky*

\*

How the masses take to an idea is the sole measure of its viability.

*M. E. Saltykov-Shchedrin*

Once a nation has emerged on the stage of history, it develops irrepressibly.

*Konstantin Ushinsky*

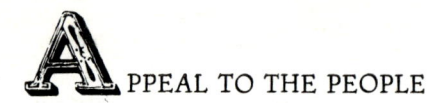

# APPEAL TO THE PEOPLE

Our idea is that a state is strong when the people are politically conscious. It is strong when the people know everything, can form an opinion of everything, and do everything consciously.

*V. I. Lenin*

∗

The chief source of our strength is the class-consciousness and heroism of the workers.

*V. I. Lenin*

∗

The real emancipation of the masses from oppression and tyranny has nowhere in the world ever been effected by any other means than the independent, heroic, conscious struggle of the masses themselves.

*V. I. Lenin*

## POLITICS AND STATESMANSHIP

The prime task of every party of the future is to convince the majority of the people that its programme and tactics are correct.

*V. I. Lenin*

*

All-sided political agitation is a focus in which the vital interests of political education of the proletariat coincide with the vital interests of social development as a whole, of the entire people.

*V. I. Lenin*

*

Personal influence and speaking at meetings make all the difference in politics. Without them there is no political activity.

*V. I. Lenin*

*

The work of political agitation is never wasted.

*V. I. Lenin*

*

You must learn to carry on agitation, otherwise your economic plans will come to nothing.

*V. I. Lenin*

Every agitator must be a state leader, a leader of all the peasants and workers in the work of economic development.

*V. I. Lenin*

*

We need every agitator and propagandist; he will be doing his job if he works in a strictly Party spirit.

*V. I. Lenin*

*

Without a clear, well-thought-out ideological content agitation degenerates into phrase-mongering.

*V. I. Lenin*

*

The flaunting of high-sounding phrases is characteristic of the declassed petty-bourgeois intellectuals.... The people must be told the bitter truth simply, clearly, and in a straightforward manner.

*V. I. Lenin*

*

I will never tire of repeating that demagogues are the worst enemies of the working class.

*V. I. Lenin*

We must learn to approach the masses with particular patience and caution so as to be able to understand the distinctive features in the mentality of each stratum, calling, etc., of these masses.

*V. I. Lenin*

*

Speak simply and clearly, in a language comprehensible to the masses, absolutely discarding the heavy artillery of erudite terms, foreign words and stock slogans, definitions and conclusions which are as yet unfamiliar and unintelligible to the masses.

*V. I. Lenin*

*

Clarity in propaganda and agitation is a fundamental condition.

*V. I. Lenin*

*

The propagators of progress must find the vital grains of Russian speech and thought, and take them to the people.

*Mikhail Kalinin*

*

Words bring people together. We must, therefore, try to be understood by everybody and to speak nothing but the truth.

*Lev Tolstoy*

We must not shirk the problem by shouting propaganda slogans.

*V. I. Lenin*

The people should be told the truth. Only then will their eyes be opened and they will *learn* to fight against untruth.

*V. I. Lenin*

The only way to speak to the masses is to speak openly and directly.

*Mikhail Kalinin*

The public speaker must not run from difficulties or evade awkward questions.

*Mikhail Kalinin*

To lead the masses you must take fire with the masses.

*Mikhail Kalinin*

Less political fireworks and more attention to the simplest but living facts of communist construction, taken from and tested by actual life—this is the slogan which all of us, our writers, agitators, propagandists, organisers, etc., should repeat unceasingly.

*V. I. Lenin*

\*

The art of every propagandist and every agitator consists in influencing the listeners effectively, making a known verity as convincing as possible, as easily comprehensible as possible, and as graphic and memorisable as possible.

*V. I. Lenin*

# THE LEADER'S AUTHORITY

Not a single class in history has achieved power without producing its political leaders, its prominent representatives able to organise a movement and lead it.

*V. I. Lenin*

\*

History long ago proved that in the course of the struggle great revolutions bring great men to the forefront and develop talents that had previously seemed impossible.

*V. I. Lenin*

To govern you need an army of steeled revolutionary Communists. We have it, and it is called the Party.

*V. I. Lenin*

Political parties, as a general rule, are run by more or less stable groups composed of the most authoritative, influential, and experienced members, who are elected to the most responsible positions, and are called leaders.

*V. I. Lenin*

Without the "dozen" tried and talented leaders (and talented men are not born by the hundreds), professionally trained, schooled by long experience, and working in perfect harmony, no class in modern society can wage a determined struggle.

*V. I. Lenin*

The great reformer comes not to destroy, but to construct through destruction.

*Vissarion Belinsky*

## POLITICS AND STATESMANSHIP

The wise politician keeps ahead of events, the unwise is led by them.

*V. I. Lenin*

*

Without revolutionary theory there can be no revolutionary movement.

*V. I. Lenin*

*

The scope of the resolutions depends on the scope of vision.

*Nikolai Chernyshevsky*

*

The Communist administrator's prime duty is to see that he is not carried away by the issuing of orders. He must learn to start by looking at the achievements of science, insisting on the verification of the facts, and studying the mistakes.

*V. I. Lenin*

*

In order to be harsh one must have the right to be so, and the right to be harsh is given by one's words not differing from one's deeds.

*V. I. Lenin*

People despise the lust for power that originates from a craving for homage and for the attributes of power.

*Konstantin Ushinsky*

\*

Second to conceit, the strongest and most savage of all human passions is the lust for power.

*Vissarion Belinsky*

\*

So easily do weak men put in high positions turn villains.

*Dmitry Pisarev*

\*

A fool is very dangerous when in power.

*Denis Fonvizin*

\*

The useless has no claim to respect.

*Nikolai Chernyshevsky*

\*

If you are called upon to govern humans, treat them humanely.

*Mikhail Kalinin*

Always take guidance in your inner motives and treat people honestly.

*Mikhail Kalinin*

※

In everything you do people must feel you are sincere and honest. You will never succeed in concealing insincerity from the people. Shy as clear of it as you can.

*Mikhail Kalinin*

# THE ART OF LEADERSHIP

Man's main duty in every sphere of activity, on every rung of the human hierarchy, is to be human.

*Vissarion Belinsky*

※

He who rejoices not at other people's success is indifferent to the interests of society and must not be trusted with public office.

*Anton Chekhov*

Only that individual will show compassion in a general misfortune who shows compassion for the particular misfortunes of every other individual.

*Felix Dzerzhinsky*

\*

The chief of a state institution must possess a high degree of personal appeal and sufficiently solid scientific and technical knowledge.

*V. I. Lenin*

\*

Management necessarily implies competency,... a knowledge of all the conditions of production down to the last detail and of the latest technology of your branch of production is required, you must have a certain scientific training.

*V. I. Lenin*

\*

Let us have less of ... intellectualist and bureaucratic complacency, and a deeper scrutiny of the practical experience being gained in the centre and in the localities, and of the available achievements of science.

*V. I. Lenin*

All administrative work requires special qualifications. You may be the very best of revolutionaries and propagandists, and yet be absolutely useless as an administrator.

*V. I. Lenin*

*Take no decision rashly,
Act not before thinking.*

*Aboul Kasim Firdousi*

No political leader has a career that is without its defeats. . . .

*V. I. Lenin*

Don't be afraid to admit defeat. Learn from defeat. Do over again more thoroughly, more carefully, and more systematically what you have done badly.

*V. I. Lenin*

He who admits defeat before the battle begins is in fact half defeated.

*Dmitry Pisarev*

It would be unworthy of a genuine socialist who has suffered grave defeat either to bluster or to give way to despair.

*V. I. Lenin*

*

We have to be able to look defeat straight in the face.

*V. I. Lenin*

*

Despair is typical of those who do not understand the causes of evil, see no way out, and are incapable of struggle.

*V. I. Lenin*

*

We must know how to change our methods of fighting the enemy to suit changes in the situation.

*V. I. Lenin*

*

We must be able to take account of the situation and be bold in adopting decisions.

*V. I. Lenin*

*

No obstacle should be considered too great, no resistance too strong; move doggedly towards your goal and show self-sacrifice to accomplish the task you have been set.

*A. V. Suvorov*

※

Nothing is more disastrous in either private or public life than to act indecisively, repelling friends and fearing enemies.

*Nikolai Chernyshevsky*

※

Over-ardent protestations very often lead one to doubt and suspect the worth of whatever it is that requires such strong seasoning.

*V. I. Lenin*

# CHIEFS AND SUBORDINATES

A political leader is responsible not only for the quality of his leadership, but also for the acts of those he leads. He may now and again be unaware of what they are about, he may often wish they had not done something, but the responsibility still falls on him.

*V. I. Lenin*

Those accept an obligation lightly who feel lightly about letting it drop.

*Janis Rainis*

\*

The trouble with most people is that they think they can what they really cannot.

*Maxim Gorky*

\*

Not our place is important, but the direction in which we move.

*Lev Tolstoy*

\*

It is impossible and unnecessary for each and everyone to be in the forefront; do your own in your own circle—there is enough work for everybody.

*Alexander Herzen*

\*

The official's heart must stand at attention before his mind.

*A. A. Bestuzhev-Marlinsky*

\*

*So many, though reluctant to admit it,*
*Shun clever men, and rather suffer fools.*

*Ivan Krylov*

Exaltation and slackness are the most dangerous enemies.

*Andrejs Upits*

\*

Once accustomed to doing everything without question or without faith in the truth and the good of it, merely obeying orders, the individual becomes indifferent to good and evil, and has no qualms about acting contrary to morality on the plea that "those were orders".

*Nikolai Dobrolyubov*

\*

He who spares the feelings of everyone, loves none and nothing save himself; he who gratifies everyone can do nothing right because doing right is impossible without wronging evil.

*Nikolai Chernyshevsky*

\*

If an individual agrees with everybody, he lacks conviction; if he likes everybody and is everybody's friend, he is indifferent to one and all.

*Nikolai Dobrolyubov*

\*

Chiefs have no right to have fits of nerves.

*V. I. Lenin*

In politics spite generally plays the basest of roles.

*V. I. Lenin*

\*

Haven't you noticed that the person who is absent-minded in the midst of his subordinates is never absent-minded in the presence of his superiors?

*Ivan Turgenev*

\*

*He who fox-like got his rank*
*Is wolf-like in his office.*

*V. A. Zhukovsky*

\*

None behaves as rudely with his subordinates as he who fawns on his superiors.

*Nikolai Dobrolyubov*

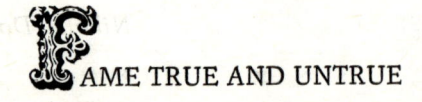

# FAME TRUE AND UNTRUE

All great men were fond of honour and praise. Lacking this, no great ventures would have been undertaken, and great deeds would have remained unaccomplished.

*Mikhail Lomonosov*

\*

True fame cannot be found: it flows out of self-dedication to the general good.

*A. V. Suvorov*

\*

Of all the different kinds of glory the most flattering and incorruptible is glory bestowed by the people.

*Vissarion Belinsky*

\*

Historical services are not judged by the contributions historical personalities *did not make* in respect of modern requirements, but by the *new* contributions they *did make* as compared to their predecessors.

*V. I. Lenin*

\*

Genius and villainy are incompatible.

*Alexander Pushkin*

\*

It is far more honest to be undeservedly ignored than to be honoured without merit.

*Denis Fonvizin*

There is always something sinister and fatal about the peak of fame.

*A. F. Pisemsky*

\*

Time is the greatest and the most brilliant and infallible of critics.

*Vissarion Belinsky*

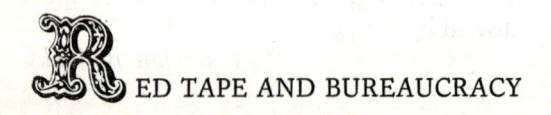

# RED TAPE AND BUREAUCRACY

Our worst internal enemy is the bureaucrat.

*V. I. Lenin*

\*

Red tape is when you disregard the substance of the matter and all your attention is on the form, the paper.

*N. K. Krupskaya*

\*

To draft and prescribe does not mean to understand and fulfil.

*Konstantin Ushinsky*

We must rule out formal bureaucratic methods of management, we must declare war on red tape of all shapes and forms.

*Sergei Kirov*

\*

The slightest tendency towards red tape must be punished ruthlessly.

*V. I. Lenin*

\*

We need to understand that the struggle against the evils of bureaucracy is absolutely indispensable, and that it is just as intricate as the fight against the petty-bourgeois element.

*V. I. Lenin*

\*

If we wish to combat bureaucratic methods, we must draw people from below into this work.

*V. I. Lenin*

\*

The fight against the bureaucratic distortion of the Soviet form of organisation is assured by the firmness of the connection between the Soviets and the "people", meaning by that the working and exploited people, and by the flexibility and elasticity of this connection.

*V. I. Lenin*

The machinery of Soviet administration must work accurately, smoothly, and swiftly.

*V. I. Lenin*

\*

The stronger the apparatus, as an auxiliary, the better and more suitable it is for manoeuvring.

*V. I. Lenin*

\*

We must reduce our state apparatus to the utmost degree of economy. We must banish from it all traces of extravagance.

*V. I. Lenin*

\*

Committee discussion must be reduced to an absolute minimum and never be allowed to interfere with swiftness and firmness of decision or minimise the responsibility of each and every worker.

*V. I. Lenin*

\*

There must be collective discussion, but individual responsibility.

*V. I. Lenin*

\*

To refer to collegiate methods as an excuse for irresponsibility is a most dangerous evil.

*V. I. Lenin*

Collective discussion and decision of all questions of administration in Soviet institutions must be accompanied by the precisely defined *responsibility of every person* holding any Soviet post for the *performance of definite*, and clearly and explicitly specified, functions and *practical* jobs.

*V. I. Lenin*

\*

We must devote our attention to business and not to resolutions.

*V. I. Lenin*

\*

To test men and verify what has actually been done—this, this again, this alone is now the main feature of all our activities, of our whole policy. This is not a matter of a few months or of a year, but of several years.

*V. I. Lenin*

\*

It will take decades to overcome the evils of bureaucracy. It is a very difficult struggle, and anyone who says we can rid ourselves of bureaucratic practices overnight by adopting anti-bureaucratic platforms is nothing but a quack with a bent for fine words.

*V. I. Lenin*

## OF PEOPLE AND HISTORY

## HISTORY AND HISTORIANS

Man's consciousness not only reflects the objective world, but creates it.

*V. I. Lenin*

\*

The history of any nation is not only a succession of events, but also a chain of ideas.

*Pyotr Chaadayev*

\*

The content of history consists of ideas as well as facts.

*Vissarion Belinsky*

\*

History deals not with individuals, but with society.

*V. O. Kliuchevsky*

## PEOPLE AND HISTORY

The supreme meaning of history is ardent struggle.

*Alexander Herzen*

\*

One may not know or want to know mathematics, Greek, Latin, chemistry or any of the thousand other sciences, and still be educated, but only a mentally undeveloped person can fail to like history.

*Nikolai Chernyshevsky*

\*

In a sense, history is the holy book of the peoples, the main one, the necessary one, the mirror of their being and activity, the scroll of revelations and rules, the behest of forebears to descendants, a supplement, an explication of the present and an example for the future.

*Nikolai Karamzin*

\*

To benefit from the lessons of history, and not to hide from the responsibility they impose, or shut ... eyes to them.

*V. I. Lenin*

\*

The purpose of history is to know the movement of mankind.

*Lev Tolstoy*

Neither humanity nor nature can be understood outside the movement of history.

*Alexander Herzen*

\*

To understand the soul of the Russian people and its greatness you must thoroughly know its past—its history, its pivotal conjunctions, and the tragic and creative epochs in which the Russian character took its beginning.

*A. N. Tolstoy*

\*

It is impossible to know the true sense of the present and the aims of the future unless you know the past.

*Maxim Gorky*

\*

To know the present you must know the past, for comparison is the key to knowledge.

*Maxim Gorky*

\*

We must learn to look upon the past and present from the summits of our future aims.

*Maxim Gorky*

Scientific socialism is that highest of intellectual plateaus from which we clearly see the past and are shown the direct and only way to the future.

*Maxim Gorky*

\*

We cannot learn to solve our problems by new methods today if yesterday's experience has not opened our eyes to the incorrectness of the old methods.

*V. I. Lenin*

\*

We interrogate the past for an explanation of our present and an intimation of our future.

*Vissarion Belinsky*

\*

Fuller insight into the past helps us apprehend the present; plumbing the meaning of the past we learn the meaning of the future; looking back we march forward.

*Alexander Herzen*

\*

Nothing could be more wrong than to ignore the past, which is the bridge to the present.

*Alexander Herzen*

If you want to go forward look back more often, lest you forget whence you came and where you are going.

*Leonid Andreyev*

\*

More than any other science, history needs to absorb contemporary ideas. It is from the standpoint of the present that we look back at the past. In the lot of our forefathers we mainly want to find an explanation of our own destiny.

*T. N. Granovsky*

\*

Respect for the past—there you have the thing that distinguishes the educated from the savage.

*Alexander Pushkin*

\*

One not only should but also must be proud of the glory of one's ancestors; lack of such pride is disgraceful.

*Alexander Pushkin*

\*

It is base and ignorant savages who do not respect the past; they grovel before the present.

*Alexander Pushkin*

PEOPLE AND HISTORY

History should be a coherent and truthful story of the life of the masses, and the place it devotes to individuals and particular events should depend on the measure to which they affect the life of the masses.

*Dmitry Pisarev*

\*

The historian must know the value and manner of uncovering the great wherever it is and not ascribe greatness to the small.

*Nikolai Karamzin*

\*

I would choose this epigraph to history: "Conceal nothing." It is not enough to avoid direct lies; try not to lie negatively, by omission.

*Lev Tolstoy*

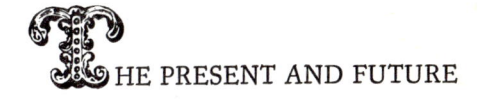

## THE PRESENT AND FUTURE

It is good to be filled with expectations of great joy.

*Maxim Gorky*

Those reluctant to part with the past should never try to peer into the better and brighter future.

*Dmitry Pisarev*

\*

He who does not see the present as being better than the past and the future as being better than the present, sees nothing but stagnation, putrefaction, and death.

*Vissarion Belinsky*

\*

Always, the art of living has mainly consisted of the ability to look ahead.

*Leonid Leonov*

\*

You cannot go against the spirit and movement of the times.

*Vissarion Belinsky*

\*

History is forever on the side of one party—the party that is in motion.

*Alexander Herzen*

## PEOPLE AND HISTORY

The present is the fruit of the past and the seed of the future.

*M. P. Pogodin*

\*

Appreciate the present. Every situation and every minute are incalculably precious for they represent eternity.

*Lev Tolstoy*

\*

The future comes sooner than the present departs.

*Effendi Kapiev*

\*

A Communist is expected to devote greater attention to the tasks of tomorrow than of yesterday.

*V. I. Lenin*

\*

Our young people should grasp this very simple point: children must be cleverer and stronger than their fathers, and will be so if they study past mistakes and absorb all the best, all the useful that was fashioned or begun by their forefathers, and that followed inevitably in ideological terms from their severe revolutionary experience.

*Maxim Gorky*

Traditions are never left in peace: they degenerate if they are not perfected.

*P. A. Pavlenko*

\*

The duty to preserve revolutionary traditions also requires that we analyse the situation in which they are used and not simply repeat revolutionary slogans which had meaning in a particular situation.

*V. I. Lenin*

\*

Cultivate the ideals of the future; in a manner of speaking they are the rays of the sun. Look closely and frequently at the glimmering spots in the perspective of the future.

*M. E. Saltykov-Shchedrin*

\*

There'd be no sense in living if mankind were not illumined by the star of socialism, the star of the future.

*Felix Dzerzhinsky*

\*

The future is bright and beautiful. Cherish it, strive and work for it, bring it closer, borrow as much as possible from it for the present.

*Nikolai Chernyshevsky*

\*

The future will admit only those who possess at least one of the qualities of the collective—joy of working, thirst of sacrifice, tirelessness of inventing, generosity of giving, and pride of humanity.

*Vladimir Mayakovsky*

# HISTORICAL ACTIVITY

Picking one's tasks and taking one's bearings, one must at least be a bit of a historian to be a consciously and conscientiously active citizen.

*V. O. Kliuchevsky*

\*

Live and behave as though the next generation is watching you.

*Mikhail Svetlov*

We must all live so that our children do not have to pay for our deeds.

*Andrejs Upits*

\*

Every individual must above all be a citizen.

*Maxim Gorky*

\*

It is undialectical, unscientific, and theoretically wrong to regard the course of world history as smooth and always in a forward direction, without occasional gigantic leaps back.

*V. I. Lenin*

\*

There can be no contest in which all the chances are known beforehand.

*V. I. Lenin*

\*

So far, history has no example of success coming without struggle.

*Nikolai Chernyshevsky*

\*

The path of history is not paved like Nevsky Prospekt; it runs across fields, either dusty or muddy, and cuts through swamps or forest thickets. Anyone who fears being covered with dust or soiling his boots, should not engage in social activity.

*Nikolai Chernyshevsky*

\*

All the genuine and all the good was acquired by people who worked for it through struggle and privation; the better future must be worked for in exactly the same way.

*Nikolai Chernyshevsky*

## OF PROBITY

# BASIC MORAL PRINCIPLES

The moral quality of its people is the most important asset of a nation.

*Nikolai Chernyshevsky*

\*

The Great October Socialist Revolution has raised the morality of all the peoples of Russia a rung higher. It has become the highest morality in human society.

*Mikhail Kalinin*

\*

Taken in their rudimentary form, the communist principles are the principles of a highly educated, honest, and progressive individual—love of the socialist Motherland, friendship, comradeship, humanity, honesty, and socialist work with a will.

*Mikhail Kalinin*

## PROBITY

Morality serves the purpose of helping human society rise to a higher level.

*V. I. Lenin*

\*

Communist morality is based on the struggle for the building and consolidation of communism.

*V. I. Lenin*

\*

Morality divorced from life is as immoral as life devoid of moral content.

*G. V. Plekhanov*

\*

What is morality? What should morality consist in? In firm and profound convictions and an ardent and unshakable faith in man's dignity and lofty mission. This is the source of all human virtues and acts.

*Vissarion Belinsky*

\*

There are values of the spirit that an individual, at least an ordinary, average individual, cannot live without. This applies first of all to his moral outlook. If you take away his ethical criteria and give him nothing new instead, you will plunge him into darkness, push him, the blinded one, into a dead end and prepare his destruction.

*V. V. Vorovsky*

\*

Convictions are the crucial element of communist morality. To cultivate enduring communist convictions is one of the main purposes of education.

*Vassily Sukhomlinsky*

\*

What our society needs is not a simple listing of ethical norms, but an orderly and practicable integral morality expressed, on the one hand, in serious philosophical studies and, on the other, in a system of ethical traditions.

*Anton Makarenko*

\*

The *finest people* are marked by the highest degree of moral development and the highest moral influence.

*Fyodor Dostoyevsky*

\*

Private morality is always dependent on public morality.

*T. N. Granovsky*

The morality of the bourgeois world is a morality of greed and is adapted to greed.

*Anton Makarenko*

\*

Morality is the relation of the power of reason to the power of feeling. The stronger his feeling and the closer his reason is to his feeling, the greater is the individual in his human activity. There is feeling that complements or obscures reason, and there is reason that dampens the impulses of feeling.

*M. M. Prishvin*

\*

No rule of morality can be dependable if it lacks common sense.

*Nikolai Pirogov*

\*

Time, hard work, honesty, knowledge, self-control, and a man's physical, intellectual, and moral powers are the sole makers of wealth.

*Konstantin Ushinsky*

\*

To my mind, virtue is the habit of acting for the common good of society.

*A. N. Radishchev*

The supreme virtue is to sacrifice your person for the good of the collective.

*M. M. Prishvin*

\*

The higher the individual's intellectual and moral development, the more free he is and the greater the satisfaction he derives from life.

*Anton Chekhov*

\*

Peace of mind is bought with moral rectitude.

*Dmitry Pisarev*

\*

There is no bliss in immorality; the supreme bliss is in morality and virtue.

*Alexander Herzen*

\*

The rational and the moral always coincide.

*Lev Tolstoy*

## THE COLLECTIVE AND THE INDIVIDUAL

One cannot live in society and be free from society.

*V. I. Lenin*

\*

The individual is inconceivable outside society.

*Lev Tolstoy*

\*

In all respects, man needs man.

*Taras Shevchenko*

\*

The individual must be a friend to people; he owes them everything he has and everything that is in him.

*Maxim Gorky*

\*

Man is created by Nature, but it is society that develops and shapes him.

*Vissarion Belinsky*

Always and everywhere, throughout history, the individual was shaped by the people around him.

*Maxim Gorky*

\*

Learn to work in a collective. First of all, working in a collective means taking criticism in the right spirit and not hesitating to criticise the mistakes of others.

*N. D. Zelinsky*

\*

Working in a collective is sticking to principle, giving the higher interests of the collective precedence over your own.

*N. D. Zelinsky*

\*

An individual cannot be happy if cast out of society any more than a plant can live if torn out of the earth and thrown on barren sand.

*A. N. Tolstoy*

\*

If you find people a nuisance, you have nothing to live for. To seclude yourself from people is suicide.

*Lev Tolstoy*

## PROBITY

Nothing but participation in collective labour can help people take the right, ethical attitude towards other people, feel friendship and brotherly affection for every working man, and rise in anger and censure against shirkers.

*Anton Makarenko*

\*

Sad is the lot of those who renounce the collective and parade as masterminds or unrecognised geniuses. The collective never fails to elevate the individual and put him firmly on his feet.

*Nikolai Ostrovsky*

\*

Individualism is emphasised weakness.

*M. M. Prishvin*

\*

In our view, individualism or fancied alienation from society is just as incongruous as suicide.

*A. N. Tolstoy*

\*

No matter how gifted the individual, the collective is always cleverer and stronger.

*Nikolai Ostrovsky*

The collective moulds people of an entirely different individual psychology—more active, more tenacious, drawing their will for action, for building, from the will of the collective.

*Maxim Gorky*

\*

The broader the collective whose perspectives coincide with those of the individual, the more noble and beautiful is the individual.

*Anton Makarenko*

\*

The collective is no faceless mass. It is a wealth of personalities.

*Vassily Sukhomlinsky*

\*

Concern for the educational effect of the collective is concern for the spiritual enrichment and development of every member of the collective, and for richness of relationships.

*Vassily Sukhomlinsky*

\*

The wealth of society is the variety of individuals comprising it, for the individual is the highest object of education.

*Vassily Sukhomlinsky*

# PROBITY

Every person knows that he must do what unites, not divides, him and other people.

*Lev Tolstoy*

\*

The person who sets himself apart from others robs himself of happiness, because the more isolated he is, the worse his life becomes.

*Lev Tolstoy*

\*

One must learn to link his life with that of society. This is not asceticism. On the contrary, one's private life is enriched by this, because the common aspirations of all become one's private aspirations. One loses nothing, and gains bright and deep experiences which philistine family life can never give.

*N. K. Krupskaya*

\*

We must do our utmost to tie our lives to the common struggle.

*N. K. Krupskaya*

\*

A Communist is first of all a social person with strongly developed social instincts, wanting all people to live well and to be happy.

*N. K. Krupskaya*

The wish to serve the common weal must in all cases be a movement of the soul, a condition of personal happiness.

*Anton Chekhov*

\*

A man is the more perfect, the more useful he is to the wide range of public interests.

*Dmitry Mendeleyev*

\*

To be a bright light for others, to emit light, is the highest joy the individual can attain. Then, he fears neither suffering nor pain nor sorrow nor need. He stops fearing death, though then only he learns to really love life.

*Felix Dzerzhinsky*

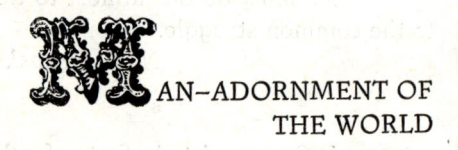

# MAN–ADORNMENT OF THE WORLD

It is a magnificent vocation to be a human being.

*Maxim Gorky*

## PROBITY

I am deeply convinced there is nothing better on earth than man. I always was, always am, and always will be a worshipper of man.

*Maxim Gorky*

\*

No bookish verity can be dearer to me than man. Man is the Universe. May he live forever, the bearer of the whole world.

*Maxim Gorky*

\*

In all difficult times, in every black hour of my life, my heart has always sung this hymn—"Long live man!"

*Maxim Gorky*

\*

Nothing in the world is more interesting than man himself.

*Vassily Sukhomlinsky*

\*

All the beauty on earth comes from the Sun and all the good from Man.

*M. M. Prishvin*

\*

*When I recall I am human*
*My soul soars into the sky.*

*V. A. Zhukovsky*

The man is the whole world, provided his main motivations are noble.

*Fyodor Dostoyevsky*

\*

It is equally good to be scholar, poet, general, or legislator, but whoever you are it is decidedly bad not to be human.

*Vissarion Belinsky*

\*

To be, not to seem, is a motto every citizen fond of his country must bear in his heart. Serve the truth—in the scientific and in the ethical sense of the word. Be human.

*Nikolai Pirogov*

\*

It is the make-up of the human being not only to worship but also to strive to excel the great.

*Vera Mukhina*

\*

Socialism is a society of science and culture. You must learn well and be knowledgeable to be a worthy member of socialist society.

*Mikhail Kalinin*

## PROBITY

No man is born ready-made, that is, fully developed; his life is a continuous development, an endless growth.

*Vissarion Belinsky*

\*

Improve yourself. Whatever your character, it can be changed. Patience, ability, even physical strength—you can cultivate anything if you put your mind to it and do not shun difficulties.

*Mikhail Frunze*

\*

The purpose of life is to improve man.

*Maxim Gorky*

\*

Dissatisfaction with oneself is a necessary condition for living sensibly. Dissatisfaction is the one and only spur to self-improvement.

*Lev Tolstoy*

\*

To improve yourself, you must first of all put yourself to a strict and impartial test to determine your faults and flaws clearly and pitilessly, and decide once and for all if you will suffer them any longer or turn over a new leaf.

*Nikolai Ostrovsky*

To know your road, to find your place—this is everything if you want to be true to yourself.

*Vissarion Belinsky*

One can understand and appreciate instantly, but one cannot become a man overnight. One must mould oneself into a real man.

*Fyodor Dostoyevsky*

You can have a hundred teachers. They will be powerless if you do not drive yourself and set your own standards.

*Vassily Sukhomlinsky*

Effort is a necessary condition for moral improvement.

*Lev Tolstoy*

To say I cannot resist an act of improbity is the same as saying I am not a man, not even an animal, but a thing.

*Lev Tolstoy*

## PROBITY

No person has so ill a disposition as to be unable to substitute an "acquired character" for his "natural temperament".

*E. I. Martsinovsky*

\*

If there is hygiene of body, there must also be hygiene of mind and character.

*Dmitry Pisarev*

\*

As physical exercises invigorate bodily powers so do exercises of the mind invigorate mental powers.

*A. N. Radishchev*

\*

The soul, like the body, must have its exercise, lacking which it wilts and runs to waste in idleness.

*Vissarion Belinsky*

\*

Be intelligent, simple, fair, brave, and kind. These terms and no other give title to the high calling of Man.

*Konstantin Paustovsky*

# PERSONAL RELATIONS

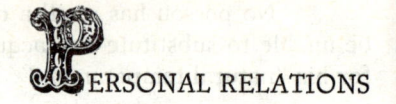

Everyday life is an overused concept; it should be freshened up, and orderliness of personal relations must be shown to be its content.

*M. M. Prishvin*

\*

Communism isn't only in the field, in the factory, in the sweat of one's brow. It is also at home, at the table, in family relations, in everyday life.

*Vladimir Mayakovsky*

\*

We must learn to be considerate to one another; we must understand that man is the most wonderful and the most noble of all the creatures on earth.

*Maxim Gorky*

\*

We shall not rid ourselves of abominations and untruths until we learn to admire man as the most beautiful and the most extraordinary phenomenon on our planet.

*Maxim Gorky*

## PROBITY

Respect one another and remember that in every man there is the sagacious power of a builder, that this power must be given scope to develop and flourish.

*Maxim Gorky*

\*

The best that I have in me are my warm feelings for good people.

*M. M. Prishvin*

\*

There are much too many wheels, bolts, and valves in each of us for us to be able to judge one another by our first impression or by the two or three most visible qualities.

*Anton Chekhov*

\*

People whom you see through at once are uninteresting; if possible, a man must have everything plus a bit more.

*Maxim Gorky*

\*

He who has not learned the man inside himself will never have deep knowledge of other men.

*Nikolai Chernyshevsky*

You are not a human being until you learn to see human beings in all others.

*A. N. Radishchev*

\*

To understand your neighbour you must learn to put yourself in his place, to feel his sorrow and his joy as he does.

*Dmitry Pisarev*

\*

Learn to feel for your neighbour, to read his mind, to see his inner world—his joys, his misfortunes, and his sorrows with his eyes.

*Vassily Sukhomlinsky*

\*

Respect and spare the vulnerability and sensitivity of others. Inflict no evil, no injury, no pain, no anxiety or trouble.

*Vassily Sukhomlinsky*

\*

There is no minute in our lives that can justify our treating another lightly or irreverently.

*Dmitry Pisarev*

## PROBITY

Respect the individual in yourself and others.

*Dmitry Pisarev*

✻

The right to be respected is won by respecting others.

*Vassily Sukhomlinsky*

✻

He who can easily lose respect for others is one who essentially has no respect for himself.

*Fyodor Dostoyevsky*

✻

Never think of anyone that he has more bad in him than good.

*Maxim Gorky*

✻

Always look for the good in other people, not for the bad.

*Lev Tolstoy*

✻

People of breeding respect the individual and are, therefore, always indulgent, mild, polite, and tractable.

*Anton Chekhov*

In its normal state, that is, blended with energy of character and a rightly developed sense of dignity, tact is one of the greatest virtues man can possess. It compounds honesty, justice, and active sympathy for the lot of one's fellows.

*Nikolai Dobrolyubov*

\*

The great are endowed with the talent of recognising the great in other people.

*Nikolai Karamzin*

\*

It is good to praise people, for it adds to their self-respect and stimulates their faith in their own powers.

*Maxim Gorky*

\*

There is never any harm in treating people well.

*Maxim Gorky*

\*

If you keep saying he is a swine, he will finally grunt like one.

*Maxim Gorky*

## PROBITY

It is a great evil to humiliate people, to consider oneself deserving respect and the other fellow a speck of dust.

*Vassily Sukhomlinsky*

\*

People aren't angels woven of light, but neither are they beasts to be driven into stalls.

*Vladimir Korolenko*

\*

Never trouble others with what you can do yourself.

*Lev Tolstoy*

\*

When you meet people think not of your own advantage but of theirs, and not of what you make of yourself but what they make of you.

*Lev Tolstoy*

## HUMANITARIANISM

Communist morality is inconceivable without elementary humanity.

*Vassily Sukhomlinsky*

# WORDS OF THE WISE

One must be fond of people. If one is fond of people, one is happier and more cheerful, for none has it as bad as the man-hater.

*Mikhail Kalinin*

\*

Love of neighbour—those are the wings that lift man up above all other things.

*Maxim Gorky*

\*

As I see it, a man lives as long as he loves; if he does not love people, what use is he?

*Maxim Gorky*

\*

Humanism is probably the one thing that has survived from long since non-existent peoples and civilisations—books, folklore, the marble of sculptures, and architectural proportions.

*A. N. Tolstoy*

\*

The natural aspirations of mankind reduced to the simplest denominator may be expressed in these words: "That everybody should have it good."

*Nikolai Dobrolyubov*

## PROBITY

Goodness is the eternal and supreme aim of our life. Whatever the meaning we put into goodness, our life is an explicit striving for it.

*Lev Tolstoy*

\*

Kindness is for the soul what health is for the body; it is inconspicuous when you have it, and it brings success to every undertaking.

*Lev Tolstoy*

\*

Great love is inseparable from a great mind; scope of mind is equivalent to depth of feeling. It is the big-hearted who attain the summits of humanism, for they are also the great minds.

*Ivan Goncharov*

\*

Rest not and be not lulled—and tire not of doing good while you are still young, strong, and full of vigour.

*Anton Chekhov*

\*

One is able to feel for a common misfortune only if one also feels for a particular misfortune of a particular person.

*Felix Dzerzhinsky*

Only he who cannot remain indifferent to the joys and sorrows of a separate individual will take close to heart joys and sorrows of his land.

*Vassily Sukhomlinsky*

\*

It may be said of some that their hearts are waterproof—impermeable to the tears of their fellow-men.

*P. A. Vyazemsky*

\*

The kind man is not he who is capable of doing good, but he who is incapable of doing evil.

*V. O. Kliuchevsky*

\*

A good deed is done with effort, but after the effort is repeated the deed becomes a habit.

*Lev Tolstoy*

\*

Nothing can more adorn one's life and that of others than the habit of being kind.

*Lev Tolstoy*

\*

Real humanity signifies justice above all.

*Vassily Sukhomlinsky*

## PROBITY

Some people turn into swine the moment they are treated like people.

*V. O. Kliuchevsky*

*

Kindness by order is no kindness.

*Ivan Turgenev*

*

Virtue under duress forfeits its value.

*Dmitry Pisarev*

*

Nothing is worse than feigned kindness. Dissembled kindness is more despicable than undisguised spite.

*Lev Tolstoy*

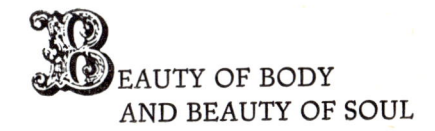

## BEAUTY OF BODY AND BEAUTY OF SOUL

The face is the mirror of the soul.

*Maxim Gorky*

Beauty elevates the moral virtues, but in the absence of moral virtues beauty is only for the eye, not the heart.

*Vissarion Belinsky*

\*

Beauty is not in the separate features of the face, but in its general expression, in the vital meaning imprinted upon it.

*Nikolai Dobrolyubov*

\*

Outward neatness and grace must express inner purity and beauty.

*Vissarion Belinsky*

\*

A foolish beauty is no beauty. Look at her, look closely at every feature of her face, look at her smile, look at her gaze–the beauty of her will gradually turn into an eyesore.

*Ivan Goncharov*

\*

A raving beauty cannot manage what a clever girl will do with ease.

*P. A. Pavlenko*

## PROBITY

Kindness is as much a gift as beauty and intellect.

*Vassily Kachalov*

\*

Beauty is good only if it is not conscious of itself.

*V. O. Kliuchevsky*

\*

No dress on earth surpasses in beauty the bronze of muscle and freshness of skin.

*Vladimir Mayakovsky*

\*

Appearance is highly important in a person, and it is hard to conceive of someone ill-kempt and slovenly who would attend to his behaviour.

*Anton Makarenko*

\*

The aesthetics of dress, room, stairway, and machine is not a whit less important than the aesthetics of behaviour.

*Anton Makarenko*

## OF MAN AND NATURE

The sense of Nature is one of the pillars of patriotism.

*Konstantin Paustovsky*

\*

I cannot conceive of a member of socialist society who'd be indifferent to Nature.

*Konstantin Paustovsky*

\*

Happiness is to be with Nature, to see it, to communicate with it.

*Lev Tolstoy*

\*

The human being cannot be unaffected by Nature; he is tied to it by a thousand threads; he is its son.

*Ivan Turgenev*

\*

The delights of contemplating Nature are greater than those of contemplating art.

*Pyotr Chaikovsky*

## MAN AND NATURE

Nature is the mother of all talent, from the sunny dewdrop that lights up with a thousand fires to the great gifts inscribed in the history of culture.

*M. M. Prishvin*

\*

Your eye is not enough. The inner senses must feel Nature, hear its music, and imbibe its quietude.

*I. I. Levitan*

\*

Nature is the everlasting model of the arts, and Man the greatest and noblest object of Nature.

*Vissarion Belinsky*

\*

Sun and life—man probably learned to associate and compare these concepts the moment he began looking intelligently at the surrounding world and at himself. Isn't the proof thereof in sun worship, which we meet both at the lowest stages of civilisation and among peoples at a high level of culture.

*K. A. Timiryazev*

\*

The plant is the link between heaven and earth, the Prometheus who stole fire from the skies. The Sun's rays which it stole set in motion the fly-wheel of the steam engine, the artist's brush, and the pen of the poet.

*K. A. Timiryazev*

\*

If the green leaf were to stop its work for a few years, all living things on earth, including humans, would perish as the tiny insect does with the coming of winter, and perish irretrievably.

*S. P. Kostychev*

\*

Forests are much more than an adornment of the Earth, much more than its magnificent and astonishing attire. They are the greatest sources of health and inspiration and huge green laboratories manufacturing oxygen and trapping toxic gases and dust.

*Leonid Leonov*

\*

Forests adorn the Earth. They inspire a sense of grandeur and teach us to appreciate beauty.

*Anton Chekhov*

\*

The forest gives me peace of mind and comfort; it helps me forget my troubles and aggravations.

*Maxim Gorky*

## MAN AND NATURE

All things in Nature are splendid, but water is the beauty of all Nature.

*S. T. Aksakov*

\*

Nature, the world is the source of knowledge.

*N. I. Lobachevsky*

\*

Before people learned the powers of Nature they submitted to them blindly; after they learned them the powers of Nature submitted to people.

*G. V. Plekhanov*

\*

Existing and acting independently of and outside our mind, a law of Nature makes us slaves of "blind necessity". But once we come to know this law, which acts (as Marx repeated a thousand times) *independently* of our will and our mind, we become the masters of Nature.

*V. I. Lenin*

\*

None can read the book of Nature whole, from beginning to end. But the purpose of being is to read as much of it as one can. The more pages one turns, the more interesting and gratifying it becomes for all who can feel and think.

*K. E. Tsiolkovsky*

\*

The source of all our wealth, the foundation of our civilisation and the real motor of world history is, of course, man's physical work, man's direct and immediate action on Nature.

*Dmitry Pisarev*

\*

We cannot wait for Nature's favours; we must take them from it.

*Ivan Michurin*

\*

Man can and must do better than Nature.

*Ivan Michurin*

\*

It is becoming ever more necessary for man to take from Nature that which it does not easily surrender.

*N. A. Umov*

\*

Nature is no temple; it is a workshop and man in it simply a labourer.

*Ivan Turgenev*

# MAN AND NATURE

Man is the source of the unprecedented in Nature.

*M. M. Prishvin*

\*

Man's action on the environment distinguishes him from other creatures. This distinction, great though it was from the very beginning, has become truly immense with the passage of time.

*V. I. Vernadsky*

\*

A new, tremendous geological force appeared on the surface of our planet with the coming of Man.

*V. I. Vernadsky*

\*

Nowhere else and, perhaps, in no other field must one consider so many different conditions for success and possess such diverse information as in agriculture, and nowhere else will a one-sided viewpoint lead to such disastrous failure.

*K. A. Timiryazev*

\*

There is no such thing as bad land, there are bad tillers.

*Maxim Gorky*

You may fell trees out of need, but it is high time to stop exterminating them. Man is endowed with reason and creative energy precisely to augment what he has been given.

*Anton Chekhov*

\*

We are the masters of Nature. For us it is the Sun's storehouse of great treasures.

*M. M. Prishvin*

\*

As a diamond is cut and polished, so must the Earth be by Man's labour.

*Maxim Gorky*

\*

The Earth must be worthy of Man. To be so, you must arrange it carefully, as you do your dwelling.

*Maxim Gorky*

\*

May the intellect celebrate victory after victory over surrounding Nature.

*Ivan Pavlov*

\*

Every person must adorn the Earth.

*Mikhail Sholokhov*

Outwardly, too, our country must be made the most beautiful in the world.

*Ivan Michurin*

\*

When I hear the rustling of the young forest I have planted with my own hands, I become aware that climate is also a little in my power and that if man is happy a thousand years hence I, too, have done my bit for him to be so.

*Anton Chekhov*

\*

If every man did everything he can on the plot that is his own, the Earth would be a place of beauty.

*Anton Chekhov*

\*

Afforestation of the southern steppes is feasible.... I think this so important for Russia's future that for me it ranks as high as defending the country from an enemy.

*Dmitry Mendeleyev*

\*

The time has come for great epoch-making measures to protect our country's natural wealth, for it has neither fist nor tooth nor thorn to protect itself from mischief.

*Leonid Leonov*

\*

When I speak of protecting Nature I have in mind the moral as well as practical side of the matter for the young. What I have in mind, if you like, is educating the rising generations in a spirit of what may be described as practical patriotism.

*Leonid Leonov*

\*

Our youth must be on the firing line of the just war against the elemental powers of Nature in order to master its wealth and break its secrets in all spheres, outer space included.

*I. P. Bardin*

\*

Nature in all shapes and forms must be protected. We must protect land, soil, plants, water, and air. We must protect the beautiful Russian landscape, which has played and continues to play so tremendous a part in moulding the character of the Russian people.

*Konstantin Paustovsky*

## MAN AND NATURE

Fish must have pure water. So let us protect our rivers, lakes, and ponds. There is valuable wild life in forests, steppes, and mountains. So let us protect our forests, steppes, and mountains.... Man must have his Motherland. To protect Nature is to protect the Motherland.

*M. M. Prishvin*

## OF THE PURPOSE OF LIFE, PURSUIT OF HAPPINESS, JOY, AND HOPE

### THE PURPOSE OF LIFE

What is dearest to man? Life is dearest, for with it come our joys, our happiness, our hopes.

*Nikolai Chernyshevsky*

\*

Setting limitless demands on life is the only thing that makes living worthwhile.

*Alexander Blok*

\*

Once an individual is aware that he is a human being, his life will mean nothing unless he feels that he is aspiring to something lofty—not in the sense of his egoistic interests, but in the sense of the lofty goal of the foremost men fighting for that common great cause which inspires him as well.

*Mikhail Kalinin*

# PURPOSE OF LIFE

Life is progressive, and the mainsprings of its progress are concentrated in the thoughts and strivings of the finest, that is, the soundest, normally organised specimens of our breed.

*Dmitry Pisarev*

*

Man is the more perfect, the more useful he is for the broad range of public and state interests.

*Dmitry Mendeleyev*

*

Nothing can justify a life without service to the general interests and purposes of society.

*Nikolai Leskov*

*

It is better not to develop at all than to develop without the influence of one's thoughts about public affairs or that of the feelings aroused by involvement in public affairs.

*Nikolai Chernyshevsky*

*

Certainly, a hungry one does not feel well; but the sated does not feel well either when hearing the groans of the hungry, for they are unbearable to the human heart.

*Nikolai Chernyshevsky*

\*

Everlasting anxiety, struggle, and privation—these are necessary conditions that no man should ever dare try to avoid. To live an honest life one must strain, flounder and err, begin and give up, begin again, give up again, and struggle forever and forever be deprived. For complacency is baseness of heart and soul.

*Lev Tolstoy*

\*

He who understands that the purpose of life is concern and anxiety ceases to be a common barbarian.

*Alexander Blok*

\*

The philistine is one who thinks in bits and pieces, disjointedly, and who commits himself to nothing and nobody.

*Mikhail Kalinin*

\*

There are many ways of making the human condition unbearable. Probably, the surest of all is to dedicate oneself to the cult of self-preservation, to suppress the turbulence of one's spirit, and to acknowledge one's life to be a senseless flutter in all the time that the lure of life endures.

*M. E. Saltykov-Shchedrin*

\*

You cannot live on earth without making sacrifices, without effort and privation, for life is no garden where only flowers grow.

*Ivan Goncharov*

\*

Faith in oneself and the wish to live for others is a formidable force.

*Felix Dzerzhinsky*

\*

The more an individual gives of himself and the less he demands, the better he is; the less he gives unto others, and the more he demands, the worse he is.

*Lev Tolstoy*

\*

What has always mattered, and always will, is the benefit of all, not the benefit of one.

*Lev Tolstoy*

If you are Man do not call him Man who is unconcerned about the needs of people.

*Alisher Navoi*

\*

To live is to fight, not only for life but also for the fullness and improvement of life. For us, therefore, Man means a fighting man, a man who feels, who revels in a fight, who does not flinch in daily struggles, who even relishes them, for where there is struggle there is the intensity of life and Man sensible to its throbbing.

*N. A. Rubakin*

\*

Men of devotion are as indispensable as the Sun. They are the most poetic and buoyant part of society. They excite, console, and ennoble. Their personalities are living proof that apart from people who argue about optimism and pessimism, write mediocre novels from boredom, or unneeded projects and cheap dissertations, or who indulge in vice to negate life, or lie to obtain a slice of bread, there are also people of a different breed, people of courage, faith, and clear purpose.

*Anton Chekhov*

## PURPOSE OF LIFE

Life is so broad and diverse that the individual will nearly always find his fill of that for which he feels the strongest and truest need.

*Nikolai Chernyshevsky*

*

Life is shallow and colourless only for those colourless people who hold forth about feelings and cravings, while they are in fact devoid of any special feeling and cravings save the craving to cut a figure.

*Nikolai Chernyshevsky*

*

Man never loses desire to improve his life.

*Nikolai Chernyshevsky*

*

Life is short and the greatest of fortunes.

*Sergei Sergeyev-Tsensky*

*

It's a true pleasure to be alive.

*Maxim Gorky*

The greatest of delights and the biggest of joys is to know that people need you and to know yourself close to them.

*Maxim Gorky*

\*

The right way to live is to be enamoured of something out of reach. Man gains in stature by stretching upwards.

*Maxim Gorky*

\*

Life is fullest and has the most meaning when you come to grips with whatever stands in your way.

*Maxim Gorky*

\*

Life flows on and he who can't keep pace with it is reduced to solitude.

*Maxim Gorky*

\*

Time is not the sole measure of life. There are people who lived but 24 years, and old men who lived a hundred. Time passed and the old men were forgotten, whereas those of 24, who had been fired by the people's cause, are remembered and live on in our hearts.

*Mikhail Kalinin*

## PURPOSE OF LIFE

Life is not the days that are gone, but the days that are remembered.

*P. A. Pavlenko*

∗

Life is not mere living; it is feeling that you are alive.

*V. O. Kliuchevsky*

∗

Many people live without living, only intending to live.

*Vissarion Belinsky*

∗

The most unbearable condition is to live uselessly.

*Nikolai Karamzin*

∗

To live in the wide world is to fight continuously and to win all the time.

*Dmitry Pisarev*

∗

Life and activity are as closely united as fire and light. Whatever is afire must, indeed, give light, and whatever is alive must, indeed, be active.

*Fyodor Glinka*

The greatest tragedy of life is to cease struggling.

*Nikolai Ostrovsky*

\*

Life teaches none but him who studies it.

*V. O. Kliuchevsky*

\*

Blessed is he who has adorned his swiftly fleeing days with memorable deeds.

*A. K. Tolstoy*

\*

Struggle—this is the joy of life.

*Leonid Andreyev*

\*

Struggle breeds pride.

*Mikhail Lermontov*

\*

Struggle is a condition of life: life ceases when struggle ends.

*Vissarion Belinsky*

\*

Life is action and action is struggle.

*Vissarion Belinsky*

## PURPOSE OF LIFE

Merit comes with struggle, reward comes with merit, and life comes with action.

*Vissarion Belinsky*

\*

The clever and energetic fight to the finish, while the empty and useless submit without struggle to all the casual pettiness of their senseless existence.

*Dmitry Pisarev*

\*

To live is to feel, to enjoy, to be constantly aware of the new that reminds us we are alive.

*N. I. Lobachevsky*

\*

To live is to feel and think, to suffer and revel. Any other life is death.

*Vissarion Belinsky*

\*

Life is endless work, and only those who see it from this angle understand it as humans should.

*Dmitry Pisarev*

\*

Life is made vital and beautiful by energetic work; it is not a burden, it is wings, creation and joy, and if anyone turns it into a burden, he is himself to blame.

*Vikenty Veresayev*

\*

One thing is never imprudent, and that is the lust for exploits. In this lust there palpitates the living human heart and the questing and never resting human spirit.

*M. E. Saltykov-Shchedrin*

\*

One who yearns for exploits will always know how to perform them and will find where they are fitting. You ought to know that in life there is always room for exploits.

*Maxim Gorky*

\*

The exploit, like talent, shortens the way to the goal.

*Leonid Leonov*

\*

It is a hard life if you have done nothing to earn your place in the Sun.

*Dmitry Venevitinov*

PURPOSE OF LIFE

A life that leaves no lasting trace recedes with every step you make.

*Alexander Herzen*

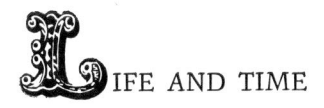

# LIFE AND TIME

Time is the cheapest and at once the most precious of our possessions, because it is with time that we get what we get.

*Janis Rainis*

\*

Money is dear, human life is dearer, and time is the dearest of all.

*A. V. Suvorov*

\*

The inability to value one's own and other people's time is rank absence of culture; it is outright ignorance and must be wiped out as soon as possible.

*N. K. Krupskaya*

\*

For us saving time is an axiom.

*Felix Dzerzhinsky*

Have a goal for your life, a goal for a fixed period, a goal for the year, for the month, for the week, for the day and the hour, and for the minute as well, sacrificing the lesser aims for the bigger.

*Lev Tolstoy*

\*

Time is endless motion without an instant of immobility, and cannot be conceived in any other way.

*Lev Tolstoy*

\*

I cannot visualise a situation where I'd have nothing to do.

*Fyodor Dostoyevsky*

\*

If you wish to have little time, do nothing.

*Anton Chekhov*

\*

A person's character is best seen from the kind of leisure is easiest for him, the kind he prefers.

*Nikolai Chernyshevsky*

\*

The word "tomorrow" is for the irresolute and for children.

*Ivan Turgenev*

## PURPOSE OF LIFE

Speed is good, haste is bad.

*A. V. Suvorov*

\*

In matters of importance one must always make haste as if everything would collapse from the loss of a minute.

*Vissarion Belinsky*

\*

To delay is criminal if you have a great mission.

*Shot'ha Rust'hveli*

\*

Sometimes delay is tantamount to death.

*Mikhail Lomonosov*

## THE PURSUIT OF HAPPINESS

Everyone needs happiness, is entitled to it, must pursue it at any cost.

*Nikolai Dobrolyubov*

Everyone wants to be happy, should be happy, has a right to be happy.

*N. V. Shelgunov*

*

The right to happiness is the most inalienable of human rights.

*Konstantin Ushinsky*

*

Man is created to be happy as the bird is created to fly.

*Vladimir Korolenko*

*

They say misfortune is a good school. Perhaps so. But good fortune is the best of universities. It completes the education of a soul pregnant with goodness and beauty.

*Alexander Pushkin*

*

Our communist ethics must work for millions of happy people, not for my happiness alone. The old logic: I want to be happy and other people are no concern of mine. The new logic: I want to be happy and the best way to be happy is to help all the others to be happy, too.

*Anton Makarenko*

## PURPOSE OF LIFE

He who wants to make his own happiness must help forge happiness for all workers and peasants. As the maker of the happiness of all he will be the maker of his own happiness.

*Mikhail Kalinin*

※

There is a way to be happy—it is to be useful to the world and especially the Motherland.

*Nikolai Karamzin*

※

Man has risen higher in the world than all other living things chiefly because the grief of others became his own.

*Vassily Sukhomlinsky*

※

The finest and also the happiest people are those who dedicate their lives to the happiness of others.

*Vassily Sukhomlinsky*

※

The supreme happiness is to fight for something more significant than one's own interest.

*Vassily Sukhomlinsky*

The wish to serve the common weal must always be an intrinsic wish, the condition of one's own happiness.

*Anton Chekhov*

\*

Personal happiness is inconceivable without the happiness of others.

*Nikolai Chernyshevsky*

\*

There is but one incontestable happiness—living for the sake of another.

*Lev Tolstoy*

\*

Happiness—whatever it consists of in the case of every individual—is inconceivable until the prime needs of man are satisfied.

*Nikolai Dobrolyubov*

\*

Wealth is something one can be happy without, but there must be wellbeing to be happy.

*Nikolai Chernyshevsky*

\*

The right to live and be happy is a mere spectre for someone without means.

*Nikolai Chernyshevsky*

## PURPOSE OF LIFE

Man must be happy. If he is not, he is himself to blame. And he must work assiduously until this discomfort or misunderstanding is removed.

*Lev Tolstoy*

*

To be happy one must first have faith that happiness is possible.

*Lev Tolstoy*

*

To be happy you must continuously strive for happiness and understand what it is. Happiness depends not on circumstances, but on yourself.

*Lev Tolstoy*

*

Happiness has to be conquered or earned. You cannot get it out of the hands of a benefactor.

*Dmitry Pisarev*

*

Happiness does not flit about in the air. It is the fruit of labour.

*Rudaki*

Awareness of the wonderful that was within grasp comes too late.

*Alexander Blok*

\*

Happiness is always on the side of the daring.

*P. I. Bagration*

\*

You cannot teach a person to be happy, but you can bring him up so that he will be happy.

*Anton Makarenko*

\*

Complete happiness does not mix with anxiety; complete happiness is as tranquil as the sea in the summer's calm.

*Alexander Herzen*

\*

He who is always cheerful is happy and he who is happy is kind.

*Vissarion Belinsky*

\*

Happiness is not carefree existence, it is a state of the spirit.

*Felix Dzerzhinsky*

## PURPOSE OF LIFE

Man is what his notions of happiness make him.

*Vassily Sukhomlinsky*

❈

Happiness is like health: you have it if you don't feel its absence.

*Ivan Turgenev*

❈

Happiness begins with a hatred for misfortune, with a physiological distaste for everything that warps and cripples people, with an inner loathing of everything that groans, wails, and yearns for the tinselled well-being that is being increasingly assailed by the tempest of history.

*Maxim Gorky*

\*

Chronic happiness does not exist any more than unmelting ice.

*Alexander Herzen*

❈

There are two wishes which, if fulfilled, make man truly happy–to be useful and to have a clear conscience.

*Lev Tolstoy*

Happiness is pleasure without remorse.

*Lev Tolstoy*

\*

An indispensable accessory of happiness is the certainty that you are living right, that your conscience is unsullied by baseness, cheating, cunning, time-serving, or some other blemish.

*Anton Makarenko*

# JOY, SADNESS, GRIEF, AND HOPE

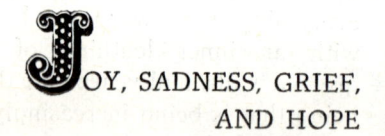

One cannot live if there is nothing joyous to look forward to.

*Anton Makarenko*

\*

Life must and can be an unceasing joy.

*Lev Tolstoy*

\*

Man should always be cheerful. If your good cheer runs out, see where you have erred.

*Lev Tolstoy*

## PURPOSE OF LIFE

If you do not conceive of life as a tremendous joy, this is solely due to your mind being on the wrong track.

*Lev Tolstoy*

\*

It is untrue that life is sombre; it is untrue that there is nothing in it but groans and grief. It has everything man wants to find in it, and man has the capacity to create what it lacks.

*Maxim Gorky*

\*

How often sadness comes on the wings of joy.

*Effendi Kapiev*

\*

He who lacks the faculty of feeling sad is as wretched as he who knows not the feeling of joy or has lost his sense of humour. Lack of any one of these speaks of an irremediable narrowness of spirit.

*Konstantin Paustovsky*

\*

Joys may be forgotten, sadness never.

*Mikhail Lermontov*

Sadness is a cruel taskmaster.

*Mikhail Lermontov*

\*

Strange that joy sometimes resembles grief and sad that grief never resembles joy.

*Pyotr Valuyev*

\*

*Joys are easy to indulge in; fortitude in adversity is better.*

*Shot'ha Rust'hveli*

\*

Anticipating a disaster is invariably more terrifying and unbearable than the disaster itself.

*Dmitry Pisarev*

\*

*Grief can never be eternal
Nor anguish incurable.*

*A. K. Tolstoy*

\*

What you need is confidence and energy; despair is the road to inactivity.

*N. P. Ogarev*

## PURPOSE OF LIFE

The sole salvation from grief is work.
*Pyotr Chaikovsky*

*

The support man leans upon most frequently is hope.
*A. F. Weltman*

*

The anticipation of happy days is sometimes far better than what these days turn out to be.
*Konstantin Paustovsky*

## OF LABOUR

### MAN'S MAIN CONDITION

Labour and science—there is nothing on earth superior to these two forces.

*Maxim Gorky*

\*

Labour has made of us a force that is uniting all the working people.

*V. I. Lenin*

\*

The worker's labour, the peasant's crop—those are the two axles of time on which life turns in top gear.

*Vladimir Mayakovsky*

\*

All the wealth of society, all of it, is reducible to the labour of this society.

*Dmitry Pisarev*

# LABOUR

All the wonders of the world were created by man's persevering and devoted labour.

*Maxim Gorky*

∗

In labour and nothing but labour is man's grandeur contained.

*Maxim Gorky*

∗

Free labour is the pivot of Archimedes required to overturn the world.

*Maxim Gorky*

∗

No heroics in the world are more majestic than the heroics of labour and creation.

*Maxim Gorky*

∗

All my life it was people fond of working and who worked well that I regarded as the real heroes.

*Maxim Gorky*

∗

Labour is the foundation of culture.

*Maxim Gorky*

The level of one's culture is always directly proportionate to one's diligence.

*Maxim Gorky*

\*

Work has always been the cornerstone of human existence and culture.

*Anton Makarenko*

\*

The most beautiful in our world is that which was created by labour, by man's clever hands; all our thoughts and ideas have their origin in the process of labour.

*Maxim Gorky*

\*

Hard work, man's work, will all things make and all ends reach. Such is the motto of history.

*Dmitry Mendeleyev*

\*

Our world has been created not by the word but by the deed, by labour.

*Maxim Gorky*

\*

We must learn to see work as creation.

*Maxim Gorky*

## LABOUR

Be fond of what you do; then your work, even the crudest, attains the level of creativity.

*Maxim Gorky*

*

He who works with a will injects poetry into all his work.

*Nikolai Chernyshevsky*

*

Physical work does not rule out mental work. It heightens its significance and also encourages it.

*Lev Tolstoy*

*

There are no talents and no geniuses in the absence of plainly intensive diligence.

*Dmitry Mendeleyev*

*

No force makes man great and wise but that of collective, concerted, and free labour.

*Maxim Gorky*

*

*Man's will and labour*
*Perform prodigious wonders.*

*Nikolai Nekrasov*

Labour, the activity of brain and muscle, constitutes a natural, inborn need.

*Nikolai Chernyshevsky*

\*

Nothing expresses man's essence better, more nobly and consummately than his deeds, his labour, and creativity.

*Alexander Fadeyev*

\*

Anything easily attained, anything attained without effort, is of highly dubious value.

*Leonid Leonov*

\*

Whatever the job, its habit and the skill it breeds are great things. He who did not sit on his hands when he had nothing to do will know what to do when the time comes for action.

*Vissarion Belinsky*

\*

The worker's physical energy can perform miracles.

*Maxim Gorky*

\*

Work ennobles man.

*Vissarion Belinsky*

## LABOUR

Nothing ennobles man more than work. Without work man cannot keep up his human dignity.

*Lev Tolstoy*

\*

Nothing save labour and struggle ensures distinctiveness and a sense of dignity.

*Fyodor Dostoyevsky*

\*

Work generates man's creative faculties.

*A. N. Tolstoy*

\*

You must put your life on a track where work becomes indispensable. No clean and joyous life is conceivable without work.

*Anton Chekhov*

\*

Everyone must work, work in the sweat of his brow whoever he may be, for this alone is the sense and purpose of life, happiness, and life's delights.

*Anton Chekhov*

\*

Develop yourself in working for the common good—that is the fundamental law.

*Janis Rainis*

Work is the strongest and the most dependable link between the man who works and the society for which he works.

*Dmitry Pisarev*

\*

You must not be ashamed of work, be it of the lowliest. Beware of just one thing: a life in idleness.

*Lev Tolstoy*

\*

Liberating oneself from work is a crime.

*Lev Tolstoy*

\*

Destruction of the indolent and glorification of labour—here you have the constant tendency of history.

*Nikolai Dobrolyubov*

\*

The future belongs to people of honest labour.

*Maxim Gorky*

## SOCIALISM AND LABOUR

Communism is the higher productivity of labour—compared with that existing under capitalism—of voluntary, class-conscious, and united workers employing advanced techniques.

*V. I. Lenin*

*

One of the basic tasks is to raise the level of labour productivity, for without this the full transition to communism is impossible.

*V. I. Lenin*

*

It will take many years and decades to create a new labour discipline, new forms of social ties between people, and new forms and methods of drawing people into labour.

It is a most gratifying and noble work.

*V. I. Lenin*

*

Capitalism can be utterly vanquished, and will be utterly vanquished by socialism's creating a new and much higher productivity of labour.

*V. I. Lenin*

We are now exercising our main influence on the international revolution through our economic policy. That is why for us questions of economic development become of absolutely exceptional importance.

*V. I. Lenin*

\*

Until the "higher" phase of communism arrives, the Socialists demand the *strictest* control by society *and by the state* over the measure of labour and the measure of consumption.

*V. I. Lenin*

\*

"He who does not work, neither shall he eat"—this is the *practical* commandment of socialism. This is how things should be organised in *practice*.

*V. I. Lenin*

\*

We shall work to inculcate in people's minds, turn into a habit, and bring into the day-by-day life of the masses, the rule: "All for each and each for all"; the rule: "From each according to his ability, to each according to his needs"; we shall work for the gradual, but steady introduction of communist discipline and communist labour.

*V. I. Lenin*

\*

Communism begins when the *rank-and-file workers* display an enthusiastic concern that is undaunted by arduous toil to increase the productivity of labour, husband *every pood of grain, coal, iron,* and other products.

*V. I. Lenin*

\*

We must organise all labour, no matter how toilsome or messy it may be, in such a way that every worker and peasant will be able to say: I am part of the great army of free labour.

*V. I. Lenin*

\*

The communist organisation of social labour, the first step towards which is socialism, rests, and will do so more and more as time goes on, on the free and conscious discipline of the working people themselves.

*V. I. Lenin*

\*

With the development of communism there will be a maximum growth of labour productivity, on the one hand, and all ablebodied members of communist society will be engaged in productive labour, on the other.

*Mikhail Kalinin*

\*

Communism inspires and infects people with great enthusiasm, communism lends inspiration to plain physical labour, giving it a profound ideological content.

*Mikhail Kalinin*

\*

Nowhere else in the world can labour so captivate people as it does here, in our country; nowhere else in the world does labour enjoy the same dignity and respect as it does here, in our country.

*Mikhail Kalinin*

\*

In the Soviet Union urban and rural labour—from the plainest to the most highly skilled—has acquired profound content, is imbued by the great socialist idea, has become that very creative principle which rejuvenates people and instils in them the spirit of communist ethics.

*Mikhail Kalinin*

# LABOUR

Every kind of labour is honoured in our country. There is no such thing here as lowly work and work of a higher kind. The work of the stonemason, carpenter, artist, swineherd, actress, tractor driver, agronomist, salesclerk, physician, and so on—work, whatever it may be, is in our country a matter of honour, glory, valour, and heroism.

*Mikhail Kalinin*

\*

Labour is inscribed on the Red Banner of the Revolution. Labour is sacred, for it gives people life and develops their minds, their will, and their hearts.

*Alexander Blok*

\*

To learn to work well you must be really fond of your work. You will not learn to work unless you like your job.

*Mikhail Kalinin*

\*

Respect for physical work is one of the strongest pillars of the proletarian morality.

*Mikhail Kalinin*

To be fond of working is one of the chief elements of communist ethics.

*Mikhail Kalinin*

\*

Love your work. More, be conscientious in what you do. Remember that if a man subsists and eats and does not work, he simply devours another's labour.

*Mikhail Kalinin*

\*

In our society the right to work is not simply a right to earn your living; it is first and foremost a right to creativity.

*Anton Makarenko*

\*

The obligation to work has already ceased to be a negative side of life. It is no longer a frigid category of human bondage. With us it is first of all *a programme of the individual's growth and development* closely linked with the joyous perspectives of life.

*Anton Makarenko*

## LABOUR

In our society work is not a mere economic concept, but also an ethical concept.

*Anton Makarenko*

\*

He who tries to shirk his work, who looks on calmly as others work and who uses the fruit of their labour is the most immoral of people in Soviet society.

*Anton Makarenko*

\*

*All our big nation wants work
To be a cult, the holiest of holies.
Where work is shirked there orchards wilt,
Where love of labour lacks the world's a desert.*

*Sergei Sergeyev-Tsensky*

\*

Far from extinguishing competition, socialism for the first time creates the opportunity for employing it on a really *wide* and on a really *mass* scale, for actually drawing the majority of working people into a field of labour in which they can display their abilities, develop their capacities, and reveal talents, so abundant among the people whom capitalism crushed, suppressed, and strangled in thousands and millions.

*V. I. Lenin*

## SENSE OF DUTY

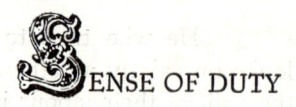

Aspire to fulfilling your duty and you will instantly learn what you are worth.

*Lev Tolstoy*

\*

We attach no practical significance to the finer aspirations of the soul so long as they are mere aspirations; yes, we value facts only and judge the worth of men only by their deeds.

*Nikolai Dobrolyubov*

\*

The old humanism postulated: "I care not for your occupation, the important thing is that you are a human being." The socialist humanism says: "If you have never done anything and are not doing anything now, I refuse to accept you as a human being no matter how clever and kind you may be."

*Alexander Fadeyev*

## LABOUR

A man is judged not by what he says or thinks about himself, but by what he does.

*V. I. Lenin*

\*

Never believe words, whether your own or another's; believe nothing but deeds—your own and another's.

*Lev Tolstoy*

\*

All of us have an anchor that never fails us, unless we break from it ourselves. It is our sense of duty.

*Ivan Turgenev*

\*

Never forget your duty. It is the only music. Without duty there is no life, no passion.

*Alexander Blok*

\*

You cannot fulfil your duty until you grow fond of it.

*Ivan Goncharov*

\*

To suppress your sense of duty and reject your obligations, while claiming all your rights, is rank swinishness.

*Fyodor Dostoyevsky*

An unflinching sense of duty is the badge of character.

*N. V. Shelgunov*

\*

In our society precise performance of obligations is a moral concept.

*Anton Makarenko*

## ACTIVENESS

Life and activity are as close as fire and light.

*Fyodor Glinka*

\*

Not to do is not to live. He who carries not in himself the source of life, the source of living activity, he who relies not on himself, is one who eternally expects things from the outward and accidental.

*Vissarion Belinsky*

\*

Once he begins, the real doer instantly sees so many things to do that he never has

# LABOUR

cause to complain he is not being given a chance to do them. He always finds something to do, and manages to do at least part of it.

*Fyodor Dostoyevsky*

∗

The chief element of reality is labour, and the truest sign of reality is activity.

*Nikolai Chernyshevsky*

∗

Nothing can justify inactivity; it is always possible to do something that is not entirely useless; one must always do everything one can.

*Nikolai Chernyshevsky*

∗

The goodness of a job isn't always in the tools, but certainly always in its maker.

*Maxim Gorky*

∗

A major success consists of a multitude of anticipated and calculated trifles.

*V. O. Kliuchevsky*

A man's activity is futile and wretched unless inspired by a lofty idea.

*Nikolai Chernyshevsky*

\*

No job can be done well if you don't know what you want to achieve.

*Anton Makarenko*

\*

To turn word into deed is much more difficult than deed into word.

*Maxim Gorky*

\*

Much too frequently people reluctant to do what they ought take cover behind high-sounding words.

*N. K. Krupskaya*

\*

Talk and words are necessary, but they are only the beginning; the substance of life is in deeds, in the ability to pass from words to deeds, in matching deeds to words.

*Dmitry Mendeleyev*

## LABOUR

In our society efficiency is becoming a virtue that all citizens must possess; it is becoming the criterion of behaviour in general.

*Anton Makarenko*

✻

The less your inner being is diffused, the more close-knit are your thought, word, and deed.

*Nikolai Pirogov*

✻

Check all your work, so that words should not remain words, but *practical* successes in economic construction.

*V. I. Lenin*

✻

Don't split hairs, don't be pompous in your communism, don't use great words to cover up your slackness, idleness, apathy, and backwardness.

*V. I. Lenin*

✻

Less political ballyhoo. Fewer highbrow discussions. Closer to life. More attention to the way in which the workers and peasants are *actually* building the *new* in their everyday work, and more *verification* so as to ascertain the extent to which the new is *communistic*.

*V. I. Lenin*

## MAN AND ACTION

To live you must at least be able to do something.

*Maxim Gorky*

\*

All his life a person must be doing something—all his life.

*Maxim Gorky*

\*

Do not spare yourself—that is the proudest and most beautiful verity on earth. Long live the man who does not spare himself.

*Maxim Gorky*

\*

The man who does not know what he will do tomorrow is a sorry sight.

*Maxim Gorky*

# LABOUR

*If you lack the knack for action
Wasted is your sound perception.*

                *Shot'ha Rust'hveli*

\*

It is never too early to ask yourself: is what I am doing worthwhile or not?

                *Anton Chekhov*

\*

Never undertake anything you are unable to accomplish. You'll bungle the task.

                *Nikolai Chernyshevsky*

\*

*Tackle but that for which you are suited
If success is to crown your endeavour.*

                *Ivan Krylov*

\*

*'Tis best you turn away a job
In which you know yourself unpractised.*

                *Nasir Khosrow*

\*

Work is a tough and headstrong beast; control it skilfully and pull the bridle tight or it will get the better of you.

                *Maxim Gorky*

If you do anything, do it well. If you cannot or do not want to do it well, don't do it at all.

*Lev Tolstoy*

\*

To be done well a job must be congenial.

*Maxim Gorky*

\*

No job will prosper in the absence of ardour and zeal.

*Ivan Pavlov*

\*

Any job is hard if you don't like it and easy if you know it is useful and necessary.

*G. V. Plekhanov*

\*

If the good you do is difficult, the difficult will pass and the good will remain; if the bad you do is pleasant, the pleasure will pass and the bad will remain.

*Mikhail Lomonosov*

\*

Deeds are governed by their aims; that deed is great which has a great aim.

*Anton Chekhov*

# LABOUR

Show no haste when you tackle a difficult task. Give yourself the time you need to summon your powers; avoid bustle.

*Ivan Pavlov*

\*

Bridle your zeal if it is out of place.

*Aboul Kasim Firdousi*

\*

In every undertaking the most important is to overcome the moment of reluctance to begin.

*Ivan Pavlov*

\*

To do what you want is not happiness. Happiness is to want what you do.

*Lev Tolstoy*

\*

Everything great is done without fanfare, in modesty, and simplicity: you cannot plough or build or graze cattle, or even think, in ostentation and lustre. The truly great is always simple and modest.

*Lev Tolstoy*

\*

In an instant of indecision hasten to act, do something, take the first step, however superfluous it may be.

*Lev Tolstoy*

*None but the fool will put his deeds off till tomorrow,
For what the morrow holds we cannot know today.*

*Aboul Kasim Firdousi*

\*

Tireless labour surmounts all obstacles.

*Mikhail Lomonosov*

\*

Perseverance is the earnest of success.

*I. I. Dmitriev*

\*

He who falters over the small is also incapable of the big.

*Mikhail Lomonosov*

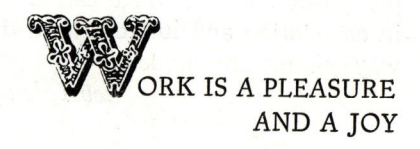

## WORK IS A PLEASURE AND A JOY

Work turns the day into a celebration.

*Janis Rainis*

# LABOUR

Nothing but work gives happiness to man and to his soul clarity, harmony, and satisfaction.

*Vissarion Belinsky*

\*

Work is the source of all joy, of all that is best in the world.

*Maxim Gorky*

\*

The intrinsic, spiritual, and vital power of work is the only source of human dignity, and of morality and happiness.

*Konstantin Ushinsky*

\*

Nothing but work, hard and cheerful work, yields soundness of spirit.

*Alexander Herzen*

\*

If a man does not put his heart into his work, that is, if he does not earn his bread in the sweat of his brow, then he cannot be happy.

*Dmitry Pisarev*

One of the most curious mistakes is to think that man derives happiness from being idle.

*Lev Tolstoy*

\*

Work is the incontestable condition for happiness—first, the work that one likes best and that is free, and, second, physical work that whets the appetite and that induces sound and refreshing sleep.

*Lev Tolstoy*

\*

Work, work! How happy I am when I work!

*Lev Tolstoy*

\*

In certain conditions physical effort is "muscular joy".

*Ivan Pavlov*

\*

Work alone is the warrant for the pleasures of living.

*Nikolai Dobrolyubov*

\*

Happiness is in the goodness of your work.

*Janis Rainis*

## LABOUR

*Work is the joy of living,*
*In the field, at the bench, at the desk.*
*Work in the sweat of your body,*
*Work in oblivion of time.*
*The joy of the world is in working.*

                *Valery Briusov*

\*

Should your choice of occupation be a happy one, and should you put your heart into your work, happiness will need no guide to find you.

                *Konstantin Ushinsky*

\*

It is an extraordinary joy to be wedded to the work you like best.

                *Vladimir Nemirovich-Danchenko*

\*

In communist society there will be no punishment more insufferable, inflicted for the basest offences, than excommunication from work.

                *Leonid Leonov*

## WORK LENGTHENS YOUTH

The most beautiful and the dearest for a man is his life. And his life is sustained by varied and tireless work. No sooner a man's work lapses than his life, too, begins to lapse.

*G. M. Krzhizhanovsky*

\*

The industrious soul must always be plying its trade; practice is as vital for it as exercise is for the body.

*A. V. Suvorov*

\*

The prime principle of a sensible life is work. The whole body must work.

*A. A. Bogomolets*

\*

All my life I have loved mental as well as physical effort, the latter probably a bit more, for physical effort is the best medicine for a disorder of the higher nervous activity.

*Ivan Pavlov*

\*

He who works is always young. In fact, it sometimes seems to me that work generates hormones that heighten the vital impulse.

*N. N. Burdenko*

\*

In work is the secret of longevity.

*Sergei Sergeyev-Tsensky*

\*

Nothing is more disabling and unbearable than inactivity.

*Alexander Herzen*

\*

Forces not refreshed by practice become blunted.

*Dmitry Pisarev*

\*

Idleness and inactivity father ignorance and are also the cause of disease.

*Avicenna*

\*

Work is the noblest healer of all ills.

*Nikolai Ostrovsky*

\*

Where work turns into creation fear of death vanishes even physiologically.

*A. N. Tolstoy*

## OF WAR AND PEACE

### THE PEOPLES WANT PEACE

The question of peace is a burning question, the painful question of the day.

*V. I. Lenin*

\*

Peace is the prime condition for the development of culture.

*A. N. Tolstoy*

\*

Every unjust war is pillage.

*N. P. Ogarev*

\*

Wars are in general cruel, exacting, and merciless.

*Mikhail Kalinin*

\*

The moral harm inflicted by wars is incalculable.

*Lev Tolstoy*

## WAR AND PEACE

We know, we know only too well, the incredible misfortunes that war brings to the workers and peasants.

*V. I. Lenin*

\*

We promise the workers and peasants to do all we can for peace.

*V. I. Lenin*

\*

What we prize most is peace.

*V. I. Lenin*

\*

Socialists have always condemned wars between nations as barbarous and brutal.

*V. I. Lenin*

\*

An end to wars, peace among the nations, the cessation of pillaging and violence—such is our ideal.

*V. I. Lenin*

\*

Disarmament is the ideal of socialism.

*V. I. Lenin*

All our politics and propaganda... are directed towards putting an end to war and in no way towards driving nations to war.

*V. I. Lenin*

※

We have all the requisites—an honest policy of peace, military power, and the unity of the Soviet people—to keep our borders inviolable in every possible contingency, and to protect the gains of socialism.

*L. I. Brezhnev*

※

As before, we have consistently upheld Lenin's principle of the peaceful coexistence of states irrespective of their social system. These days, the coexistence principle has become a real mover of international progress.

*L. I. Brezhnev*

※

Outside of socialism there is *no* deliverance of humanity from wars, from hunger, from the destruction of still more millions and millions of human beings.

*V. I. Lenin*

※

The workers' movement will triumph and will pave the way to peace and socialism.

*V. I. Lenin*

## WAR AND PEACE

Communism puts an end to predatory motivations in the movement of nation states.

*M. M. Prishvin*

\*

I refuse to believe that humanity will not finally understand the senselessness and cruelty of war.

*Alexander Pushkin*

\*

Two hundred or three hundred years hence life on earth will be unimaginably beautiful and astonishing. That is the life man wants, and since it has not yet come he must anticipate it, wait, dream, and prepare for it.

*Anton Chekhov*

\*

Humanity is on the road to the highest truth, the highest happiness possible on earth.

*Anton Chekhov*

\*

We have won conditions in which we can exist alongside the capitalist powers.

*V. I. Lenin*

Forever prevail in our republic—Work, Peace, May!

*Vladimir Mayakovsky*

\*

The flag of peace has been hoisted over our country—a magnificent flag, the hope of all mankind.

*Nikolai Ostrovsky*

\*

Our peace policy is approved by the vast majority of people all over the world.

*V. I. Lenin*

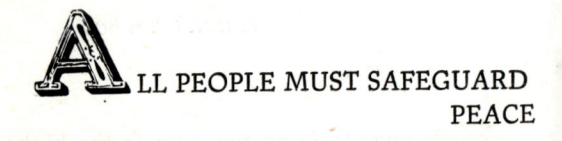

# ALL PEOPLE MUST SAFEGUARD PEACE

Every effort must be made to establish peace and affection among people of different nationalities.

*Hassan-bek Zardabi*

\*

Mankind must not let clouds of destructive radioactive dust envelop the Sun and make the air deadly. We are born to live and we shall live!

*Mikhail Sholokhov*

✻

Peace shall not be stolen from those whose hands carried arms, whose inflamed lips dried the tears on the cheeks of orphaned children, and whose eyes saw and forever imprinted on their memories the horrors of the past war.

*Mikhail Sholokhov*

✻

Humankind must not let itself be deceived. While facing the future, we must not forget the bloody lessons of the past.

*Mikhail Sholokhov*

✻

Let us see to it that our children should breathe air uncontaminated either by atomic radiation or the vile self-interest of predators.

*Leonid Leonov*

✻

If you don't want to become a soldier or victim of a new war, be a faithful soldier of peace.

*Leonid Leonov*

In substance, war is a beastly way of settling vital difficulties, a method unworthy of human reason and its immeasurable resources.

*Ivan Pavlov*

\*

The war which the imperialists are lusting to unleash would be equally perilous for all nations. This is why they are rising as one man against the warmongers and for the cause of peace and international co-operation.

*Nikolai Tikhonov*

\*

The peace movement will not be killed. It lives as naturally as the Sun, rising each day over the world.

*Nikolai Tikhonov*

\*

The one guarantee of peace is the organised, conscious movement of the working class.

*V. I. Lenin*

\*

We fully anticipate a peaceful attitude not only on the part of the workers and peasants ... but also on the part of a huge section of reasonable bourgeoisie and the governments.

*V. I. Lenin*

# THE CAUSES AND NATURE OF MODERN WARS

All wars are inseparable from the political systems that engender them.

*V. I. Lenin*

*

It is fundamentally wrong, un-Marxist, and unscientific to separate "foreign policy" from policy in general, let alone counterpose foreign policy to home policy.

*V. I. Lenin*

*

Wars and all their calamities are produced by capitalism, which keeps millions of working people in bondage, sharpens the struggle between nations, and turns the slaves of capital into cannon fodder.

*V. I. Lenin*

*

War is no chance happening ... but an inevitable stage of capitalism, just as legitimate a form of the capitalist way of life as peace is.

*V. I. Lenin*

Wars are rooted in the very essence of capitalism; they will end only when the capitalist system ceases to exist.

*V. I. Lenin*

\*

A favourable soil for wars are nationalist prejudices, which are systematically cultivated in the civilised countries in the interests of the ruling classes, with the object of diverting the proletarian masses from their own class objectives and making them forget the duty of international class solidarity.

*V. I. Lenin*

\*

For the capitalists war is pure gain; they sell arms and profit colossally by the blood spilt by the workers.

*Maxim Gorky*

\*

When their class profits are at stake, the bourgeoisie will sell their country and strike a bargain with any foreigner against their own people.

*V. I. Lenin*

\*

The proletariat struggles against war and will always struggle against it unremittingly.

*V. I. Lenin*

## WAR AND PEACE

There are wars and wars. There are adventurist wars, fought to further dynastic interests, to satisfy the appetite of a band of freebooters, or to attain the goals of the knights of capitalist profit. And there is another kind of war—the only war that is *legitimate* in capitalist society—war against the people's oppressors and enslavers. Only utopians and philistines can condemn such a war on principle.

*V. I. Lenin*

\*

We regard civil wars, i.e., wars waged by an oppressed class against the oppressor class, as legitimate, progressive, and necessary.

*V. I. Lenin*

\*

Only stern battles, namely civil wars, can free humanity from the yoke of capital.

*V. I. Lenin*

\*

The social revolution can come only in the form of an epoch in which are combined struggle by the proletariat against the bourgeoisie in the advanced countries and a *whole series* of democratic and revolutionary movements, including national liberation movements, in the undeveloped, backward, and oppressed nations.

*V. I. Lenin*

\*

Revolution is war. Of all the wars known in history it is the only lawful, rightful, just, and truly great war.

*V. I. Lenin*

# OF HEROISM, COURAGE, AND BRAVERY

We won because the best people from the entire working class and from the entire peasantry displayed unparalleled heroism... performed miracles of valour, withstood untold privations, made great sacrifices, and got rid of scroungers and cowards.

*V. I. Lenin*

\*

Our victories were due to our ability to arouse the energy, heroism, and enthusiasm of the masses and to concentrate every ounce of revolutionary effort on the most important task of the hour.

*V. I. Lenin*

\*

Our Motherland is a cradle of heroes, a crucible where the souls of men are made as hard as diamonds and steel.

*A. N. Tolstoy*

The hero is the living embodiment of everything that is best in man, and the very best is to work for the might, prosperity, and wellbeing of country and nation.

*A. N. Tolstoy*

\*

A hero is he who creates life in the teeth of death, he who conquers death.

*Maxim Gorky*

\*

Valour is the virtue of those aspiring to a lofty aim.

*Aboul Kasim Firdousi*

\*

He who strives for a great aim must give up all thoughts of himself.

*Ivan Turgenev*

\*

It is not reckless, the thirst for an exploit. In it throbs the human heart and the questing and never resting human reason.

*M. E. Saltykov-Shchedrin*

\*

Bravery is one of the finest qualities of the human soul, less which noble deed,

## HEROISM, COURAGE, AND BRAVERY

sense of decency, and independence of character are impossible.

*Konstantin Ushinsky*

\*

So long as man lives he fights and never admits defeat. Hence, clever and energetic people fight to the end, while empty and worthless people submit without a fight to the trivialities of their senseless existence.

*Dmitry Pisarev*

\*

Natural daring is that rock of precious marble out of which fear sculpts the majestic statue of courage.

*Konstantin Ushinsky*

\*

We are all born heroes and live as heroes. Once the majority understands this, all life will be heroic.

*Maxim Gorky*

\*

We hail courage delightedly, we take pride in the brave, we respect the honest and loathe liars, we admire heroes and despise cowards.

*Nikolai Ostrovsky*

Bravery is nothing if not a sense of confidence.

*Konstantin Ushinsky*

\*

True courage is sparing of words: it needs so little to show itself that it considers heroism a duty not an exploit.

*A. A. Bestuzhev-Marlinsky*

\*

For the individual who has self-respect death is far easier than humiliation.

*Nikolai Chernyshevsky*

\*

It is better to die in glory than to live in shame!

*Shot'ha Rust'hveli*

\*

Death in honesty is better than life in shame.

*Dmitry Donskoi*

\*

Dare and dare again to glorify your land by courage.

*Mikhail Lomonosov*

## HEROISM, COURAGE, AND BRAVERY

Courage is bred day after day in dogged resistance to difficulties.

*Nikolai Ostrovsky*

\*

In a struggle the victory is his who is strong in spirit.

*K. N. Bestuzhev-Riumin*

\*

To look death in the eye, to anticipate its coming and not to seek escape in self-deception, to be true to yourself to the last breath, not to weaken and not to betray fear—this is the hallmark of character.

*Dmitry Pisarev*

\*

You are better advised to meet danger face on than to sit and wait for it.

*A. V. Suvorov*

\*

Life will take you by the throat and crush the breath out of you if you face it in mystical terror and servility; look it in the eye.

*Vissarion Belinsky*

The man of resolve leans on his courage as on a rock of granite.

*N. V. Shelgunov*

\*

He who is brave stays alive, he who is daring stays unharmed.

*A. V. Suvorov*

\*

Like the bullet, life spares the brave and slays the coward.

*Vissarion Belinsky*

\*

*He whom the hammer-blows of fate*
*Make cry for mercy is a wretch.*

*N. P. Ogarev*

\*

It is cowards who speak most of bravery and rogues who speak most of honour.

*A. N. Tolstoy*

\*

Precise performance of one's duties in all circumstances is also heroic.

*Mikhail Kalinin*

Courage usually goes with softness of character; the man of courage is more likely than others to be magnanimous.

*N. V. Shelgunov*

※

Please, do not believe him who says that he was unafraid and that the whistling of bullets was for him the sweetest music. He is either demented or a braggart. All people are afraid to die. But some wilt from fear, while others keep themselves in hand.

*Alexander Kuprin*

※

He is brave who can suppress his fear. There is no other kind of bravery. Do you think marching into a hail of bullets and shells means to feel nothing, to fear nothing? No, it means just that–to feel and to fear–but also to suppress your fear.

*Anton Makarenko*

※

Not he is brave who courts danger without a sense of fear, but he who can suppress the strongest fear and think of danger without submitting to fear.

*Konstantin Ushinsky*

The difference between the brave and the coward is that the former knows danger without sensing fear, while the latter senses fear without knowing danger.

*V. O. Kliuchevsky*

\*

Bravery is fathered by a fully apprehended responsibility.

*P. A. Pavlenko*

\*

He who risks his life out of vanity, curiosity, or greed should not be considered brave.

*Lev Tolstoy*

\*

Mad courage and mad cowardice are equally fatal.

*Konstantin Ushinsky*

\*

Every man's life belongs to his country, but only true courage, not reckless daring, benefits the Fatherland.

*P. S. Nakhimov*

## HEROISM, COURAGE, AND BRAVERY

For courage you need willpower, fortitude, and the ability to subdue your weaknesses; it takes no brains to cut a caper.

*N. K. Krupskaya*

*He who attacks a ferocious lion
No hero is he, but a madman.
Valour steeped in discretion is the warrior's virtue.*

*Aboul Kasim Firdousi*

Insensate valour, they say, is nothing.

*Denis Davydov*

All virtue and strength is calm—precisely because it is confident.

*Vissarion Belinsky*

Strength alone is nothing; it must have deeds to show itself.

*Vissarion Belinsky*

The essence that determines an individual's behaviour must be in him, in his intellect; should this essence be outside of him, then he is a slave despite all his bravery.

*Alexander Herzen*

*

Fear is, probably, the most agonising of all the psychic sensations to which human nature is susceptible.

*Dmitry Pisarev*

*

Fear is the most depressing of human feelings.

*Konstantin Ushinsky*

*

Fear is the most fecund source of vice.

*Konstantin Ushinsky*

*

A coward is the next thing to a traitor today and certainly a turncoat in battle.

*Nikolai Ostrovsky*

*

In a man all deeds must be imbued with courage.

*Alexander Kazbegi*

## HEROISM, COURAGE, AND BRAVERY

A man of effeminate character is the most noxious parody of a human being.

*Vissarion Belinsky*

✳

Show more courage. For the coward things are hard and fearful, while for the brave the hard, too, looks easy.

*Fyodor Gladkov*

## OF CONVICTIONS, CRITICISM, AND MISTAKES

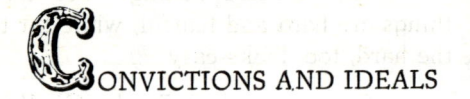

### Convictions and Ideals

An ideologically oriented purposeful life saturated with the public interest is the best and the most interesting life on earth.

*Mikhail Kalinin*

\*

He who has no ideals is a sorry sight.

*Ivan Turgenev*

\*

Every individual must have something he can love, something he can believe in, something that gives meaning to his life.

*Leonid Andreyev*

\*

Man needs an ideal, but it must be a human ideal corresponding to nature and not a supernatural ideal.

*V. I. Lenin*

An ideal is like a guiding star. In its absence there can be no set course, and in the absence of a set course there can be no life worth living.

*Lev Tolstoy*

※

Lacking an ideal, that is, without some even vague aspiration to something better, there will never be a better world.

*Fyodor Dostoyevsky*

※

When Nature deprived man of the ability to perambulate on all fours, it gave him a staff to lean on—the ideal. And he has unconsciously striven for a better world ever since.

*Maxim Gorky*

※

Life seeks perfection, spurred by the ideal, by that which is still non-existent but already conceived by the mind and pictured as attainable.

*Maxim Gorky*

※

Love of the ideal is an active feeling ardently inclining towards sacrifice.

*Maxim Gorky*

The moment an ideal loftier than the previous one is put before humankind, all previous ideals lose their lustre like stars beside the Sun, and people can no more fail to accept that loftier ideal than they can fail to see the Sun.

*Lev Tolstoy*

٭

A man's work is petty if not inspired by an idea.

*Nikolai Chernyshevsky*

٭

Humankind cannot survive without generous ideas.

*Fyodor Dostoyevsky*

٭

What would all the aspirations and all the labours of humankind be without love?

*Mikhail Lermontov*

٭

He who has an ideal and is alive cannot be useless, unless he disavows his ideal.

*Felix Dzerzhinsky*

٭

Clear and conscious convictions develop in a person either under the influence of society or with the help of literature.

*Nikolai Chernyshevsky*

## CONVICTIONS AND CRITICISM

An individual must have strong convictions. All people promote their convictions save those who have none; to have none you must be either dense or unscrupulous.

*Nikolai Chernyshevsky*

\*

Honesty is not enough to be right and useful; you also need consistency of thought.

*Nikolai Chernyshevsky*

\*

Have the courage to voice your convictions.

*Ivan Sechenov*

\*

A conviction must be cherished for its verity, not for being yours.

*Vissarion Belinsky*

\*

If you deny that people can have sincere, deep-seated, and selfless convictions, I shall have every reason to conclude that you have no convictions yourself.

*Nikolai Dobrolyubov*

Convictions are no convictions unless they are translated into deeds.

*Vassily Sukhomlinsky*

\*

By their very nature convictions cannot be an inactive spiritual value.

*Vassily Sukhomlinsky*

\*

Ideas become a power when they grip the people.

*V. I. Lenin*

\*

Many people, weak of nature, become altogether vile because they lack the ability to be themselves and to dissociate from a general chorus singing an alien tune.

*Dmitry Pisarev*

\*

A man without convictions is empty, and without principles he is a contemptible wretch.

*Ilya Repin*

\*

Frequently people's convictions are no more than skindeep–the skin of their tongues.

*V. I. Lenin*

He who does not stand up for his opinions is a traitor to his conscience.

*Vissarion Belinsky*

\*

Someone who changes his views to please another is for us a worthless creature without convictions of his own.

*Nikolai Dobrolyubov*

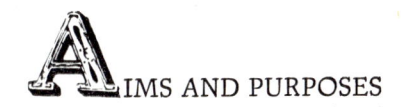

# AIMS AND PURPOSES

*One's purpose* in life is the pivot of one's human dignity and happiness.

*Konstantin Ushinsky*

\*

Though you satisfy a man's every wish, he will be unhappy and wretched if you deny him his aim in life.

*Konstantin Ushinsky*

\*

To lessen the mass of human suffering and to increase the mass of human joys—

it is towards this aim that all clever and honest people have gravitated consciously or unconsciously, directly or indirectly.

*Dmitry Pisarev*

※

When his life's struggle turns into a conscious striving for a definite goal, the individual can consider himself happy.

*Dmitry Pisarev*

※

The sense of life is in beauty and in the drive for an aim; it is necessary, therefore, that every moment should have its lofty aim.

*Maxim Gorky*

※

Man must set himself lofty aims.

*Maxim Gorky*

※

The purpose of life is in the drive forward.

*Maxim Gorky*

※

As I see it, only he can be happy who sets himself big goals and fights for them might and main.

*Mikhail Kalinin*

Valour is the possession of those striving for lofty aims.

*Aboul Kasim Firdousi*

٭

The measure of men are the aims they set themselves.

*N. N. Miklukho-Maklai*

٭

It is bad if a man hasn't something for which he is ready to die.

*Lev Tolstoy*

٭

People have long since likened the world to a stormy ocean, but that is nothing for someone who sails it with a compass.

*Nikolai Karamzin*

٭

You must set yourself a goal in life. But, certainly, have the good sense to set one that you can achieve.

*Nikolai Ostrovsky*

٭

The worst among men is he who has no aspirations.

*Abai Kunanbayev*

Without interest there is no aim, without aim there is no activity, and without activity there is no life. Interest, aim, and activity have their source in the life of society.

*Vissarion Belinsky*

\*

Set yourself positive aims. We must fight not only *against* something, but also and mainly *for* something.

*E. I. Martsinovsky*

\*

If an aspiration originates from a pure source, it will do lots of good even if it does not entirely succeed and falls short of the goal.

*Ivan Turgenev*

\*

To differentiate strictly between stages that are essentially different, to examine soberly the conditions in which they occur does not mean postponing one's ultimate aim indefinitely, or deliberately slowing down one's progress.

*V. I. Lenin*

\*

He who sets himself a great aim must abandon all thoughts of himself.

*Ivan Turgenev*

If a road leads to the goal, its length is immaterial.

*E. I. Martsinovsky*

\*

In evil surroundings a great idea is warped and can result only in absurdity.

*V. O. Kliuchevsky*

\*

Aimless is not just that which is short of the aim, but also that which overreaches the aim.

*V. O. Kliuchevsky*

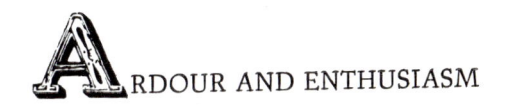

# ARDOUR AND ENTHUSIASM

To instil communist ideas you must have ardour.

*Mikhail Kalinin*

\*

No great advance in history has ever been achieved without ardour, which multiplies the moral strength and sharpens the mental faculties and is, therefore, a great progressive force in its own right.

*G. V. Plekhanov*

\*

Energy is the power of love for the set goal.

*P. A. Pavlenko*

\*

It is from buoyant and fiery ardour, from ardent love of one's country, from courage and energy that victory is born. And this not only through a separate action, but also, and more, through a dogged rallying of all forces, through a constant dedication which moves mountains slowly but surely, and thrusts into unexplored chasms, opening them to the brilliant radiance of the Sun.

*Mikhail Lomonosov*

\*

Passion becomes a vice when it turns into a habit or a virtue when it resists habit.

*V. O. Kliuchevsky*

\*

Ardour is the poetry and flower of life, but what good is ardour if the heart lacks will?

*Vissarion Belinsky*

Beneath blazing passion we often find nothing but a weak will.

*V. O. Kliuchevsky*

# INDIFFERENCE

Nothing is more dangerous than a man for whom the human is foreign, who cares not for the fate of his country or the lot of other people.

*M. E. Saltykov-Shchedrin*

※

If one honest face is slapped, all honest faces must feel the sting, the outrage, and the agony of mortified human dignity.

*Leonid Andreyev*

※

Indifference is a paralysis of the soul, a premature death.

*Anton Chekhov*

Beware of indifference, for it is deadly for the soul.

*Maxim Gorky*

\*

Indifference is tacit support of the strong, of those who rule.

*V. I. Lenin*

\*

Life is so devilishly artful that lacking the ability of hating neither can one love.

*Maxim Gorky*

\*

Indulging evil borders closely on indifference to goodness.

*Nikolai Leskov*

# CRITICISM

Criticism is a revolutionary's duty.

*V. I. Lenin*

# CONVICTIONS AND CRITICISM

Working in a collective means taking criticism in the right spirit and not hesitating to criticise the mistakes of others.

*N. D. Zelinsky*

\*

Criticism to the face must cut down all evil. And that is the best of proofs of our purity and strength.

*Vladimir Mayakovsky*

\*

The Party of the revolutionary proletariat is strong enough to openly criticise itself, and unequivocally call mistakes and weaknesses by their right names.

*V. I. Lenin*

\*

Self-criticism is vitally essential to every live and vigorous party. Nothing is more disgusting than smug optimism.

*V. I. Lenin*

\*

Do not cover up existing evil ... but draw the Party's attention to it, and call on all Party members to work on remedying the evil.

*V. I. Lenin*

To treat a disease you must first diagnose it and bring it into the open; that is the most radical and the most effective approach.

*Felix Dzerzhinsky*

\*

To find the cause of an evil is nearly as good as finding its antidote.

*Vissarion Belinsky*

\*

I can condone tolerance of a misconception, at least in others if not in myself, but I shall never absolve tolerance of baseness.

*Vissarion Belinsky*

\*

If everything were kept quiet and proper, with polite compliments and nods, there would be boundless scope for dishonesty, deceit, and ignorance: there would be no one to accuse and no one to speak the warning word of truth.

*Vissarion Belinsky*

\*

Criticism is like sound blood circulation. In its absence there is inevitable turgidness and morbidity.

*Nikolai Ostrovsky*

## CONVICTIONS AND CRITICISM

Criticism is a dangerous enemy of error and of hollow though revolutionary exhortations; it is the most dependable pillar of the truth. It is its mother and its midwife, its friend and guardian. The truth thrives on criticism.

*G. V. Plekhanov*

\*

Even genius needs criticism, for criticism reveals its accomplishments and shortcomings.

*N. A. Bestuzhev*

\*

We must not delude ourselves with lies. That is harmful.

*V. I. Lenin*

\*

We must courageously look the bitter, unadorned truth straight in the face.

*V. I. Lenin*

\*

We must learn to admit an evil fearlessly in order to combat it the more firmly.

*V. I. Lenin*

Only the putrid fears the touch of criticism, for it is like an Egyptian mummy that crumbles unto dust from a movement of air.

*Dmitry Pisarev*

\*

If we are not afraid to speak the sad and bitter truth straight out, we shall learn, we shall unfailingly and certainly learn to overcome all our difficulties.

*V. I. Lenin*

\*

Criticism of faults is governed by construction. What we need is to climb more steeply, and we criticise because our construction is being retarded by all kinds of negative things.

*Mikhail Kalinin*

\*

Publicity is a sword that itself heals the wounds it makes.

*V. I. Lenin*

\*

Evil must be combatted. Evil is intolerable. To be reconciled to evil is immoral.

*Vassily Sukhomlinsky*

## CONVICTIONS AND CRITICISM

Man feels better when you show him what he is really like.

*Anton Chekhov*

\*

The truth is above pity.
*Maxim Gorky*

\*

Criticism of faults, as you know, is absolutely free and vitally necessary in our country. Certainly, it must be based on fact.

*Mikhail Kalinin*

\*

Not all people are able to speak the truth.

*Maxim Gorky*

\*

To have the right of criticising you must believe in some truth.

*Maxim Gorky*

\*

Only he who loves may censure or scold.

*Ivan Turgenev*

To spot a flaw in something does not go to say that this something is wrong.

*Vissarion Belinsky*

※

Unless there is a particular reason for it, it is wrong to recall mistakes which have been completely set right.

*V. I. Lenin*

※

An inapposite truth is worse than a lie, and an inapposite question can only confuse and hinder.

*Ivan Turgenev*

※

To learn to speak the truth to others you must first learn to speak the truth to yourself.

*Lev Tolstoy*

※

Show the misconceptions of the human mind with noble ardour, but without anger.

*Nikolai Karamzin*

※

Criticism is worthless unless it shows how to remedy the wickedness that it reproves.

*Lev Tolstoy*

It is of little avail to notice mistakes; a man of worth should offer something better instead.

*Mikhail Lomonosov*

※

To say "this isn't right" is not enough; you must add, "here is how".

*Maxim Gorky*

※

A mind that is all negation grows barren and dries up.

*Ivan Turgenev*

※

The fortitude of years and years of daily work is, probably, the most remarkable kind of fortitude. It does not take much intelligence howl about faults. Demagogy and word-slinging are contemptible. It is better *to do* than to talk.

*Vassily Sukhomlinsky*

※

He who speaks harshly of another's deeds commits himself to doing better.

*Vissarion Belinsky*

Be hard on yourself if you don't want others to be hard on you.

*Leonid Leonov*

\*

Learn young to forgive the faults of others, but never forgive your own.

*A. V. Suvorov*

\*

For some people every word of truth sounds harsh even though it is moderate.

*Nikolai Chernyshevsky*

\*

To demand the truth while disregarding the conditions that breed untruth is like demanding that there should be no mud in an unpaved street during a downpour.

*Dmitry Pisarev*

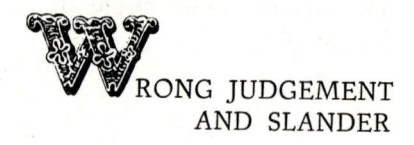

# WRONG JUDGEMENT AND SLANDER

Criticism would, of course, be a terrible weapon if, fortunately, it were not itself subject to criticism.

*Vissarion Belinsky*

## CONVICTIONS AND CRITICISM

Slander is not always an act of spite: more often it results from the innocent desire to indulge in chatter, and sometimes from well-intentioned compassion as sincere as it is awkward.

*Vissarion Belinsky*

\*

To portray nothing but the shady side of life is not slander but one-sidedness; to slander is to lay blame on what exists for faults that do not exist.

*Vissarion Belinsky*

\*

Clumsy bunglers are usually the most demanding critics: not knowing how and what to do, incapable of the simplest that is possible, they expect the impossible of others.

*V. O. Kliuchevsky*

\*

He who has much knowledge knows how cautious one must be to avoid error in expressing judgement. It is the superficial dabbler who judges all things with extraordinary audacity.

*Lev Tolstoy*

\*

*Slander is for the ear what wormwood is for the tongue.*

*Shot'ha Rust'hveli*

Slander is as dangerous a weapon as firearms.

*Anton Rubinstein*

\*

Even though it is unproven, calumny leaves all but everlasting traces.

*Alexander Pushkin*

\*

Lies and slander are the legitimised arm of the philistine. Hardly any great men in the world have escaped being spattered with mud.

*Maxim Gorky*

\*

Philistinism is like a creeping vine; it can multiply to infinity and wants its tentacles to strangle everything it meets on its way.

*Maxim Gorky*

\*

Philistinism is a great evil; like a river dam it serves no other purpose but stagnation.

*Anton Chekhov*

## THE ATTITUDE TO ERRORS

He errs not who acts not, though, to be sure, precisely this is his monumental error.

*A. N. Tolstoy*

\*

There are those whose only merit is that they do nothing.

*V. O. Kliuchevsky*

\*

Have no fear of mistakes, they are unavoidable.

*Maxim Gorky*

\*

Mistakes educate the mind.

*Lev Tolstoy*

\*

Mistakes are lessons. They teach us. They are the road to the truth. It is wrong to fear mistakes. We must learn to draw lessons from them.

*M. N. Strepetova*

By analysing the errors of yesterday, we learn to avoid errors today and tomorrow.

*V. I. Lenin*

\*

Man may err. An error is not a lie. Even several mistakes cannot make a good cause collapse. At least the idea on which everything is built will survive unblemished. Your first try may fail, your second will succeed.

*Fyodor Dostoyevsky*

\*

If we are not afraid of admitting our mistakes, not afraid of making repeated efforts to rectify them, we shall reach the very summit.

*V. I. Lenin*

\*

It is not a matter of never making a mistake, but of admitting mistakes and following your conscience with courage and generosity.

*Vissarion Belinsky*

\*

The stronger is the individual and the higher is his ethics, the more bravely does he see his own faults and weaknesses.

*Vissarion Belinsky*

## CONVICTIONS AND CRITICISM

A man has trust in himself only if he hides nothing from himself.

*P. A. Pavlenko*

\*

None but the strong admits his faults. None but the strong is modest. None but the strong is forgiving. And none but the strong can laugh, though often his laughter is tinged with tears.

*Alexander Herzen*

\*

Those reluctant to admit their faults will in due course, shamelessly, vindicate their ignorance, and ignorance is the greatest evil.

*G. S. Skovoroda*

\*

In learning you must repeat your lessons to remember them; in ethics you must remember your mistakes not to repeat them.

*V. O. Kliuchevsky*

\*

It is much better to admit a mistake than to let it become irremediable.

*Lev Tolstoy*

## WORDS OF THE WISE

A minor error can always assume monstrous proportions if it is persisted in, if profound justifications are sought for it, and if it is carried to its logical conclusion.

*V. I. Lenin*

\*

A lie to others will only confuse matters and delay a solution; a lie to yourself disguised as the truth will destroy your life.

*Lev Tolstoy*

\*

Do not hesitate to laugh at yourself. Self-criticism is as vital as washing.

*Maxim Gorky*

\*

Honest self-criticism is the voice of the conscience.

*Vassily Sukhomlinsky*

## OF KNOWLEDGE, UPBRINGING, AND EDUCATION

### KNOWLEDGE

The working people are thirsting for knowledge because they need it to win.

*V. I. Lenin*

\*

Without knowledge the workers are defenceless, with knowledge they are a force!

*V. I. Lenin*

\*

It takes knowledge to participate in the revolution with intelligence, purpose, and success.

*V. I. Lenin*

\*

Socialism is a society of science and culture. To be a worthy member of socialist society you must learn hard and well, and amass a store of knowledge.

*Mikhail Kalinin*

For a nation that has won its freedom nothing but the torch of knowledge will light the way to a happy future.

*L. I. Brezhnev*

Succeeding their fathers and mothers and helping their elder brothers and sisters in their great undertakings, the young must cram themselves with knowledge.

*Maxim Gorky*

To live well you must work well, and to have a firm footing you must accumulate knowledge.

*Maxim Gorky*

Nothing is more powerful than knowledge: a knowledgeable man is unconquerable.

*Maxim Gorky*

# KNOWLEDGE AND UPBRINGING

The more one knows, the stronger one is.

*Maxim Gorky*

\*

And if it is true, as is often said, that no man can live without faith, then there should be no other faith than faith in the omnipotence of knowledge.

*Ilya Mechnikov*

\*

Knowledge and nothing but knowledge makes man free and great.

*Dmitry Pisarev*

\*

Our task is to learn and learn, to try and accumulate as much knowledge as possible, because the serious social currents are those that thrive on knowledge and because the future happiness of humankind grows from knowledge.

*Anton Chekhov*

\*

We need clever and educated people; as humanity draws closer to a happy life their numbers will grow, until one day they will be the majority.

*Anton Chekhov*

The goal is for everybody to see and know more than was seen and known by their fathers and forebears.

*Anton Chekhov*

\*

Be a man when learning, young fellow! Your virtue is in learning to the best of your ability. Your masculine dignity requires you not to be a parasite or sponger. Have contempt for mental sloth.

*Vassily Sukhomlinsky*

\*

Knowledge is your armour against adversity.

*Rudaki*

\*

Knowledge is strength. No petrified prejudice can resist it any more than the inertia of surrounding Nature.

*Alexander Herzen*

\*

The knowledge produced by the labour of men and amassed by science keeps accumulating and growing deeper, broader, and sharper; it is the foundation for the endless development of our cognitive faculties and creative energies.

*Maxim Gorky*

## KNOWLEDGE AND UPBRINGING

Proving the need for learning is like explaining the usefulness of eyesight.

*Maxim Gorky*

\*

Knowledge is the absolute value of our world. We must learn, we must quest for knowledge. Nothing is unknowable, though some things are still unknown.

*Maxim Gorky*

\*

The fount of knowledge never runs dry: no matter what success humanity achieves there will still be something left to seek, to discover, and to learn.

*Ivan Goncharov*

\*

Never brag of ignorance: ignorance is impotence.

*Nikolai Chernyshevsky*

\*

Not knowing is tantamount to not developing and not moving.

*Maxim Gorky*

Knowledge is man's companion wherever he goes.

*David Guramishvili*

\*

The need for improving one's life inevitably creates the need for mental effort.

*Nikolai Chernyshevsky*

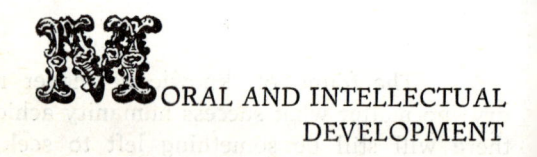

# MORAL AND INTELLECTUAL DEVELOPMENT

Nothing is richer and more complex than the human personality. Its all-sided development and moral perfection is the ultimate aim of communist education.

*Vassily Sukhomlinsky*

\*

The entire purpose of training, educating, and teaching the youth of today should be to imbue them with communist ethics.

*V. I. Lenin*

## KNOWLEDGE AND UPBRINGING

The craving for an education sits in every man; people crave and seek an education as they crave and seek air for breathing.

*Lev Tolstoy*

\*

Education is the source from which come the wellbeing or misfortune of the entire people.

*N. I. Novikov*

\*

One of the chief purposes of all education is to draw the continuously rising generations into humanity's common and endless pursuit of the absolute good.

*Konstantin Ushinsky*

\*

Knowledge must serve man's creative purposes. It is not enough to gather knowledge; it must be spread as broadly as possible and applied in practice.

*N. A. Rubakin*

\*

General education is the link and the means of bringing home the natural connection between the individual and humanity.

*Dmitry Pisarev*

Thought! A great thing! What else if not thought makes man great!

*Alexander Pushkin*

\*

An educated person is a person with his or her own outlook, his or her own opinion on all the aspects and spheres of the surrounding world.

*N. A. Rubakin*

\*

There are many kinds of education and development, and each is important, but first place should go to ethical education.

*Vissarion Belinsky*

\*

The prosperity of the state and the wellbeing of the nation depend invariably on good morals and good morals invariably on good upbringing.

*N. I. Novikov*

\*

Inexhaustible springs of creation are sealed in man or he would not have become man. They must be unsealed and released. And this must be done not with pleas for justice, but by putting man in the right social and material conditions.

*A. N. Tolstoy*

\*

Education must not be confined to just producing educated citizens; education that does not end in school and continues in public life should have the requisite resources to help the exercise and development of the creative faculties, energy, and initiative of the individual.

*N. A. Umov*

\*

In addition to developing the mind and giving a certain amount of information, education must also stimulate a thirst for serious work, for without this life is neither useful nor satisfying.

*Konstantin Ushinsky*

\*

Education consists in the adult generation passing on its experience, ardour, and convictions to the younger generation.

*Anton Makarenko*

The upbringing of a child must foster the habit of, and a liking for, work, and help it to find its vocation.

*Konstantin Ushinsky*

\*

Education is a great thing: every man's lot depends on it.

*Vissarion Belinsky*

\*

The more enlightened the person, the more useful he is to his Motherland.

*Alexander Griboyedov*

\*

The man we are bringing up must have on him a blend of moral purity, spiritual wealth, and physical perfection.

*Vassily Sukhomlinsky*

\*

The people of a socialist country must have a highly developed sense of beauty.

*Mikhail Kalinin*

\*

No man must leave his childhood without the rudiments of the constructive and beautiful; no generation must set out on its journey without the rudiments of the constructive and beautiful.

*Fyodor Dostoyevsky*

\*

He who has a sense of beauty can understand the essence of the life of real people.

*Felix Dzerzhinsky*

\*

No man can be cultured unless he knows the history of culture.

*Maxim Gorky*

\*

Culture is the cement that binds all achievements. Socialism is inconceivable without a steep rise of culture.

*N. K. Krupskaya*

\*

Music is a powerful stimulant of thought. Truly valid mental development is impossible without a musical education.

*Vassily Sukhomlinsky*

\*

As physical exercise straightens the body so does music straighten the soul.

*Vassily Sukhomlinsky*

Music is the most miraculous and sensitive means of wedding people to kindness, beauty, and humanism.

*Vassily Sukhomlinsky*

\*

Music wakens in man an awareness of the lofty, majestic, and beautiful in the surrounding world, and also within oneself.

*Vassily Sukhomlinsky*

\*

Need one prove that education is the greatest of blessings? Without an education people are crude, poor, and miserable.

*Nikolai Chernyshevsky*

\*

To be educated in the full sense the individual must have three things—extensive knowledge, the habit of thinking, and nobility of feelings. He who has little knowledge is an ignoramus; he whose mind is unpractised is crude or dull-witted, and he who lacks noble feelings is wicked.

*Nikolai Chernyshevsky*

\*

To be educated, intellectual, and refined you must be so to the marrow, showing your education, intellect and refinement in small things as well as big, in the casual, and in all your life.

*N. A. Rubakin*

\*

The educated sees different sides where the ignorant sees but one and by it judges of all the others.

*N. A. Rubakin*

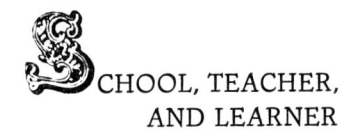

## SCHOOL, TEACHER, AND LEARNER

The school is a tremendous force that shapes the life and future of nations and states depending on the main subjects and principles of the educational system.

*Dmitry Mendeleyev*

\*

Our schools must provide the youth with the fundamentals of knowledge, the ability to evolve communist views independently; they must make educated people of the youth.

*V. I. Lenin*

We could not believe in teaching, training, and education if they were restricted only to the schoolroom and divorced from the ferment of life.

*V. I. Lenin*

\*

Education divorced from life and politics is lies and hypocrisy.

*V. I. Lenin*

\*

The school must fight for communism with the same will, the same courage, and the same determination as the rest of our society. And with the same enthusiasm.

*Anton Makarenko*

\*

The purpose of our Soviet school is not only to provide a definite body of knowledge, but also to show how this knowledge is linked with, and can change, everyday life.

*N. K. Krupskaya*

\*

We must build a school that teaches work, a school that shows how to make our work collective and how our work must draw on the achievements of modern science.

*N. K. Krupskaya*

An ideal future society cannot be conceived without combining education with the productive labour of the younger generation.

*V. I. Lenin*

∗

One of the up-to-the-minute aims of modern education is to teach children to work and live collectively.

*N. K. Krupskaya*

∗

Education must organise our children's lives on the foundation of collective and diverse work illumined by the lights of science.

*N. K. Krupskaya*

∗

Socialist society is founded on the collectivist principle. There must be no loners in it who either protrude in the shape of a pimple or crumble into roadside dust.

*Anton Makarenko*

∗

I am in favour of production in school, be it of the simplest, the cheapest, the most boring, because only the process of production can mould the human character and shape the individual into a good member of the production group.

*Anton Makarenko*

\*

The introduction of productive work for children in school intimately associated with formal instruction will make classes a hundred times more practical and appealing.

*N. K. Krupskaya*

\*

If discipline is cultivated in the process of work, good behaviour ceases to be superficial.

*N. K. Krupskaya*

\*

No weapon is sharper than knowledge based on work processes.

*Maxim Gorky*

\*

The social and cultural development of people cannot be normal unless the hands teach the head, whereupon the wisened head teaches the hands and thereby helps the brain to develop even more.

*Maxim Gorky*

The teacher's pride is all in his pupils, in the growth of the seeds he has sown.

*Dmitry Mendeleyev*

\*

The teacher does the most responsible work there is—he shapes the individual.

*Mikhail Kalinin*

\*

Good teachers make good pupils.

*M. V. Ostrogradsky*

\*

The teacher is the architect of human souls.

*Mikhail Kalinin*

\*

Schooling is but one of the petals of the flower called education.

*Vassily Sukhomlinsky*

\*

Unless the teacher wins the trust of his pupils learning will yield no fruit.

*Dmitry Mendeleyev*

I would like our young people to read the ancient philosophers. They would see how respectful and reverent pupils were to their teachers.

*Mikhail Kalinin*

\*

The teacher must pass on to the rising generation all the valuable assets of past centuries and withhold the prejudices, faults, and ills.

*A. V. Lunacharsky*

\*

In education everything hinges on who is the educator.

*Dmitry Pisarev*

\*

The educator must himself be what he wants to make of his pupil.

*V. I. Dahl*

\*

Teachers, who are local beacons of science, must be wholly abreast of modern knowledge in their respective fields.

*Dmitry Mendeleyev*

The educator must know life thoroughly in order to train people for it.

*Lev Tolstoy*

\*

The educator must himself possess intellect, great self-control, kindness, and a high sense of morality.

*M. I. Dragomanov*

\*

If he is honest, the teacher must always be an attentive pupil.

*Maxim Gorky*

\*

It is a sorry teacher who does not learn or learns but little.

*Maxim Gorky*

\*

For his influence on the whole mass of pupils to be beneficial, the teacher must himself be strong in science, possess learning, and like it.

*Dmitry Mendeleyev*

\*

To be a good teacher you must like what you teach and be fond of those whom you teach.

*V. O. Kliuchevsky*

# WORDS OF THE WISE

*If teachers want* to cultivate people in all respects, they *must first know* human nature in all respects.

*Konstantin Ushinsky*

\*

To be a teacher it is essential, first, to know your pupil inside and out and, second, to establish complete trust between yourself and your pupil.

*Dmitry Pisarev*

\*

To respect children does not mean to be indulgent and let them have their way. Children respect the teacher who stands firm on his educational demands.

*N. K. Krupskaya*

\*

The style of our education is an alloy of tremendous trust and tremendous exactingness.

*Anton Makarenko*

\*

If you do not demand much of your pupils, you will not get much out of them.

*Anton Makarenko*

## KNOWLEDGE AND UPBRINGING

The educator must always be convinced that the power of education is so great that he cannot even avail himself of all of it.

*Konstantin Ushinsky*

\*

The educator is no bureaucrat; if he were, he would be no educator.

*Konstantin Ushinsky*

\*

Tasks that are beyond the pupil's ability are corrupting, for they rob him of conscientiousness in learning.

*N. K. Krupskaya*

\*

Man is not an empty bottle into which you can pour whatever liquid you choose.

*Dmitry Pisarev*

\*

You can no more reform a person overnight than quickly clean a dress that hasn't known a brush.

*M. E. Saltykov-Shchedrin*

There are verities that, like political rights, cannot be bestowed before a definite age.

*Alexander Herzen*

\*

We have no need for cramming, but we do need to develop and perfect the mind of every student with a knowledge of the fundamental facts.

*V. I. Lenin*

\*

The thing in education is not only what the child is taught, but also how it is taught. The simplest and most trivial subjects skilfully presented will be a hundred times more useful to the child in future than lofty verities badly presented and unadapted to the child's understanding.

*Nikolai Pirogov*

\*

There is no such thing as a difficult subject, there is only incomprehensible and indigestible teaching.

*Alexander Herzen*

\*

In all things where the word is the medium, and especially in teaching, it is improper to overstate as well as to understate.

*V. O. Kliuchevsky*

The teacher is given the word not to deaden his thoughts, but to waken the thoughts of another.

*V. O. Kliuchevsky*

\*

No tutor must ever forget that his prime duty is to accustom his wards to mental work and that this duty is more important than imparting his subject to them.

*Konstantin Ushinsky*

\*

Knowledge is dead unless initiative and self-reliance is developed in our pupils: pupils must be taught to want, as well as to think.

*N. A. Umov*

\*

The true object of learning is to train the human being to be human.

*Nikolai Pirogov*

\*

The most important part of education is to mould the character.

*Konstantin Ushinsky*

Concern yourself most of all with making your pupil a man in the true sense of the word.

*Nikolai Chernyshevsky*

※

Persuasion is the mainstream of human education.

*Konstantin Ushinsky*

※

Convictions are shaped by theory, whereas behaviour is shaped by example.

*Alexander Herzen*

※

The educator influences his pupil not only by imparting knowledge, but also by his behaviour, his way of life, and his attitude to simple things.

*Mikhail Kalinin*

※

None but a personality can effectively shape another personality, and only a strong character can mould a strong character.

*Konstantin Ushinsky*

# KNOWLEDGE AND UPBRINGING

It is the living example that educates the child—not words, be they ever so virtuous, if they are not backed by deeds.

*Anton Makarenko*

\*

You cannot rear a man of courage unless you put him in circumstances where he can display courage, be it through restraint or continence, upright and honest speech, some privation, through patience or through bravery.

*Anton Makarenko*

\*

No matter how many good ideas you impart of what must be done, I shall be in my rights to say you have imparted nothing if you fail to impart the habit of overcoming prolonged hardship.

*Anton Makarenko*

\*

Nothing is more useless or even harmful than instruction, be it the most well-intentioned, if it is not backed by examples and not justified in the pupil's eyes by the whole surrounding environment.

*Vissarion Belinsky*

No man is so bad that good education will not make him better.

*Vissarion Belinsky*

\*

It is always hard to espy the good in a person. The good in a person has always to be projected, and it is the teacher's duty to do so. He must approach every person with an optimistic hypothesis, be it even at the risk of erring.

*Anton Makarenko*

\*

Wasted time at lessons and absence of mental effort where mental effort is expected is the main reason for the absence of free time and leisure.

*Vassily Sukhomlinsky*

\*

Dig for knowledge by yourself. It is dishonest to exploit the hard work of your mates. Cribbing is the first step to becoming a sponger.

*Vassily Sukhomlinsky*

\*

He who has not mastered the technique of some craft, science, or art will never be able to create anything worthwhile.

*Ivan Michurin*

KNOWLEDGE AND UPBRINGING

Attention is that one door to our soul through which everything reaching our consciousness must inevitably pass.

*Konstantin Ushinsky*

\*

To repeat your teacher's words does not mean being his successor.

*Dmitry Pisarev*

\*

Only those blame their ignorance on the incompetence of their teachers who cannot make anything out of themselves and expect to be dragged by their ears where they should go by themselves.

*Nikolai Dobrolyubov*

# SELF-IMPROVEMENT

Education is not the business of the school alone. The school merely gives you the keys to knowledge. All your life should be out-of-school education. A person must educate himself all his life.

*A. V. Lunacharsky*

As long as a man lives, though his hair may be grey, he can, must, and wants to gather knowledge. Hence, all learning obtained out of school, since life cannot be squeezed into the framework of the school, is a process of out-of-school education.

*A. V. Lunacharsky*

\*

No man on earth is born ready-made, that is, fully developed. Whatever his life may be, it is unintermittent development and ceaseless formation.

*Vissarion Belinsky*

\*

You must learn in school, but you must learn much more on leaving school; the consequences and influence on your personality and on society of this second learning are immeasurably more important.

*Dmitry Pisarev*

\*

All real education is obtained exclusively by self-education.

*N. A. Rubakin*

\*

What makes a man educated is his own inner work—what he himself thinks, experiences, and feels in digesting what he learns from other people or from books.

*N. A. Rubakin*

\*

Never end your self-education and never forget that no matter how much you learn and no matter how much you know, knowledge and education has neither borders nor limits.

*N. A. Rubakin*

\*

To be unable to express your thoughts articulately is a fault, but to have no thoughts of your own is a much bigger one; yet thoughts of your own come only from knowledge acquired on your own.

*Konstantin Ushinsky*

\*

The instructions of another are nothing but a consultative opinion.

*N. A. Rubakin*

\*

None has ever reached his goal without effort of his own. Outside help cannot substitute for your own effort.

*N. A. Rubakin*

Ready-made convictions can neither be borrowed from good friends nor bought in a bookshop. They must be the result of an independent mental process in our own heads.

*Dmitry Pisarev*

\*

Learn the ABC of science before trying to scale its summits. Never take the next step before completing the one before it. Never try to disguise gaps in your knowledge with even the boldest guesses and hypotheses. Learn to do the spadework of science.

*Ivan Pavlov*

\*

If your children want to be truly educated people, they must acquire an education by self-learning.

*Nikolai Chernyshevsky*

\*

There can be neither talent nor genius in the absence of an obviously prodigious diligence.

*Dmitry Mendeleyev*

\*

Beware of thinking that you know everything and that there is nothing left for you to learn.

*N. D. Zelinsky*

## KNOWLEDGE AND UPBRINGING

You will never extend your knowledge unless you look your ignorance straight in the eye.

*Konstantin Ushinsky*

\*

Knowledge is not knowledge unless it is acquired through the efforts of your mind, not your memory.

*Lev Tolstoy*

\*

Talent springs from a liking for your work, and it is even possible that in substance talent is no more than a liking for one's work, for the process of work.

*Maxim Gorky*

\*

Anything you want to reach you must reach by yourself through hard experience.

*Alexander Serov*

\*

Knowledge is composed of tiny grains of everyday experience.

*Dmitry Pisarev*

\*

Nothing can teach better than experience.

*Anton Makarenko*

Ability, like muscle, grows through practice.

*Vladimir Obruchev*

\*

Learn always, know everything! The more you learn, the stronger you will be.

*Maxim Gorky*

\*

Man is born to be lord and master of Nature. But the wisdom that keynotes his rule is not inborn. It is acquired by learning.

*N. I. Lobachevsky*

\*

Learn, read, think, and extract the useful from everything.

*Nikolai Pirogov*

\*

A career made with one's own head is always more dependable and always broader than that made by bowing and scraping or by the protection of an important uncle.

*Dmitry Pisarev*

## IGNORANCE

There is but one evil in humankind—ignorance, and but one remedy against it—learning.

*Dmitry Pisarev*

\*

These days ignorance and paucity of mind and feeling are becoming a moral flaw.

*Vassily Sukhomlinsky*

\*

Where precise knowledge is lacking guesses take its place, and out of ten guesses nine are wrong.

*Maxim Gorky*

\*

Those who pluck off the chains from man's reason are the only real people.

*Maxim Gorky*

\*

Ignorance makes man indifferent to the world, and indifference grows slowly but irremediably, like a malignant tumour.

*Konstantin Paustovsky*

Prejudices are the debris of outdated truths.

*Maxim Gorky*

## THE USELESSNESS OF TOO MUCH KNOWLEDGE

Human knowledge is boundless. But man need not know everything. Out of the ocean of human knowledge he must pick out the most important, just the knowledge that makes men strong, gives them power over Nature and events, that teaches them how to use the forces and riches of Nature, and how to transform the life of human society.

*N. K. Krupskaya*

\*

It is a mistake to think that much knowledge is a virtue. Its quality not its quantity is important.

*Lev Tolstoy*

\*

Wisdom is not in knowing much. We cannot conceivably know everything. Wisdom is not in knowing as much as possible, but in knowing what knowledge is more useful, what knowledge is less useful, and what knowledge is still less useful.

*Lev Tolstoy*

\*

A head full of fragmentary, disconnected knowledge is like a storehouse in disorder where the keeper can never find what he wants; a head that is all system and no knowledge is like a shop with labels on all boxes, but with the boxes empty.

*Konstantin Ushinsky*

\*

Genius is the supreme ability to concentrate attention on the subject of study.

*Ivan Pavlov*

\*

It is good to know a little about everything and everything about a little.

*K. A. Timiryazev*

\*

There are no difficult subjects, but a multitude of things we simply do not know, and still more of those that we know badly, incoherently, fragmentally, even incorrectly. And this incorrect knowledge holds us back more and confuses us more than that which we do not possess.

*Alexander Herzen*

\*

Fear not lack of knowledge, but fear false knowledge. It is the source of all the world's evil.

*Lev Tolstoy*

\*

It is neither shameful nor harmful not to know. No man can know everything. It is shameful and harmful to pretend to know what you do not know.

*Lev Tolstoy*

\*

For me not to know something and to say nothing is not ignorance: the ignoramus is he who speaks of things he does not know.

*M. M. Prishvin*

\*

Very few people, and only the best people, can simply and frankly say, "I do not know".

*Dmitry Pisarev*

## OF WISDOM, INTELLIGENCE, AND STUPIDITY

### WISDOM AND REASON

You must understand that reason is our sun. Nothing is more miraculous than the human brain, nothing more astounding than the results of scientific search.

*Maxim Gorky*

\*

Wisdom is the sum total of verities amassed by the brain through observation and experience, and applied to life; it is the harmony of ideas and life.

*Ivan Goncharov*

\*

Wisdom is limitless. The farther you go with it, the more necessary it becomes.

*Lev Tolstoy*

Thoughts are the be-all. They are the beginning of everything. And thoughts can be controlled. Hence, the main thing in bettering yourself is to better your thoughts.

*Lev Tolstoy*

\*

Many things are evils, but nothing more evil than an evil mind. An evil mind is the primary evil.

*Lev Tolstoy*

\*

Reason is strength. A head without brains is like a lamp without light.

*Lev Tolstoy*

\*

A wise man's wisdom is in three things: first, to do himself what he advises others; second, never to contradict justice, and, third, to be tolerant of the weaknesses of those around him.

*Lev Tolstoy*

\*

Wisdom shuns not ignorance, nor doubt, nor work, nor search; it shuns but one thing–claming it knows what it does not know.

*Lev Tolstoy*

## WISDOM AND STUPIDITY

Nothing in the world is more precious than thought.

*N. E. Karonin-Petropavlovsky*

\*

Before the act comes cogitation; an individual may cogitate for a few hours or minutes; society cogitates for decades on end.

*Dmitry Pisarev*

\*

The most wretched of all are not those with wrong thoughts, but those with no definite or consistent thoughts, those whose thoughts are a collection of incoherent fragments.

*Nikolai Chernyshevsky*

\*

When thoughts swirl in the heads of thinkers, the heads of non-thinkers begin to spin.

*V. O. Kliuchevsky*

\*

The mind suffers no bondage.

*Dmitry Pisarev*

The sage submits not to the insensate crowd, but himself gives it direction.

*I. I. Lazhechnikov*

\*

Thoughts that entail momentous consequences are always simple.

*Lev Tolstoy*

\*

There can be no harm in the repetition of good ideas.

*Mikhail Kalinin*

\*

Reason is by far the highest of faculties, but to acquire it you must first conquer your passions.

*Nikolai Gogol*

\*

An intellect not organised by an idea cannot enter life creatively.

*Maxim Gorky*

\*

It seems to me that wisdom in all things does not consist in knowing what must be done, but in knowing what must be done first and what later.

*Lev Tolstoy*

\*

Man is endowed with reason to live reasonably, not merely to know he is living unreasonably.

*Vissarion Belinsky*

# INTELLIGENCE

The mind is man's spiritual weapon.

*Vissarion Belinsky*

\*

Be it a little mind, but be it your own.

*Maxim Gorky*

\*

Man is born to live by his own mind.

*Lev Tolstoy*

Not the mind is primary, but what directs it—the character, the heart, the noble qualities, and development.

*Fyodor Dostoyevsky*

\*

Give your mind as much food as possible.

*Lev Tolstoy*

\*

To be clever is not to ask questions that cannot be answered.

*V. O. Kliuchevsky*

\*

You have a mind precisely in order to achieve what you want.

*Fyodor Dostoyevsky*

\*

The mind is a precious gem that sparkles more brilliantly when framed in modesty.

*Maxim Gorky*

\*

One more point of difference is that some people think before they speak and act, while others speak and act before they think.

*Lev Tolstoy*

## WISDOM AND STUPIDITY

The difference between the clever and the foolish is that the former always thinks and rarely speaks, while the latter always speaks and never thinks. The tongue of the former is always within reach of the thought, while the thought of the latter is beyond the reach of the tongue. In the former case the tongue is the handmaid of the thought, in the latter it is a gossip and tattletale.

*V. O. Kliuchevsky*

\*

Intelligence is the same everywhere; intelligent people, like fools, have common qualities irrespective of nationality, clothes, language, religion, and even outlook.

*Ivan Goncharov*

## HUMOUR

The most precious gift of Nature is a cheerful, jesting, and kind mind.

*V. O. Kliuchevsky*

\*

A man's good cheer is the best of his qualities.

*Fyodor Dostoyevsky*

If a man laughs well, he is good.

*Fyodor Dostoyevsky*

\*

Only a profound and kind soul will burst into kind and sparkling laughter.

*Nikolai Gogol*

\*

Laughter is affection.

*Lev Tolstoy*

\*

Good laughter is a sure sign of mental balance.

*Maxim Gorky*

\*

He is merry who has a joyous present and a joyous future.

*Lev Tolstoy*

\*

Humour is a great force. Nothing brings people closer than sound, inoffensive laughter.

*Lev Tolstoy*

## WISDOM AND STUPIDITY

Humour is the wit of profound feeling.

*Fyodor Dostoyevsky*

\*

None but the fool can live without humour.

*M. M. Prishvin*

\*

A merry soul is invariably a good soul. Scoundrels are hardly ever merry people.

*Maxim Gorky*

\*

Good laughter heals the soul.

*Maxim Gorky*

\*

Laughter mothers good cheer.

*Lev Tolstoy*

\*

A smile is always good, because it raises the veil on the person's simple inner world.

*N. I. Novikov*

The merriest laughter is laughter at someone who laughs at you.

*V. O. Kliuchevsky*

*

A man's laughter may betray, so that you suddenly learn everything about him. Even unquestionably clever laughter may sometimes be disgusting. Above all, laughter must be sincere.

*Fyodor Dostoyevsky*

*

Nothing is more tiresome than a cheerless mind.

*Ivan Turgenev*

*

It is bad if irony, allegory, and jest are no longer appreciated.

*Fyodor Dostoyevsky*

*

If he cannot take a joke consider him lost. His is not a genuine mind, be he even a great intellect.

*Anton Chekhov*

## WISDOM AND STUPIDITY

I am always suspicious of the eternally gloomy and strait-laced; either he is dissembling or his mind or stomach must be upset.

*Alexander Herzen*

※

Laughter often helps distinguish truth from untruth.

*Vissarion Belinsky*

※

Laughter is great: it deprives neither of life nor of possessions, but before it the culpable is like a trussed-up hare.

*Nikolai Gogol*

※

Laughter is one of the most effective weapons against the outdated that still clings on heaven only knows how, pretending importance, hindering new life, and frightening the weak.

*Alexander Herzen*

※

The funny awakens our sense of dignity.

*Nikolai Chernyshevsky*

Clever laughter is a splendid generator of energy.

*Maxim Gorky*

\*

To fear laughter is to dread the truth.

*Ivan Turgenev*

\*

Laughter is not merely a sign of strength, but strength itself. And since we have it, we must direct it along the right course.

*A. V. Lunacharsky*

\*

If you've got to laugh, laugh loudly and direct your laughter against that which deserves public ridicule.

*Nikolai Gogol*

\*

Smiles and jests must permeate seriousness as nylon threads permeate woollen fabrics. Then people's relations will need no ironing.

*Mikhail Svetlov*

\*

Many people like jesting more than thinking.

*Maxim Gorky*

## WISDOM AND STUPIDITY

In sarcasm our derision attains the highest degree of sharpness.

*Nikolai Chernyshevsky*

## STUPIDITY

Wisdom has a limit, stupidity has none.

*Janis Rainis*

\*

Neither government decree nor literary theory will ever weed out stupid and petty people.

*Dmitry Pisarev*

\*

Our stupidity is tenacious and its asylums are countless; even the cleverest assign a cosy corner for it.

*Dmitry Pisarev*

\*

Subtleness is not yet proof of intelligence. Dolts and even demented people are sometimes astonishingly subtle.

*Alexander Pushkin*

If nothing can surprise a person, this is, of course, a sign of stupidity, not cleverness.

*Fyodor Dostoyevsky*

\*

Nothing is more unbearable than the knowledge of having just committed a stupidity.

*Ivan Turgenev*

\*

Not he is stupid who does not know, but he who does not want to know.

*G. S. Skovoroda*

\*

Fools ask more questions than the inquisitive.

*Maxim Gorky*

\*

If every fool were to insist on understanding everything he utters many fools would be consigned to perpetual silence.

*Dmitry Pisarev*

\*

A fool who has admitted he is a fool is no longer a fool.

*Fyodor Dostoyevsky*

## WISDOM AND STUPIDITY

The greatest weakness of the mind is mistrust of the powers of the mind.

*Vissarion Belinsky*

✻

It is a great consolation for human ignorance to consider everything it does not know a foolishness.

*Denis Fonvizin*

✻

Scold what is beyond your comprehension, what you do not understand: this is mediocrity's general rule.

*Vissarion Belinsky*

✻

Some people think that if they call all people fools, they will be considered clever.

*V. O. Kliuchevsky*

✻

Ancient wisdom has willed us so many aphorisms that a whole indestructible wall of them has risen stone by stone.

*M. E. Saltykov-Shchedrin*

There has never yet been a case of a fool liking a clever one.

*P. A. Pavlenko*

\*

However stupid a fool's words may be, they are sometimes enough to confuse a clever man.

*Nikolai Gogol*

\*

The clever are always strangers among fools.

*Vissarion Belinsky*

# OF THE CONTINUITY OF CULTURE

Proletarian culture must be the logical development of the store of knowledge mankind has accumulated.

*V. I. Lenin*

\*

Far from rejecting the most valuable achievements of the bourgeois epoch, Marxism has assimilated and refashioned everything of value in the more than two thousand years of the development of human thought and culture.

*V. I. Lenin*

\*

Not empty negation, not futile negation, not *sceptical* negation, not vacillation or doubt are characteristic and essential in dialectics—which undoubtedly contains the element of negation and indeed as a most important element—no, but negation *as a moment* of connection, as a moment of development, retaining the positive, i.e., without any vacillations, without any eclecticism.

*V. I. Lenin*

\*

In order to raise the level of culture we must turn to the history of culture, to the entire cultural heritage of humankind.

*Mikhail Kalinin*

\*

Only a precise knowledge and transformation of the culture created by the entire development of mankind will enable us to create a proletarian culture.

*V. I. Lenin*

\*

Communist ethics does not negate, but rather encompasses, the past experience of people.

*Vassily Sukhomlinsky*

\*

We know that mankind is divided into hostile groups, first of all into classes, but we also know that despite all obstacles and contradictions there is a great line connecting the foremost fighters of all classes when these classes were young, when they were straining forward.

*A. V. Lunacharsky*

\*

Human history is marked by a continuity of thought stretching across the ages.

*Ivan Sechenov*

\*

We have the fruit of the thinking of the greatest thinkers who distinguished themselves over the millennia among billions upon billions of people, and this fruit of their thinking has been sifted through the sieve of time.

All mediocrity has been rejected. What has remained is original, profound, and useful.

*Lev Tolstoy*

\*

Our time is monumental precisely because it takes all the most valuable from the centuries-old human culture. It does not bury these values, which sparkle across the ages from under the dusty film of oblivion. The foremost people of by-gone generations have enough to show to be admitted to the communist society.

*Konstantin Paustovsky*

# WORDS OF THE WISE

The people is like a gold-miner or seeker of gems: decade after decade it selects, preserves, polishes, and takes only the most valuable and the most brilliant.

*Mikhail Kalinin*

*

We would be very clever and very happy people if we did not treat many of the verities that have become proverbial or that adorn our spellingbooks and readers as dead and trite phrases.

*Dmitry Pisarev*

## OF APHORISMS

There are certain winged words which most aptly express rather complex phenomena.

*V. I. Lenin*

*

Folk wisdom usually speaks in aphorisms.

*Nikolai Dobrolyubov*

*

It is a common trait to think in aphorisms.

*Maxim Gorky*

*

I have learnt a lot from proverbs or, in other words, from thinking in aphorisms.

*Maxim Gorky*

*

Incalculable treasures of human thought and experience accumulate over the millennia and live eternally in the word.

*Mikhail Sholokhov*

An immeasurable diversity of human relations is depicted in the precise sayings and aphorisms coined by the people.

*Mikhail Sholokhov*

\*

To all circumstances in our lives we apply the aphorisms of Pushkin, Krylov, and Griboyedov—no longer thinking of the authors of the lines, but using their word as a nugget of folk wisdom.

*Yakub Kolas*

\*

Aphorisms are, probably, the best manner of expressing philosophical ideas.

*Lev Tolstoy*

\*

There are thoughts whose application is infinitely varied; therefore, the more general the manner in which they are expressed, the more food they afford to the mind and heart, and the more deeply can they be apprehended.

*Lev Tolstoy*

\*

Words belong to the age and thoughts to the ages.

*Nikolai Karamzin*

## APHORISMS

Thoughts and sayings embellish the soul like flowers embellish the room.

*Effendi Kapiev*

\*

Far from suppressing the independent workings of the brain, books of proverbs stimulate mental activity.

*Lev Tolstoy*

\*

Terse thought is good, for it makes the serious reader think for himself.

*Lev Tolstoy*

\*

Good thoughts make others, too, think up good thoughts.

*Vissarion Belinsky*

\*

You often hear young people say: I don't want to live by another's brain, I want to think for myself. But why ponder what others have already pondered? Take what is ready and carry on. That is humanity's greatest asset.

*Lev Tolstoy*

## OF ART AND LIFE

### THE SIGNIFICANCE AND PURPOSE OF ART

Art is mankind's gigantic song about itself and its environment.

*A. V. Lunacharsky*

\*

The arts of our time are expression and embodiment in fine images of the modern consciousness and modern thought about the meaning and purpose of life.

*Vissarion Belinsky*

\*

For man art is as vital as eating and drinking.

*Fyodor Dostoyevsky*

\*

Art makes people good and moulds the human soul.

*Konstantin Paustovsky*

## ART AND LIFE

Books make people better, and that is one of the main, even *the* main and, perhaps, the sole purpose of art.

*Ivan Goncharov*

*

The arts are one of the means of communication.

*Lev Tolstoy*

*

Art is Nature plus Man.

*K. A. Timiryazev*

*

Art is the supreme manifestation of man's might.

*Lev Tolstoy*

*

The prime purpose of art, which applies to all its works without exception, is to reproduce Nature and Life.

*Nikolai Chernyshevsky*

*

Art, like science, is knowledge of life.

*Lev Tolstoy*

Poetry and art are a special form not only of expression, but also of cognition.

*Janis Rainis*

*

Poetry, like the arts and sciences in general, is composed in accordance with life, not life in accordance with poetry; everything in poetry that is contrary to life, i.e., if it does not flow directly and naturally from life, is senseless and ugly.

*Nikolai Dobrolyubov*

*

Art is thought in images.

*Vissarion Belinsky*

*

The ideal is the aim of art.

*Alexander Pushkin*

*

Art must impart faith in life and in the powers of man.

*Alexander Herzen*

*

The purpose of literature is to help man understand himself, to buttress his faith in himself, and to foster his yearning for the truth, to fight evil in people, to spot the good in them, to arouse shame, anger, and courage in their souls, and to make people nobly strong.

*Maxim Gorky*

*

As we grow richer, art will enter the life of the mass of people more and more broadly not only in the form of a great social art, but also penetrating the dwellings of worker and peasant, and filling them with joy.

*A. V. Lunacharsky*

*

Art is connected with morality.

*Alexander Blok*

*

It is no more possible to separate the question of morality from the question of art than it is to divide fire into light, heat, and intensity of combustion.

*Vissarion Belinsky*

*

Art must ennoble people.

*Maxim Gorky*

Art (the serious kind) must elevate people and give them strength to rise, to hold high their spirits.

*Ivan Kramskoi*

\*

It is a terrible mistake to think that the beautiful can be senseless.

*Lev Tolstoy*

\*

Nowhere is literature assessed by its vilest specimens, but on the merits of those of its makers who truly lead society forward.

*M. E. Saltykov-Shchedrin*

\*

Thoughtless art is like soulless man. The thought and the idea are the living soul and true content of a work of art.

*Vissarion Belinsky*

\*

Consciously or not, all art sets itself the aim of arousing the feelings and of cultivating one or another attitude towards a specific condition of life.

*Maxim Gorky*

## ART AND LIFE

The essential significance of art is its reproduction of everything that is of interest to man; frequently, especially in poetry, explication of life and judgement of its phenomena are also in the foreground.

*Nikolai Chernyshevsky*

\*

If we say that literature is the mirror of life, we must add that it is a very peculiar and magic mirror. Not only does it reflect life, but it also endows life with its own light and warmth, and gives it an elevated and noble identity.

*Hovannes Toumanian*

\*

Literature is not the mirror of the historical struggle, but a weapon of that struggle.

*Vladimir Mayakovsky*

\*

For the true artist there is life where there is poetry.

*Vissarion Belinsky*

\*

Talent's supreme task is to help people understand the sense and price of life.

*V. O. Kliuchevsky*

The artist's bounden duty is to show, not to prove.

*Alexander Blok*

\*

He is no writer if he has not added at least a grain of insight to man's vision.

*Konstantin Paustovsky*

\*

Only those are fated to pronounce a new word in art who can spot the new in life and, possessing skill, embody this new in their works.

*Dmitry Kabalevsky*

\*

A work of art is not a work of art unless it injects a new feeling into the daily round of human existence.

*Lev Tolstoy*

\*

Underlying a true work of art there must be an entirely new thought or a new feeling, but expressed to the minutest everyday detail with truly slavish precision.

*Lev Tolstoy*

## ART AND LIFE

Art performs the work of the memory: from the stream of time it selects the most vivid, exciting, and significant, and portrays it in the crystal of books.

*A. N. Tolstoy*

\*

A great art expressive of the great revolutionary forces is a mighty agitator of revolution.

*A. V. Lunacharsky*

\*

Literature and propagation of ideas is one and the same thing.

*M. E. Saltykov-Shchedrin*

\*

Literature is a servant, and its significance is in the propagation of ideas, while its worth depends on what and how it propagates.

*Nikolai Dobrolyubov*

\*

Art is the expression of verity, and reality is the sole and the supreme verity; everything outside it, that is, all realities invented by a "construer" are a lie and a slander of verity.

*Vissarion Belinsky*

Our art must rise above the reality and elevate man above that reality without separating him from it.

*Maxim Gorky*

\*

In substance, art is motion and begins with a yearning for better things—things better than what exists.

*M. M. Prishvin*

\*

There is no art for art's sake, only art for life's sake.

*Dmitry Furmanov*

\*

Art is a means of conversing with people, not an aim.

*M. P. Mussorgsky*

\*

"Art for art's sake" is for people who have not exercised their brains, who have not learned a trade, for doltish and impertinent dandies. It is absurd and senseless.

*P. P. Chistyakov*

\*

The gravitation towards art for art's sake occurs wherever artists are at odds with their social environment.

*G. V. Plekhanov*

## ART AND LIFE

A writer must not stand aloof from life and struggle.

*Nikolai Ostrovsky*

❊

If a writer sidesteps the motion of life, people will not understand him.

*Mikhail Glinka*

❊

The artist cannot dissociate himself from the life of society.

*N. P. Ogarev*

❊

Only that is art which responds to real feelings and thoughts, and is not a sweet dessert one can go without.

*V. V. Stasov*

❊

We need the word for living. We disavow useless art.

*Vladimir Mayakovsky*

❊

Literature is the imaginative expression of the ideologies—the feelings, opinions, intentions, and hopes—of social classes and groups.

*Maxim Gorky*

Russian literature was very strongly democratic, strong in its ardent wish to resolve the problems of social being, its plea for humanity, its praises of freedom, its profound interest in the life of the plain people, its chaste treatment of women, and its persevering search for the universal, all-illuminating truth.

*Maxim Gorky*

\*

The power of real art derives from its taking a plain and common phenomenon, showing its profound dramatic social significance and its close dependence on the general conditions of life and life's basic roots.

*Maxim Gorky*

\*

Literature must be like the daily bread.

*Alexander Blok*

\*

The closer attachment of art and reality, literature's active involvement in the life of the epoch has now become a prime necessity.

*Maxim Gorky*

## ART AND LIFE

Every work of art must inevitably bear the stamp of the times.

*Pyotr Chaikovsky*

\*

Only those currents of literature can rise to brilliance that are shaped under the influence of strong and vital ideas responding to the insistent needs of the epoch.

*Nikolai Chernyshevsky*

\*

The true artist always puts the idea of the times at the base of his works.

*Nikolai Chernyshevsky*

\*

In an artist modernity is a great virtue.

*Vissarion Belinsky*

\*

We accept the extent to which a writer or a work of art are expressive of the natural aspirations of a period or of a people as the measure of their virtue.

*Nikolai Dobrolyubov*

\*

Modernity is the most difficult and the most beautiful in art.

*V. V. Stasov*

Modernity is at the centre of our creative endeavours.

*Dmitry Kabalevsky*

\*

If you do not keep pace with the times you cannot write.

*Alexander Blok*

\*

There is no art without a sense of modernity.

*Sergei Konenkov*

\*

An artist who has no feeling of the times will remain unrecognised.

*M. M. Prishvin*

\*

The artist must feel eternity and yet keep abreast of the times.

*M. M. Prishvin*

\*

The artist must keep pace with the concepts of his time.

*Alexander Ivanov*

## ART AND LIFE

No artist can fail to submit to the spirit of his time.

*Alexander Serov*

\*

Real art is always up-to-date, vital, and useful; that, indeed, is its hallmark.

*Fyodor Dostoyevsky*

\*

Literature always exercises an influence on the development of nations, and always plays a more or less important role in the march of history.

*Nikolai Chernyshevsky*

\*

Not all that is modern is eternal, but that which is eternal is always modern.

*Yevgeny Vakhtangov*

\*

The appreciation of our country as a great country which has preserved its old values and is creating new ones is the chief motor in the work of the historian of literature and the writer of historical novels.

*Yuri Tynianov*

No person, be he a writer, artist, composer, scientist, or cultural worker can create in isolation from society, from life. There can be no creativity in the absence of impressions, delights, inspirations, and experience.

*Dmitry Shostakovich*

\*

Surprisingly, we have writers, even famous ones, who prefer to write without ardour, without risk, listlessly, a bit boringly and, what is worst, on the fringe of events, keeping their nose out of the boiling pot we call life.

*A. N. Tolstoy*

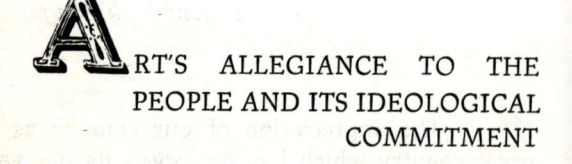

# ART'S ALLEGIANCE TO THE PEOPLE AND ITS IDEOLOGICAL COMMITMENT

Art and the people prosper and rise together.

*Maxim Gorky*

## ART AND LIFE

The people is not only the force that creates material values; it is also the only inexhaustible source of spiritual values, the first philosopher and poet in time, in beauty, and in genius, the maker of all the great poems, of all the tragedies on earth, and of the greatest of them all—the history of world culture.

*Maxim Gorky*

*

Folk art, that which has been enshrined by the people, which has been preserved, and that which the people brought down through the ages, is the highest type of art, the most gifted, the closest to genius.

*Mikhail Kalinin*

*

Literature is the consciousness of the people, the flower and fruit of its spiritual world.

*Vissarion Belinsky*

*

Art that did not grow out of the roots of the people's life, though not always useless and worthless, is in any case sure to be impotent.

*V. V. Stasov*

Art must open our eyes to the ideals created by the people.

*Konstantin Stanislavsky*

\*

The great objects of art are great solely because they are within the reach of all and intelligible to all.

*Lev Tolstoy*

\*

Literature must on all accounts be of and for the people if it is to be forceful and eternal.

*Vissarion Belinsky*

\*

Literature is the ultimate and supreme expression of the people's thoughts clothed in the word.

*Vissarion Belinsky*

\*

Art is precious for humanity precisely because it absorbs the most *winning features of the nation*.

*Vladimir Nemirovich-Danchenko*

\*

What does national form mean in art? Mainly, it means the native tongue. It also means the spirit and pattern of speech peculiar to the nation, speech that has absorbed the folklore of the nation over the centuries.

*Alexander Fadeyev*

\*

Art is not like science. It cannot be forceful unless it is national. What about old art, you will ask? Yes, but its universal quality is inevitably clothed in national dress.

*Ivan Kramskoi*

Cosmopolitanism is nonsense; a cosmopolite is nothing, worse than nothing; there is no art, no truth, no life, nothing, in the absence of national identity.

*Ivan Turgenev*

\*

The writer must be the spokesman of his people's wishes, the leader, and protector of his people.

*Nikolai Chernyshevsky*

\*

I hold the conviction that the composer, like the poet, sculptor, and artist, must serve man and the people. He must adorn and protect human life. In art, his prime duty is to be a citizen.

*Sergei Prokofiev*

\*

We must choose work as the main hero of our books, that is, the individual organised by the processes of work which in our country has behind it the power of modern equipment, the individual who, for his part, makes his work easier, more productive, giving it the dimension of an art. We must learn to see work as creation.

*Maxim Gorky*

\*

By the attractiveness of its characters literature illumines the way to all fields of human activity and labour. In this sense it is capable of directing people and helping them to find their vocation, their life's work.

*Alexander Tvardovsky*

\*

Art is real only where the audience feels at home and is conscious of being part of the action.

*V. V. Stasov*

\*

Only that literature is truly national which is at once universal, and only that literature is universally human which is a literature of the people.

*Vissarion Belinsky*

\*

For the artist, for the scientist, for the journalist, for anyone and everyone, there is a great and common rule: the idea comes first! Those who break this rule instantly forfeit the ability to be useful to people and become contemptible parasites.

*Dmitry Pisarev*

\*

Literature can do good exclusively through new ideas; that is its real vocation, and in this respect it has no rivals.

*Dmitry Pisarev*

\*

The Soviet reader is a reader who seeks wisdom, knowledge, and ideas in books.

*Anton Makarenko*

\*

Far from harming technology, thought and tendency stimulate its improvement.

*V. V. Vereshchagin*

We want the artist to be historian, philosopher, politician, organiser, and prophet. The artist is the architect of humanity's spiritual world.

*A. N. Tolstoy*

\*

To rob art of the right to serve the public interest is to depreciate it, not to raise it, because it is then deprived of its lifeblood, that is, of thought, and becomes an object of sybaritic indulgence and a toy of idle wastrels.

*Vissarion Belinsky*

\*

The great is the only object worth thinking about; the writer must set himself nothing but great assignments—boldly, undaunted by his own modest strength.

*Alexander Blok*

\*

The idea is the soul of a work of art.

*Vladimir Korolenko*

\*

Art cannot live without an idea.

*G. V. Plekhanov*

A work of art lacking a clearly conceived idea is an agglomeration of trivialities.

*M. E. Saltykov-Shchedrin*

\*

An unclear view of the world is so grave a deficiency that it reduces the creative activity of the artist to nought.

*M. E. Saltykov-Shchedrin*

\*

Works of art must respond to some great thought, for only that is beautiful which is serious.

*A. F. Koni*

\*

Every artistic gift will augment its power to a very great degree if it absorbs the great emancipative ideas of our time.

*G. V. Plekhanov*

\*

If artists are blind to the social currents of their time, the intrinsic value of the ideas they express in their works is very greatly depreciated.

*G. V. Plekhanov*

Art gains from turning its back on the trite. But when it turns its back on the great movements of history it acquires elements of triteness itself.

*G. V. Plekhanov*

\*

The Soviet writer's work has no sense unless it is illumined by the great and universal ideals of our age.

*Alexander Fadeyev*

\*

By virtue of his thought and talent, the writer must create new life.

*Leonid Andreyev*

\*

What you write must indirectly or directly serve the movement forward.

*Dmitry Furmanov*

\*

The better the book, the more it is ahead of events.

*Vladimir Mayakovsky*

\*

Poetry needs ardour, it needs your idea, and inevitably it needs the pointing finger, a finger raised in passion. Indifference

## ART AND LIFE

and mirror-like reproduction of reality, on the other hand, is worthless.

*Fyodor Dostoyevsky*

∗

In substance, art is a struggle *for* or *against*. There is no indifferent art, nor can there be, because we humans are not cameras and cannot photograph reality. We either assert or change reality, or destroy it.

*Maxim Gorky*

∗

The great writer is a politician. Though it may seem that even a magnifying glass will show no trace of politics in a writer's works, he, too, is really a politician.

*A. V. Lunacharsky*

∗

Literature must become *part* of the common cause of the proletariat.

*V. I. Lenin*

∗

We estimate every social and cultural event as a plus or minus for our construction.

Our Soviet literature, too, must be a mighty and highly competent collaborator in building socialism.

*A. V. Lunacharsky*

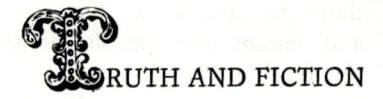

# TRUTH AND FICTION

Seeing the main purpose of literature in explicating the phenomena of life, we want it to have a quality without which it can have no virtues at all, namely, truthfulness.

*Nikolai Dobrolyubov*

\*

Truly great art does not suffer falsehood.

*Konstantin Stanislavsky*

\*

The truth of life has been and will always be the rule for the literature of socialist realism, the literature which is part of the people's life and which serves the people.

*Konstantin Fedin*

## ART AND LIFE

Concisely defined, socialist realism is a truthful portrayal of life as it develops. It is the skill of seeing the tomorrow in what you see today. It is the acknowledgement of literature's educational role in relation to the people in the spirit of socialism.

*Alexander Fadeyev*

\*

We must know not only the two realities—the past and the present, the one in the creation of which we are taking part. We must also know a third reality—that of the future. Without it we shall never understand the method of socialist realism. To know clearly and precisely what you are fighting against, you must know what you want.

*Maxim Gorky*

\*

We must learn to look at the past and present from the summits of our future goals.

*Maxim Gorky*

\*

Scientific socialism has created for us a lofty intellectual plateau from which we clearly see the past and where we are shown the direct and only path to the future.

*Maxim Gorky*

Any and all narrowness is foreign to the art of socialist realism. It has never excluded either history or world literature, either the epic or the fable, from its range of interests.

*Dmitry Kabalevsky*

\*

Literature owes its greatness to its truthfulness.

*Maxim Gorky*

\*

One must seek beauty and the truth of life together. The truth of life is simple, severe, and sometimes unattractive, but if you succeed in mastering it, beauty, too, will be the more lasting.

*Vladimir Korolenko*

\*

The artistic truth is the immediate goal of art.

*Ivan Goncharov*

\*

Art is the truth. The truth alone is convincing and irrevocable. Where truth is absent, art, too, is absent.

*Mikhail Kalinin*

## ART AND LIFE

The writer must be able to tell his reader the truth directly to his face no matter how bitter it is. This is why in assessing every work of art we must first of all approach it from the standpoint of its credibility and truthfulness.

*Mikhail Sholokhov*

\*

No art can exist without the truth.

*Mikhail Glinka*

\*

The power of talent lies in the truth; a mistaken course destroys the strongest of talents.

*Nikolai Chernyshevsky*

\*

The truth wants simplicity, the lie complexity. This is proved very well by the history of literature.

*Maxim Gorky*

\*

*The moment* an artist wants to turn his back on the truth, he instantly becomes barren and for this minute loses all his talent.

*Fyodor Dostoyevsky*

## WORDS OF THE WISE

The truest token of the truth is simplicity and clarity. A lie is always complicated, pretentious, and garrulous.

*Lev Tolstoy*

\*

The artist must be colossally truthful and must take his characters from real life. Any writer who substitutes a fabrication for the true-to-life image is a liar.

*A. V. Lunacharsky*

\*

In the written or spoken arts nothing is more unpleasant than falsehood. What you write must be truthful.

*Alisher Navoi*

\*

To say what you have to say intelligibly speak sincerely, and to say it sincerely speak as the thought comes to you.

*Lev Tolstoy*

\*

Sincerity is one of the main conditions of art.

*N. P. Ogarev*

## ART AND LIFE

The highest quality of any of the arts is sincerity.

*Sergei Rachmaninov*

\*

Only that which is the writer's confession, that in which he *consummates himself*—only that can be great.

*Alexander Blok*

\*

He who ventures to be a writer must be always and entirely sincere.

*Maxim Gorky*

\*

In art everything unfaithful to reality is a lie and speaks of failure, not talent.

*Vissarion Belinsky*

\*

Reality consists not only in the naturalness of what you see, but more in the naturalness and simplicity and depth of what you make of the purport of an event.

*P. P. Chistyakov*

\*

Realism is material, and if this is applied to the word, it means that the realist's word is not hollow, but filled with the matter of truth. A realist writer is a truthful writer.

*M. M. Prishvin*

\*

A true realist, as I see him, is someone who sees the sombre as well as the bright, but gravitates towards the bright and considers as realistic only the path travelled towards the bright.

*M. M. Prishvin*

\*

I am driven forward by the power of my faith in something better, and I clear the path to it with my doubts.

*M. M. Prishvin*

\*

The artistic truth must speak for itself, and not with the help of commentaries and interpretations.

*M. E. Saltykov-Shchedrin*

\*

Consummate and full-blooded art is not a dead copy of Nature; no, art is a product of the soul and the human spirit.

*P. P. Chistyakov*

# ART AND LIFE

To write a scene from history or from life is not everything. It will be an ordinary photograph, a study, unless it is illuminated by the author's philosophical outlook and unless it carries—no matter in what form—the profound sense of life.

*Ilya Repin*

\*

Truth is a necessary element, but not yet the virtue of a work of art. We measure the virtue of a work of art by the author's breadth of vision, his correct understanding, and lively portrayal of the things he writes about.

*Nikolai Dobrolyubov*

\*

The imagination is always the artist's helper.

*Ivan Goncharov*

\*

In art the intellect must be allied to phantasy.

*Ivan Goncharov*

\*

Imagination is one of the most essential tools in the literary armorarium which creates the image.

*Maxim Gorky*

Artistism is impossible without phantasy.

*Maxim Gorky*

\*

Art thrives on invention, science puts it into practice.

*Maxim Gorky*

\*

In the art of depicting life by means of the word, the brush, or the sculptor's chisel, "invention" is apposite and useful if it improves the depiction, making it more convincing or deepening its meaning, showing it as socially true and inevitable.

*Maxim Gorky*

\*

There is much in common between science and fiction; in both cases the main role is played by observation, comparison, and study; like the scientist, the writer must have imagination and the knack of conjecture, that is, "intuition".

*Maxim Gorky*

\*

Only very naive people think that fiction is hostile to reality.

*Konstantin Paustovsky*

## ART AND LIFE

It is not invention that creates a tale, but reality. Yet an invention can be more real than reality.

*Mikhail Svetlov*

\*

Never will a writer invent anything more beautiful and forceful than the truth.

*Yuri Tynianov*

\*

Fiction differs from history not by virtue of any "fabrication", but by virtue of its greater, closer, and more vital understanding of people and events, and its greater concern for them.

*Yuri Tynianov*

\*

The fact is not all the truth, it is only the raw material out of which the real truth of art must be smelted or extracted.

*Maxim Gorky*

\*

The truth without invention is like an aircraft without fuel. The truth is prostrate. When the tanks are filled, the truth flies, crossing the meridians and poles of our planet. There is no truth without invention. On the contrary. Invention saves the truth, and exists solely for the sake of the truth.

*M. M. Prishvin*

\*

The invention is all the better the more credible it is, and the more pleasant, the closer it is to the probable and possible.

*M. M. Prishvin*

\*

Anything can be invented save psychology.... And it is terrible when in novels and stories people are made to do what they are quite unlikely to do in view of their mentality. In art falsehood destroys the ties between events, and everything turns into powder.

*Lev Tolstoy*

\*

In works of a historical nature the truth must be factual; in fiction, where the events are invented, it is replaced by the logical truth, that is, a reasonable possibility and correspondence to the existing course of events.

*Nikolai Dobrolyubov*

## ART AND LIFE

# HARMONY OF CONTENT AND FORM

Harmony of thought and word–very important and often even climacteric. Sometimes a wretchedly trivial thought is clad in such resplendent garb that it becomes entangled in the vain folds of its own frippery and is hard to get at, while sometimes a sound and original thought is so expressed that it wilts and loses colour like a flower trodden upon by a heavy boot.

*V. O. Kliuchevsky*

\*

Form is beauty, that is, harmony of the parts composing a balanced whole.

*Mikhail Glinka*

\*

A profound idea impresses if clad in consummate form. It is through the form that it acquires its great significance. Attacks on lofty ideas by lowly means are loathsome.

*Ilya Repin*

\*

Even gifted with genius, one must work very hard to attain absolute perfection of form. This unassuming devotion to hard work is the foundation of genius.

*Ilya Repin*

\*

Even though advocating a great and profound thought, a work is not a work of art unless it expresses its message in images that have a direct and stimulating effect on the senses.

*A. V. Lunacharsky*

\*

Great works of art are valued less for their immediate power and more for the perfection of form in which this power is expressed.

*Pyotr Chaikovsky*

\*

A work embodying a valid idea is artistic only if its form is in complete accord with that idea.

*Nikolai Chernyshevsky*

\*

The lame and undeveloped character of the form makes any serious step in the further development of the content impossible; it causes a shameful stagnation, leads to a waste of energy, to a discrepancy between word and deed.

*V. I. Lenin*

\*

Creative endeavour is a passion that expires in form.

*M. M. Prishvin*

\*

Formalism is a recognised evil, but form is goodness. All too often, consciously or not, some of our writers sweep out form on the pretext of fighting formalism.

*M. M. Prishvin*

\*

Even a simple arranging of things and instilling of order yields harmony, and the resulting form yields satisfaction.

*M. M. Prishvin*

\*

Formalism is where the means are paraded as the aim, and this not only in art, but also everywhere else—even where the literary prospector describes an excavator instead of the man for whom it works.

*M. M. Prishvin*

Science and art wash the gold of reality and beat it into exquisite forms.

*Vissarion Belinsky*

*

Art is meant to instil harmony and order in the soul, not confusion and turmoil.

*Nikolai Gogol*

*

Beauty is the correspondence of form to content.

*G. V. Plekhanov*

*

It is an axiom that beauty is the essential condition of art and that there is no art without beauty.

*Vissarion Belinsky*

*

Time has no power over the truly beautiful in art.

*Alexander Serov*

*

We must distinguish three elements in every literary work. The most important is content, then the author's devotion to his subject, and lastly technique. Harmony of content and devotion gives the work fullness, whereupon the third element—technique—usually attains a certain perfection by itself.

*Lev Tolstoy*

٭

The artist engaged in arts that give form and character to word, sound, or colour must seek to strike an equilibrium between his powers of imagination and his powers of logic, between the intuitive and the rational.

*Maxim Gorky*

٭

The challenge facing every real master possessing content is to express this content in the most convincing, striking, and simple manner.

*A. V. Lunacharsky*

٭

In the case of a writer, form is inseverably connected with, and conceived by, the content.

*Ivan Bunin*

٭

Above all, art must be clear and simple, for its significance is much too great to allow for "eccentricities".

*Maxim Gorky*

In art nothing must be vague or unintelligible.

*Vissarion Belinsky*

\*

Every deliberate attempt at originality results in tawdry garishness.

*Nikolai Chernyshevsky*

\*

The finish, the so-called technical gloss, must never be seen as a value in itself. Yet this very finish makes poetry fit for consumption.

*Vladimir Mayakovsky*

\*

For me form and content are one, and I never know what the one is without the other. Precision of thought conditions precision of expression and is, in fact, itself precision of expression.

*Maxim Gorky*

\*

When the form is an expression of the content they are so closely attached that to separate the form from the content is to destroy the content; conversely, to separate the content from the form is to destroy the form.

*Vissarion Belinsky*

## ART AND LIFE

The concept of artistic skill applies equally to the realm of form and the realm of content.

*Dmitry Kabalevsky*

\*

Even works of art by authors who cherish form and are unconcerned about content are bound to express some idea.

*G. V. Plekhanov*

\*

One begins working on the form when one lacks a content.

*A. V. Lunacharsky*

\*

Technique is a means; when treated as an aim it is reduced to a very lowly state, to mere jugglery.

*Alexander Serov*

\*

Strange though it may seem, art requires even greater precision than science.

*Lev Tolstoy*

\*

Like any other art, literature needs painstaking preparation and perseverance; its technique, though less conspicuous, is no less difficult to master than that of painting or music.

*Ivan Turgenev*

＊

Precision in the use of words is not merely a requirement of style and good taste, but first of all a requirement of sense.

*Konstantin Fedin*

＊

Exterminate needless words as you would exterminate lice.

*Maxim Gorky*

＊

The art of writing consists not in the art of writing, but in the art of striking out what is badly written.

*Anton Chekhov*

＊

The art of writing is the art of deleting.

*Anton Chekhov*

＊

The writer's greatest skill is the skill of deleting.

*Fyodor Dostoyevsky*

## ART AND LIFE

Language is the writer's weapon like the rifle is the soldier's, and the better the weapon, the stronger is the warrior.

*Maxim Gorky*

\*

Write without conceits and extravagances which mislead both the reader and the author himself.

*V. I. Lenin*

\*

Those who write obscurely either involuntarily betray their ignorance or are trying ineffectually to conceal it. Those who write obscurely write of things that are obscure to them.

*Mikhail Lomonosov*

\*

One writes elaborately only if one does not understand what one is writing about.

*V. O. Kliuchevsky*

\*

There are two kinds of nonsense, one deriving from a deficiency of feelings and thoughts replaced by words, the other from an abundance of feelings and thoughts and a deficiency of words to express them.

*Alexander Pushkin*

Comprehensibility and readability are not just a necessary condition for something to be eagerly read by the people; as I see it, they are the check against anything foolish, inapposite, and trashy.

*Lev Tolstoy*

\*

For a literary work to earn the title of artistic it must be given consummate literary form. A story or novel acquires this form through simple, precise, clear, and concise language.

*Maxim Gorky*

\*

The writer's art is judged ultimately by his style, and style is primarily language.

*Konstantin Fedin*

\*

Every thought can be expressed in simple and clear terms.

*Alexander Herzen*

\*

Real good taste is not indiscriminate rejection of a word or phrase, but a sense of proportion and fitness.

*Alexander Pushkin*

## ART AND LIFE

The richer the language is in expressions and turns of the phrase, the better for a skilled writer.

*Alexander Pushkin*

✶

In a writer lack of variety speaks of a one-sided though, perhaps, profound mind.

*Alexander Pushkin*

✶

Good writing wants the word to be fitting, to be indispensable and unavoidable, and it wants as few words as possible. Good writing must be terse.

*Nikolai Chernyshevsky*

✶

Our word must be clear, loud, and intelligible for as many as possible.

*M. M. Prishvin*

✶

We must sharpen our words. We must demand speech that portrays every movement tersely and precisely ... so that words should now explode like a bomb, now smart like a wound, and now reverberate like a bellow of triumph.

*Vladimir Mayakovsky*

The important thing in art is not to say more than is necessary.

*Lev Tolstoy*

\*

False notes and lack of a sense of proportion are terribly harmful to a work of art.

*Lev Tolstoy*

\*

Precision and brevity are the prime virtues of prose. It wants thoughts and more thoughts, for without them the most striking of expressions is meaningless.

*Alexander Pushkin*

\*

Brevity is the cardinal condition of the artistic.

*Fyodor Dostoyevsky*

\*

Brevity is the sister of talent.

*Anton Chekhov*

\*

Literary verbosity is, doubtless, the most abominable of all verbosity.

*M. E. Saltykov-Shchedrin*

ART AND LIFE

Brevity does not consist in a piece of writing just being short, but in a terse crowding of ideas, so that much is said in little and so that there are no hollow words.

*G. R. Derzhavin*

\*

The literary gift is an ability to say or express well what the ungifted will say or express badly.

*Fyodor Dostoyevsky*

\*

In literature, as in life, one must always remember the rule: people repent a thousand times that they have spoken much, and never that they have spoken little.

*A. F. Pisemsky*

\*

Man dies, his thoughts live on. This long life of ideas should commit people to a certain restraint when putting their vague emotions into words and thoughts.

*Maxim Gorky*

## OF INSPIRATION AND TORMENT OF CREATION

For him who has tasted the joy of creation, other joys no longer exist.

*Anton Chekhov*

*

All sincere enjoyment of beauty is itself a source of moral beauty.

*Konstantin Ushinsky*

*

Creativity is the finest that there is in any man; it yields the most sublime of joys and the wisest of thoughts, and arouses the noblest of passions.

*Vera Mukhina*

*

Without creativity there can be no true rapture, unmixed with fear, suffering, qualms of conscience, and shame.

*Lev Tolstoy*

# INSPIRATION

The days of writing at leisure are over; give yourself whole to the people. That is what art requires of you these days.

*M. P. Mussorgsky*

※

Without preparation, without passion, without hard work and perseverance in developing your sense of beauty, art is bound to elude you.

*Vissarion Belinsky*

\*

What is needed are positive values, inordinate feelings, and thoughts geared to the great whole. And this is what the writer must now produce.

*M. M. Prishvin*

※

It is a terrible hindrance if the subject is imposed on you.... It breeds high- or low-grade hack writing and divests the writer of quality.

*Konstantin Paustovsky*

\*

The development of art needs initiative, and for this it must be free.

*Konstantin Stanislavsky*

In substance, art must have unconditional freedom in the choice of subjects—from the artist himself, as well as the critics.

*Vissarion Belinsky*

\*

True criticism never imposes on the artist. The sole demand it makes on him may be expressed in a word: be truthful.

*G. V. Plekhanov*

\*

Any work of art, if a true work of art, is an expression of the artist's innermost feelings in a singular manner that has no resemblance to anything else.

*Lev Tolstoy*

\*

To produce a good portrayal, the artist must see distinctly, must even foresee, let alone know.

*Maxim Gorky*

\*

The beginning, the first sentence, is the hardest of all. As in music, it sets the tune for the rest of the piece, and one usually has to look for it a long time.

*Maxim Gorky*

## INSPIRATION

Writing is not the hardest part of a writer's trade; writing is the easiest. The hardest is the time when you cannot write.

*M. M. Prishvin*

\*

Inspiration wells exclusively from hard work and during work.

*Pyotr Chaikovsky*

\*

Inspiration is a guest that does not visit the lazy.

*Pyotr Chaikovsky*

\*

Inspiration is a sudden perception of the truth.

*Vissarion Belinsky*

\*

A writer must write and write, but must never hurry.

*Anton Chekhov*

\*

The slower you go, the more you see of the movement of life.

*M. M. Prishvin*

The only good time for writing is when you leave a piece of your flesh in the inkwell each time you dip your pen in it.

*Lev Tolstoy*

\*

The pen does not write well unless you add at least a few drops of your own blood to the ink.

*V. F. Odoyevsky*

\*

No passage in a book will ever reach the reader's heart unless it stirred the author five times as strongly.

*P. A. Pavlenko*

\*

Only he can ignite others who is himself afire.

*P. A. Pavlenko*

\*

When legitimate discussion and concern arise over the weakness of literature and the mediocrity of books, the answer should be sought first of all in the background of every separate writer.

*Konstantin Paustovsky*

# INSPIRATION

Why do we keep scrawling tediously when our ideas, our thoughts, and images should blazon abroad like the golden horn, carrying word about the new world?

*A. N. Tolstoy*

\*

A thought that you forget to record is a lost treasure.

*Dmitry Mendeleyev*

\*

Love the art in you, not yourself in art.

*Konstantin Stanislavsky*

\*

Look harder, draw longer, write simpler.

*Ilya Repin*

\*

If the artist is to acquaint us with interesting aspects of life, he must himself be perspicacious and developed enough to distinguish between the interesting and uninteresting.

*Dmitry Pisarev*

If you want to serve society, you must know and understand it and all its interests in every detail, and for this you must be a most enlightened and educated person.

*Ivan Kramskoi*

\*

A brilliant pen and a bright thought are not the same thing.

*V. O. Kliuchevsky*

\*

The less a work of art tends to be didactic and the more impartially the artist picks the figures and situations for the setting to his idea, the more balanced and true his portrayal will be, and the surer will he achieve the desired effect.

*Dmitry Pisarev*

\*

Mediocrities like to lay on the paint thickly, brightly, and strikingly, so that it catches the eye and is seen from afar. Instead of a painting they get a signboard.

*Dmitry Pisarev*

# INSPIRATION

Simplicity is the essential condition for a work of art, which by nature rejects all outward adornments and refinements.

*Vissarion Belinsky*

\*

The highest degree of artistry is that where one does not see the effort and forgets the artist.

*Lev Tolstoy*

## OF THE WRITER AND ARTIST

A real writer is like the prophet of olden times: he sees more clearly than ordinary people.

*Anton Chekhov*

\*

The artist is the sensorium of his country and his class—their ear, eye, and heart; he is the voice of his time.

*Maxim Gorky*

\*

The artist is the mirror of his environment: he reflects his society, the nation, and the times.

*Ilya Repin*

\*

While paying due tribute to his age, every true artist also creates for eternity; contemporary beauty vanishes, while the universal, that which is rooted in the human heart and the nature of things retains its relevance.

*Nikolai Karamzin*

# THE WRITER AND ARTIST

When a writer writes he must feel equal to the highest-ranking political leader, not to an apprentice or hireling.

*Alexander Dovzhenko*

*

The writer must have a big heart. Indifferent people rarely become writers. A writer must be intelligent and, doubly so, warm-hearted.

*P. A. Pavlenko*

*

The writer transfuses himself whole into his book and the composer into his music; here they stay alive for the rest of time. Open a book, listen to music, and if you can read you will be confronted by their makers.

*V. O. Kliuchevsky*

*

A book is its author's confession, it is the man. By a book you can judge of its writer.

*Mikhail Kalinin*

*

The content of a work of art depends entirely on the comportment of the artist: the content is the artist himself, his own soul enshrined in the form.

*M. M. Prishvin*

Books are people in paper binding.

*Anton Makarenko*

\*

The creator can bestow upon his creation only those qualities that he himself possessses.

*Dmitry Pisarev*

\*

Every piece of fiction represents its author and his inner world no less than a learned treatise. As we read a novel, story, satire, or article, it is easy for us to determine their authors' degree of insight or ignorance, as well as their outlook.

*M. E. Saltykov-Shchedrin*

\*

Every work of art is a faithful mirror of its creator and none has ever succeeded in disguising his nature.

*V. V. Stasov*

\*

The works of a gifted author are bound to reflect his personality, because creative writing consists precisely in that the objective outer material is processed quite individually by the author's psyche.

*V. V. Vorovsky*

## THE WRITER AND ARTIST

Art is personal experience rendered in images and sensations, and aspiring to be a generalisation.

*A. N. Tolstoy*

\*

Live as you write and write as you live or the sounds struck by your lyre will be false.

*K. N. Batyushkov*

\*

Our era will bow in homage to just those artists whose lives are the truest illustration of their works and whose works are the truest justification of their lives.

*Vissarion Belinsky*

\*

Writing is neither trade nor occupation. It is a vocation. Probing some of the words, their very sound, we find their original meaning. The word "vocation" originated from the word "voice"—primarily the voice of our hearts.

*Konstantin Paustovsky*

\*

Only he who has something new, significant, and interesting to say can be a writer —he who sees many things others do not notice.

*Konstantin Paustovsky*

Write only when you feel something entirely new, an important content clear to you but unintelligible to people, and when the need to express it gives you no peace.

*Lev Tolstoy*

\*

Art, like life, is not for the weak.

*Alexander Blok*

\*

For me literature is a battlefield.

*S. M. Stepniak-Kravchinsky*

\*

By judging how deep the writer's vision penetrates the essence of things and how broadly he covers the various aspects of life in his portrayals one can also judge of his talent.

*Nikolai Dobrolyubov*

\*

Every real talent is something entirely unique.

*Nikolai Chernyshevsky*

Talent is rare. It should be systematically and carefully tended.

*V. I. Lenin*

*

It has long been observed that talent always appears where the social conditions are favourable for its development.

*G. V. Plekhanov*

*

Talent is a sense of the truth.

*Nikolai Dobrolyubov*

*

Talent has that precious quality of not being able to lie or to distort the truth.

*Ivan Goncharov*

*

A man's gift is a diamond. Having found it, lose no time to polish it and show its brilliance.

*A. V. Suvorov*

*

Talent is nothing more than an ability to do; the virtue of what is done depends on its purpose and content.

*Nikolai Chernyshevsky*

It takes perseverance and patience to develop a gift.

*Alexander Herzen*

\*

Much talent requires much diligence.

*Pyotr Chaikovsky*

\*

Talent is like a precious stone—the more labour is put into polishing it, the more beautiful it will be.

*Pyotr Chaikovsky*

\*

Even a person with the stamp of genius will create nothing great, even nothing mediocre, unless he labours with hellish persistence.

*Pyotr Chaikovsky*

\*

Talent without diligence will achieve little, diligence without talent will create much, though nothing that would make us marvel. This is why the gifted often go under, while the hardworking attain fame.

*Anton Rubinstein*

## THE WRITER AND ARTIST

Talent is faith in oneself, in one's powers.

*Maxim Gorky*

\*

Neither talent nor love of art are enough to become an artist; to be worth anything they must be compounded with hard work.

*Alexander Herzen*

\*

Continuous labour, without which nothing truly great can result, is a necessary condition for artistic pursuits.

*Alexander Pushkin*

\*

He who does not love literature enough to sacrifice his wellbeing will do better to leave it alone.

*Nikolai Leskov*

\*

The first step in all the creative arts is self-renouncement.

*M. M. Prishvin*

\*

People still think the writer and poet can work only at times of inspiration. Isn't this why many writers wait for inspiration to come and write nothing for years? I am convinced that inspiration comes in the act.

*Nikolai Ostrovsky*

\*

Talent is a divine spark whereby its bearer burns himself to cinders, lighting the way for others with the flame that consumes him.

*V. O. Kliuchevsky*

\*

Talent proves itself when the time is right, while genius proves itself before its time.

*P. A. Pavlenko*

\*

Genius is first and foremost kin of the people.

*Alexander Blok*

\*

Genius' name is million, because in his breast he bears the agony, joy, hope, and aspirations of millions of people.

*Vissarion Belinsky*

## THE WRITER AND ARTIST

In literature low ranks are just as indispensable as they are in the army.

*Anton Chekhov*

\*

No poet in world literature has ever, at least to some extent, escaped the influence of his predecessors. Influence is like the rung of a ladder whereby the novice ascends to the summits of originality.

*Hovannes Toumanian*

\*

In the art of writing all are one another's apprentices, but each goes his own way.

*M. M. Prishvin*

\*

To create is to sing one's very own song.

*Mikhail Kalinin*

\*

Repeating the same ideas clothed merely in other words without feeling is not just needless, but also unagreeable. The great secret is to arouse ever fresh curiosity in the quick and inquiring soul.

*G. R. Derzhavin*

Tradition is not mere repetition, but the projection of already accumulated experience.

*Dmitry Shostakovich*

*

The most modest original work is more precious and more important than the most excellent of copies. He who is not bent on producing his own, should not even touch the arts.

*V. V. Stasov*

# OF MUSIC, POETRY, ARCHITECTURE, ART AND THEATRE

## MUSIC

Music is the most sublime art in the world.

*Lev Tolstoy*

\*

From the cradle of humanity and as long as it exists there will be music.

*A. V. Lunacharsky*

\*

Music is the intellect embodied in beautiful sounds.

*Ivan Turgenev*

\*

Through music you will discover in yourself new powers you did not know before.

*Dmitry Shostakovich*

Is there anyone on earth, unless he be deaf of mind, who is indifferent to a song?

*Mukhtar Auezov*

*

Music has many meanings. You can endow it with diverse content, depending on the pattern of your own soul.

*A. V. Lunacharsky*

*

Music has extraordinary purifying and animating powers.

*A. V. Lunacharsky*

*

The Russians are one of the most musical nations in the world. They were known as such since antiquity. The people of Russia, unshakable and unchanging in this respect, have borne their folk songs through the ages.

*V. V. Stasov*

*

Nowhere else has the folk song played so great a part in the people's life as it has in our land, and nowhere has it been preserved in such abundance, force, and diversity.

*V. V. Stasov*

In music beauty is achieved not through a cumulation of effects and oddities of harmony, but through simplicity and naturalness.

*Pyotr Chaikovsky*

\*

Great composers have always and above all paid attention to melody as the prime principle of music. Melody *is* music, the main fabric of all music.

*Anton Chekhov*

\*

To banish melody is to renounce truthful expression of great feeling, content, and reality.

*Tikhon Khrennikov*

\*

Melody is the thought, movement, and soul of a musical composition.

*Dmitry Shostakovich*

\*

There is no poetry without an idea and no music without a melody.

*V. V. Stasov*

Lovers and connoisseurs of music are developed, not born. To grow fond of music one must first of all listen to it.

*Dmitry Shostakovich*

\*

Dissonance is a great force in music.

*Pyotr Chaikovsky*

\*

Music is the material daughter of material sound; music and only music can transmit the palpitations of one soul to another, can confer blissful, unaccountable emotion.

*Alexander Herzen*

\*

Music, like literature, must be ideologically committed.

*Tikhon Khrennikov*

\*

Good music is always revolutionary in spirit for it unites people, arouses them, and urges them forward.

*Dmitry Shostakovich*

## MUSIC, POETRY, ART, AND THEATRE

Good music arouses only humane feelings, only progressive and humane ideas.

*Dmitry Shostakovich*

## POETRY

The poetry of today is a poetry of struggle. Its every word must be like a soldier of an army.

*Vladimir Mayakovsky*

\*

The times call for heroic poetry.

*Maxim Gorky*

\*

Among the essential qualities that make a true poet there must definitely be modernity. More than anyone else, the poet must be a son of his time.

*Vissarion Belinsky*

\*

To be a poet you must think in poetic images, not warble melodious sounds. To be a poet you need a powerful sense of involvement in contemporary problems, not a trivial longing to shine, not the musing of an idle fancy, not affected feelings, not primped-up sorrow.

*Vissarion Belinsky*

\*

All poetry must be an expression of life. But to express life, poetry must first of all be poetry.

*Vissarion Belinsky*

\*

The language of poetry is terse, condensed, picturesque, and musical.

*Vladimir Korolenko*

\*

Poetry is the inner flame of all talent.

*Fyodor Dostoyevsky*

\*

Poetry is the soul of the deed that turns beauty into virtue.

*M. M. Prishvin*

\*

Poetry is a flame lighting up man's soul. It burns, warms, and illumines. A true poet sears himself and others quite unavoidably with scorching pain, and that is the whole thing.

*Lev Tolstoy*

\*

Poets come not from somewhere across the sea, but from the midst of their own people. They are lights emanating from their people, and are the most advanced heralds of its powers.

*Nikolai Gogol*

\*

A poet has no age. A true poet is the contemporary of all generations—his own and that of his grandchildren.

*Alexander Tvardovsky*

\*

In poetry, as in prose, the thought comes first; you may conceal its absence with fantastic arabesques and obfuscate it with the smoothness and tunefulness of the rhyme, but what is devoid of thought will never make a lasting impression.

*Dmitry Pisarev*

\*

Poets whose verse contains few thoughts are not likely to win much importance.

*Nikolai Dobrolyubov*

Dashing off rhymes does not make a poet.

*Alexander Pushkin*

\*

To be able to write verse does not mean to be a poet; bookshops are piled high with proof of this.

*Vissarion Belinsky*

\*

Poetry must be novel; nothing is more deadly for it than repetition.

*Afanasy Fet*

\*

There can be neither life nor poetry without passions and contradictions.

*Vissarion Belinsky*

\*

Poetry and chatter are at opposite poles. The essence of poetry is concentrated content; to dilute it is to kill it.

*Nikolai Chernyshevsky*

\*

*I allow*
> *poetry*
>> *one form only:*
*brevity,*
*the precision of mathematical formulae.*

*Vladimir Mayakovsky*

> *Mint verse like coin,*
> *Austere, distinct, and true.*
> *Never fail the rule*
> *That words be few*
> *And thoughts be many.*
>
> *Nikolai Nekrasov*

*

> *The poet's pride is silvery rhyme,*
> *But rhyme abhors a hollow word.*
>
> *Suleiman Stalsky*

*

Poetry, like everything else, sheds its sacred beauty and naturalness the moment it becomes a trade.

*Maxim Gorky*

*

The fashionable is transient, especially in writing verse.

*A. N. Radishchev*

# ARCHITECTURE

Every great period has its great architecture.

*A. V. Lunacharsky*

Architecture is one more chronicle of the world; it speaks when songs and traditions have already fallen silent.

*Nikolai Gogol*

# PAINTING

Out of all the arts that nature has gifted the human race, painting is the most pleasing and usefully indulges the eye and mind.

*Alexander Ivanov*

\*

Painting is an art that uses lines and paints on a flat surface to depict all visible objects.

*Alexander Ivanov*

\*

The art of drawing and painting is nothing but an instrument that assists literature and, consequently, the enlightenment of the people.

*A. G. Venetsianov*

Images are the life of the memory, the memory of those who had once lived, the evidence of by-gone days, a homily of virtue, and an expression of might, resurrection of the dead, immortality of praise and glory, a reminder of past exploits. Images make visible that which is far away, and that which is in different places they portray together.

*S. F. Ushakov*

\*

Smearing and scribbling–doing as best you can–is not art.

*P. P. Chistyakov*

\*

To wield the brush is not enough by far for a painter. A painter must be educated and knowledgeable.

*Alexander Ivanov*

\*

It seems only right to me that the artist should be among the most highly educated people of his time; he must know the point of development reached today, and must also have opinions of his own on all matters that animate the finest members of society–opinions that go farther and deeper than those reigning at the time.

*Ivan Kramskoi*

The artist must be historian, poet, philosopher, and observer all at once.

*A. A. Bestuzhev-Marlinsky*

# THEATRE

The theatre is a pulpit from which the world can be told many virtuous things.

*Nikolai Gogol*

\*

Like every great artist, the theatre must respond to the noblest currents in modern life, lest it become a worthless institution.

*Vladimir Nemirovich-Danchenko*

\*

The theatre is the highest instance for the solution of life's problems.

*Alexander Herzen*

\*

If the purpose of the theatre were reduced to mere entertainment, it would, probably, warrant less effort. But the theatre is the art of mirroring life.

*Konstantin Stanislavsky*

\*

Not that which blinds and befuddles the spectator with its histrionics is beautiful, but that which ennobles the life of the human spirit on the stage and from the stage, that is, the thoughts and feelings of actor and audience.

*Konstantin Stanislavsky*

\*

What the theatre needs is to be simple, forceful, and unaffected.

*Lev Tolstoy*

\*

The actor must above all possess culture and must understand and learn to reach up to the geniuses of literature.

*Konstantin Stanislavsky*

\*

The actor must learn to make the difficult habitual, the habitual easy, and the easy beautiful.

*Konstantin Stanislavsky*

## OF SATIRE

Art invariably contends for virtue either positively or negatively—showing us either the beauty of what is best in man or deriding the hideousness of all that is worst. If you put the rubbish on display, and if you display it so that it awakens the spectator's disgust, then I ask you: isn't this the same as praising the good, isn't this the same as praising virtue?

*Nikolai Gogol*

\*

Sometimes you cannot direct society or even the whole generation to the beautiful, unless you show it the deepness of its iniquity.

*Nikolai Gogol*

\*

In the recesses of frigid laughter there may be burning sparks of powerful, everlasting love.

*Nikolai Gogol*

## SATIRE

Laughter visible to the world is frequently tinged with tears the world cannot see.

*Nikolai Gogol*

\*

Describing human frailties, misconceptions, and passions is no more reprehensible than dissecting is murderous.

*Alexander Pushkin*

\*

To depict nothing but the good, bright, and gratifying in human nature is to trim the truth, that is, to depict incompletely and hence incorrectly. The result is monotonous, cloying, and sugary. Light cannot be depicted unless you show the shadows.

*Ivan Goncharov*

\*

Art aims at exaggerating the good so that it should become still better, and at exaggerating the bad so that it should excite disgust.

*Maxim Gorky*

\*

Organic tissue, if viable, is bound to react to irritations. And I do react! I respond to pain with screams and tears, to evil with indignation, and to vileness with loathing. In substance, as I see it, this is called life.

*Anton Chekhov*

\*

The life about us speaks so loudly of injustice and evil that it is positively impossible not to hear it or to seek refuge in illusions. We must speak up about these things.

*Gleb Uspensky*

\*

There are more ways than one of serving the common weal, but exposing evil, falsehood, and vice is equally useful, I daresay, and doubly so because it implies complete sympathy with virtue and verity.

*M. E. Saltykov-Shchedrin*

\*

Literature is something that has over centuries and millennia inscribed on its scrolls great deeds and abominations, exploits of self-sacrifice and infamous incitements, and frivolity.

*M. E. Saltykov-Shchedrin*

## SATIRE

Nothing so discourages vice as the knowledge that it has been discovered and that ridicule has already resounded on its account.

*M. E. Saltykov-Shchedrin*

\*

For satire to be real satire and to achieve its purpose it is necessary, first, that it should let the reader feel the ideal of its author and, second, that it should wholly and distinctly understand the object against which it is aiming its darts.

*M. E. Saltykov-Shchedrin*

\*

Voltaire used the tool of ridicule to extinguish the fires of fanaticism and ignorance in Europe.

*Vissarion Belinsky*

\*

We must require that art show us life as it is, because, whatever life is like, it will tell us and teach us more than all the figments and harangues of the moralists.

*Vissarion Belinsky*

None but wretched hacks whitewash and prim up life, seeking to conceal its darker sides and exhibiting only the consoling.

*Vissarion Belinsky*

\*

When the time comes, the habit of faithfully portraying the negative sides of life will enable the same people or their successors to portray its positive developments just as faithfully.

*Vissarion Belinsky*

\*

The shriek of indignation that escapes the artist at the sight of social iniquities is as precious as his tranquil contemplation of beauty.

*Dmitry Pisarev*

\*

Literature is a great social force that tends to corrupt society the moment it ceases to prod it forward or to exhibit its acute and chronic ailments.

*Dmitry Pisarev*

\*

There are ulcers of the people's life which sensible people can laugh at only in an abrasive and sarcastic way; he who laughs at

## SATIRE

them merely to help his digestion distracts the public consciousness, lulls public outrage, and abuses man's sacred personality.

*Dmitry Pisarev*

\*

Satire is good only if it is topical.

*Dmitry Pisarev*

\*

The art of inciting laughter is more difficult than the art of inciting emotion.

*Vissarion Belinsky*

\*

Satire that bites is rich in morals.

*Vissarion Belinsky*

\*

None cares to recognise himself in a satire.

*Ivan Krylov*

\*

Laughter is among the most effective weapons against anything no longer fit to survive.

*Alexander Herzen*

## OF LITERARY CRITICISM

Among us, especially in Russia, literary criticism is being wrongly understood by the masses: for many to criticise means to scold. To so understand criticism is tantamount to confusing justice with accusation and punishment, and overlooking acquittal. In the broader sense, criticism is the same as judgement.

*Vissarion Belinsky*

\*

Literature without criticism is like a street without lanterns.

*Samuel Marshak*

\*

Where love of art is lacking, criticism is lacking too.

*Alexander Pushkin*

\*

Criticism is the science of discovering the beauties and faults in a work of art or literature.

*Alexander Pushkin*

## LITERARY CRITICISM

Criticism is not the middleman or conciliator between art and science: it is an application of theory to practice, it is a science in its own right, one created by art but not creating art.

*Vissarion Belinsky*

*

The purpose of criticism is to interpret the creations of good writers, to distinguish the relevant, to single out the best out of the large amount of trash written by all of us. As for the critics, their treatment often turns good writers into bad, profound ones into shallow, and wise ones into foolish.

*Lev Tolstoy*

*

Literary criticism must encourage, intensify, and direct those workings of the mind that a piece of fiction stimulates in the reader.

*Dmitry Pisarev*

*

If the critic wishes to avoid pouring water into a sieve, he must present his views on the vital issues reflected in the book.

*Dmitry Pisarev*

Critics must measure current literature by its ability to stimulate the people's will for creative, cultural-revolutionary activity.

*Maxim Gorky*

\*

Literature can arouse the public's mental activity, but it can neither substitute for the public nor exist without the public's support.

*Nikolai Chernyshevsky*

\*

For literature, the public is the supreme court of justice, the highest tribunal.

*Vissarion Belinsky*

\*

When evaluating a book you must think not of the book, but primarily of the life it reflects and expresses.

*N. A. Rubakin*

\*

Frequently, they scold a writer simply because they cannot write as he does.

*V. O. Kliuchevsky*

\*

A mediocrity will jump at being a critic if only because he does not see himself as a mediocrity.

*Dmitry Pisarev*

## LITERARY CRITICISM

A critic's severity will not kill true talent any more than a critic's acclaim will elevate a nonentity.

*Vissarion Belinsky*

*

Human works can never attain absolute perfection, but there can also be beauty in imperfect works.

*Anton Rubinstein*

*

I maintain that the writer is entitled to experiment and to the errors that go with it. A writer's experiment must be respected, for there can be no art without daring.

*A. N. Tolstoy*

*

I try to be cautious in my judgements, because the history of literature and art shows that the condemned often survive the judges and their tribunals.

*Maxim Tank*

*

A spurious work of art praised by critics is a door through which art's hypocrites hasten to slip in.

*Lev Tolstoy*

## OF TRASH AND HACKS

Great art transcends its limits, whereas mediocre art cannot fit its limits.

*Janis Rainis*

\*

If you bore the reader you will never make him apprehend the world, no matter how hard you try.

*A. N. Tolstoy*

\*

Artificiality demeans and debases everything it touches.

*Dmitry Pisarev*

\*

Trash, of course, is invariably devoid of principles; it creates indifference to the subject, and sidesteps difficult subjects.

*Vladimir Mayakovsky*

\*

One author of a piece of printed trash creates the impression in another two that they can write no worse. Having written and having been printed, these two provoke the envy of another four.

*Vladimir Mayakovsky*

\*

We are not very good at separating worthwhile writing from commercial trash. Both have the appearance of a book. In fact, trash is often printed much more lavishly than good books.

*Alexander Blok*

\*

Let there be fewer books, but let them be brighter. A lacklustre book has no business to be on a bookshelf. An honest workingman's time must not be frittered away.

*Nikolai Ostrovsky*

\*

It is as disgusting to see a lavishly produced shallow book as it is to see a shallow person enjoying all the blessings of wealth.

*Vissarion Belinsky*

\*

Haste is harmful. How much passion has been put to paper in vain. A book flashes by, creates a sensation, and is then consigned to oblivion, and this merely because everything in it is hasty, unconsidered, and unfinished.

*A. N. Tolstoy*

\*

*The muses suffer no haste:
Beauty must be majestic.*

*Alexander Pushkin*

\*

Humanity must by all means be delivered from reading trashy and worthless books.

*S. I. Vavilov*

## OF LANGUAGE AND WORDS

### THE BASIC MEDIUM

Words are given to man not for self-indulgence, but for the embodiment and communication to other people of thoughts and feelings, and of the share of the truth and of inspiration that is in him.

*Vladimir Korolenko*

\*

The summits of human thought, the most profound knowledge, and the most ardent emotions remain unknown to people until they are put into words clearly and precisely. Language is a tool for the expression of ideas.

*Mikhail Kalinin*

\*

Language is a living body created gradually by millions of generations.

*A. N. Tolstoy*

Language is the outcome of gigantic productive labour by human society. It consists of the deposited crystals of a myriad movements made in work, of gestures, and of the spiritual energy they generated.

*A. N. Tolstoy*

\*

The country's nature and the history of its people, reflected in people's souls, were put into words. People went to their graves, but the words they created remained as an everlasting and inexhaustible treasury of the national language; every word of the language, and every one of its forms, are the result of the thoughts and feelings through which the country's nature and the history of its people were reflected in words.

*Konstantin Ushinsky*

\*

Language gives spiritual expression to the people and its Motherland. It is the most vital, most abundant, and most lasting bond joining the past, present, and future generations of a people into one great, historical, and living whole.

*Konstantin Ushinsky*

## LANGUAGE AND WORDS

Without language neither individual nor nation could communicate their thoughts and feelings to others, and especially to the succeeding generation.

*Khachatur Abovian*

\*

Language and literature are not just a means, but the principal means of public enlightenment.

*Nikolai Karamzin*

\*

Learning a foreign language develops the mind, making it flexible and capable of understanding the outlook of other peoples.

*Dmitry Pisarev*

\*

Learning foreign languages enriches one's own tongue, making it more vivid, flexible, and expressive.

*N. K. Krupskaya*

\*

Language grows together with culture.

*A. N. Tolstoy*

\*

Richness of language is richness of thought.

*Nikolai Karamzin*

It is entirely safe to say that a person speaking a choice, pure, and rich language thinks more diversely than those who speak inarticulately and exhibit paucity of language.

*A. N. Tolstoy*

\*

Language is a tool of the mind. To treat it negligently is to think negligently—inexactly, approximately, incorrectly.

*A. N. Tolstoy*

\*

All resources, especially language, require a thorough sifting of the best they contain—the clear, precise, colourful, and resonant—and its further fond and careful development.

*Maxim Gorky*

\*

If in its speech a nation strives for nothing but a striking effect, when it speaks in ready-tailored phrases filled incontinently with declamatory words that leave you cold as ice, then this nation is in utter decline.

*Alexander Herzen*

## LANGUAGE AND WORDS

All languages aspire to precision, and precision demands brevity and terseness.

*Maxim Gorky*

\*

Vague words are invariably a sign of vague thoughts.

*Lev Tolstoy*

\*

To fight for the purity, semantic precision and incisiveness of language is to fight for the instrument of culture. The sharper and the more precisely aimed this instrument is, the more surely it is triumphant.

*Maxim Gorky*

\*

There is nothing in the world that cannot be put into simple and clear words.

*Maxim Gorky*

\*

It would be good to keep the language, all its departments, pure; not to make it uniform but, on the contrary, to avoid that uniform and stiff literary language which invariably conceals a vacuum.

*Lev Tolstoy*

\*

Language progresses towards precision and expressiveness through simplicity and frugality.

*A. N. Tolstoy*

\*

Flexible and rich, and beautiful for all its imperfections, is the language of every nation whose intellectual life has attained a high level of development.

*Nikolai Chernyshevsky*

\*

What a delight to hear the speech of the plain people! It is picturesque, moving, and serious.

*Lev Tolstoy*

\*

Keep closer to the language of the plain people, strive for the simplicity, brevity, and robust force that creates an image in two or three words.

*Maxim Gorky*

Language is the soul of the nation. It is the living medium of ideas, feelings, and thoughts.

*A. N. Tolstoy*

# THE RUSSIAN LANGUAGE

The Russian language—for thousands of years the people elaborated on this flexible, effervescent, inexhaustibly rich, clever, poetic, and industrious implement of its social life, its thoughts, feelings, hopes, vexations, and great future.

*A. N. Tolstoy*

\*

The Russian language is above all Alexander Pushkin, that indestructible pillar of the Russian language. It is also Lermontov, Lev Tolstoy, Leskov, Chekhov, and Gorky (*qq. v.*).

*A. N. Tolstoy*

\*

The language used by Russia to rule over a large part of the world has commensurate to her might a natural abundance, beauty, and force, conceding nothing in this respect to any other European language. And there is not the slightest doubt that the tongue of the Russians can be raised to the level of excellence which astounds us in other languages.

*Mikhail Lomonosov*

\*

Lord over many other languages, Russian is great *beside all the other tongues of Europe* not only by virtue of the vast spaces in which it reigns, but also by virtue of its own amplitude and abundance.

*Mikhail Lomonosov*

\*

The beauty, grandeur, force, and richness of the Russian language are made clear by books written in past ages, when our ancestors knew no rules of composition and, more, were hardly aware that any such existed or could exist.

*Mikhail Lomonosov*

\*

The Russo-Slavonic tongue, as foreign aesthetes testify, concedes nothing to Latin in virility or to Greek in fluency.

*G. R. Derzhavin*

Russian is, probably, closer to the classical languages in richness, force, structural freedom, and abundance of form than any of the other modern languages.

*Nikolai Dobrolyubov*

٭

There is no doubt that the Russian language is one of the richest in the world.

*Vissarion Belinsky*

٭

It (the Russian language.–*Ed.*) is astonishingly good for its native simplicity and uninhibited force.

*Ivan Turgenev*

٭

In days of doubt, of painful reflection on the lot of my Motherland, you alone, o great, mighty, veracious, and free Russian language, is my pillar of support! It is inconceivable that such a language should be given to a nation that is not great.

*Ivan Turgenev*

٭

One marvels at the preciousness of our language. Every sound of it is a gift: everything is granular and sumptuous as a pearl; indeed, a word is sometimes even more precious than the thing it stands for.

*Nikolai Gogol*

\*

No word can be as penetrating, exuberant, soulful, blazing and vibrant as an aptly chosen Russian word.

*Nikolai Gogol*

\*

In skilled hands and on practised lips the Russian language is beautiful, mellifluous, expressive, flexible, obedient, nimble, and spacious.

*Alexander Kuprin*

\*

Our language is expressive not only for lofty rhetoric or for resounding and picturesque poetry, but also for chaste simplicity, for sounds of the heart and the senses. It is more harmonious than French, more suited in tone for the outpourings of the soul, and encompasses more analogous words, that is, words compatible with the articulated action—an advantage that only the basic languages happen to possess.

*Nikolai Karamzin*

# LANGUAGE AND WORDS

As a material of literature the Russo-Slavonic language is incontestably superior to all the European ones.

*Alexander Pushkin*

\*

Throughout the eighteenth century the new Russian literature was fashioning that rich scientific language which we now possess—a flexible and forceful language capable of expressing the most abstract ideas of German metaphysics and the effervescent sparkle of French wit.

*Alexander Herzen*

\*

The principal characteristic of our language consists in the extraordinary lightness with which everything can be expressed in it—abstract ideas, innermost lyrical emotions, life's mousey bustle, bellows of indignation, ebullient frolic, and devastating passion.

*Alexander Herzen*

\*

The Russian literary language is closer to colloquial speech than any other European tongue.

*A. N. Tolstoy*

# WORDS OF THE WISE

The Russian language is so rich in verbs and nouns, so diverse in forms expressing inner movements, gestures, shades of feeling and thought, colours, smells, the material of things, and the like, that in developing the scientific linguistic culture we must deeply examine this brilliant legacy of "muzhik power".

*A. N. Tolstoy*

\*

Glory to our language which in its native richness, with practically no alien admixtures, flows along like a proud and magnificent river, thundering and booming, and can suddenly, if need be, turn soft and ripple like a tender runnel, pouring sweetly into the soul and forming all the cadences that exist in the drop or rise of the human voice.

*Nikolai Karamzin*

\*

For us nothing seems as ordinary or as simple as our speech, but in substance there is nothing more astonishing and marvellous.

*A. N. Radishchev*

\*

Among the splendid qualities of our language there is one which is entirely marvellous and inconspicuous: it is so diverse in its

## LANGUAGE AND WORDS

sounds that it covers the sounds of nearly all the other languages of the world.

*Konstantin Paustovsky*

٭

We are endowed with the richest, the most incisive, forceful, and truly enchanting Russian language.

*Konstantin Paustovsky*

٭

The Russian language reveals its truly wondrous qualities and wealth only to those innately fond of their people, who know it "root and branch", and who feel the native loveliness of our land.

*Konstantin Paustovsky*

٭

There are no sounds, colours, images, or thoughts—profound or simple—for which a precise expression would be lacking in our language.

*Konstantin Paustovsky*

٭

There is this one momentous fact: in our as yet unaccomplished and young language we can convey the most profound forms of the spirit and intellect of the European languages.

*Fyodor Dostoyevsky*

The natural wealth of the Russian language and speech is so great that, without going far out of your way, keeping your finger on the pulse of the times, in close association with the plain people, and with a volume of Pushkin in your pocket, you can become a competent writer.

*M. M. Prishvin*

\*

Our speech is predominantly aphoristic and distinguished by its terseness and vigour.

*Maxim Gorky*

\*

The Russian language is infinitely rich and growing richer all the time at an astonishing rate.

*Maxim Gorky*

\*

Protect our language, our splendid Russian language—it is a treasure, an asset willed to us by our ancestors. Treat this mighty weapon with due respect.

*Ivan Turgenev*

\*

Adoption of foreign words, especially without need, is not enrichment, but corruption of the language.

*A. S. Sumarokov*

## LANGUAGE AND WORDS

The Russian language is rich enough, it has all the means for expressing the most subtle sensations and shades of meaning.

*Vladimir Korolenko*

\*

I do not consider foreign words good or appropriate if there are purely Russian or more Russified ones to be used in their stead. We must safeguard our rich and splendid language against corruption.

*Nikolai Leskov*

\*

New words of foreign origin are being continuously introduced in the Russian press, often quite needlessly; deplorably, these harmful exercises are seen in the very publications that crusade most hotly for the Russian nationality and its distinctive features.

*Nikolai Leskov*

\*

Using a foreign word when there is an equivalent Russian word is an insult to common sense and good taste.

*Vissarion Belinsky*

\*

The habit of sprinkling Russian speech with foreign words needlessly, without sufficient cause, is contrary to common sense and good taste; but it harms only those who indulge in it, and not the Russian language or Russian literature.

*Vissarion Belinsky*

\*

For us our native tongue must be the principal basis for our general level of education, as well as the education of each of us.

*P. A. Vyazemsky*

\*

We must cherish and safeguard the samples of Russian that we have been gifted by our great writers.

*Dmitry Furmanov*

\*

For the patriot language is important.

*Nikolai Karamzin*

\*

One can judge very accurately of a person's cultural level and civic worth by his attitude towards his language.

*Konstantin Paustovsky*

## LANGUAGE AND WORDS

True love of one's country is inconceivable without true love of one's language.

*Konstantin Paustovsky*

\*

Language is the history of the people. It is the road-way to civilisation and culture. This is why study and protection of the Russian language is not an idle occupation, but a vital necessity.

*Alexander Kuprin*

\*

The Russian language must become a world language. The time will come (and it will come soon) when Russian will be learned in all latitudes.

*A. N. Tolstoy*

\*

The Russian language is the language of Lenin.

*Mikhail Kalinin*

\*

The language of Turgenev, Tolstoy, Dobrolyubov, and Chernyshevsky (*qq. v.*) is a great and mighty one. And we, of course, are in favour of every inhabitant of Russia having the opportunity to learn the great Russian language.

*V. I. Lenin*

\*

Thanks to the Russian language we, members of different national literatures, have learned to know one another. The mutual enrichment of literary experience occurs through the Russian language and Russian books. Publishing a book by any writer of our country in Russian means reaching a very broad readership.

*Yuri Rytkheu*

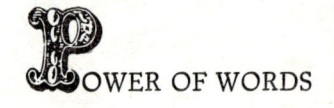

# Power of Words

The word is the marshal of human energy.

*Vladimir Mayakovsky*

\*

The word is a great tool of life.

*Vladimir Korolenko*

# LANGUAGE AND WORDS

The word is one of the greatest tools man has. Powerless by itself, it becomes strong and irresistible when spoken skilfully, sincerely, and suitably. It can carry away its speaker, and its brilliance can blind him and those around him.

*A. F. Koni*

\*

A thought expressed in words is a force of infinite effect.

*Lev Tolstoy*

\*

Words can prevent death, words can resurrect the dead.

*Alisher Navoi*

\*

Where the word has not perished there the cause, too, is still alive.

*Alexander Herzen*

\*

Words are the cloth for the coat and trousers of thoughts and feelings.

*Maxim Gorky*

\*

A word from the heart works miracles.

*N. N. Burdenko*

A kind word is a maker of marvellous marvels.

*Vladimir Mayakovsky*

\*

The word is great. It is great, because it can unite people, can disunite them, can serve love, and can pander to strife and hatred. Beware of the word that sows dissension.

*Lev Tolstoy*

\*

A word is no more important than the action to which it leads.

*Alexander Herzen*

\*

It is much harder to turn word into deed than deed into word.

*Maxim Gorky*

\*

Word is not deed; a spoken verity, however incontestable, is but a word, an empty sound, a lie and nothing more, unless it materialises in deeds and action by those who pronounce it.

*Vissarion Belinsky*

## LANGUAGE AND WORDS

If you want to use a word, be mindful of the reality behind it.

*Ivan Pavlov*

*

The general mass have no idea of eloquence; this is why they do not like to, and cannot, seize upon a word and take pleasure in its sound as it fades in space. Their words are never barren; for them words are a call to action, a condition for the job at hand.

*Nikolai Dobrolyubov*

*

A word is no toy balloon soaring with the wind. It is an implement, and is meant to lift a definite weight. We measure its significance and force by how it captivates people and rouses their feelings.

*Vladimir Korolenko*

*

We have no use for dissolute and idle words that envelop you in self-indulgent slumber and fill the heart with pleasant dreams; what we need are fresh and proud words that fill the heart with civic courage and summon to broad and original activity.

*Nikolai Dobrolyubov*

What we need are words that ring like a fog-bell, calling to action, stirring the senses and prodding us forward.

*Maxim Gorky*

## ELOQUENCE

Richness of language and the art of oratory went hand in hand at all times.

*Anton Chekhov*

\*

In a society where true eloquence is scorned it is replaced by grandiloquence, stuffy bombast, and flatulent rhetoric. Now, as in ancient times, oratory has been among the strongest movers of culture.

*Anton Chekhov*

\*

Language is an instrument probably no less difficult to master than the violin. One can only add that mediocrity is insufferable in the case of either of these instruments.

*P. Y. Vyazemsky*

## LANGUAGE AND WORDS

It should be remembered that the gift of speech is the sole priceless means of penetrating to the heart of things.

*Nikolai Pirogov*

\*

Short speeches are always of more consequence and more able to create a deep impression.

*Maxim Gorky*

\*

Truthfulness and fluency of speech is good, but how magnificent is brevity in truthful words.

*Alisher Navoi*

\*

Like a pearl, eloquence derives its glitter from its content. Real wisdom is brief.

*Lev Tolstoy*

\*

In speech, precision is not only a point of style, a point of good taste, but also, and above all, a point of meaning. Where there are many words, where the words are drab, there the thinking, too, is drab.

*Konstantin Fedin*

People become entangled in a maze of redundant words.

*Maxim Gorky*

\*

The sharp mind will not tolerate verbose colloquy: who needs verbosity if we are at ease without it. Prolixity is a sign of dull-wittedness. Speeches and letters containing more words than thoughts betray stupidity.

*A. P. Sumarokov*

\*

Demagogy and grandiloquence hold in contempt. Concentrate all your thinking and all your deeds on the triumph of virtue and justice.

*Vassily Sukhomlinsky*

\*

Shy clear of mannered speech. Your language must be simple and elegant.

*Anton Chekhov*

\*

Beauty of language derives exclusively from clarity and expressiveness.

*Dmitry Pisarev*

## LANGUAGE AND WORDS

Every idea can be put simply and clearly.

*Alexander Herzen*

\*

The simpler is the word, the more it is precise, the more appropriately it is used, the more forceful and convincing it makes the phrase.

*Maxim Gorky*

\*

The truly wise is always simple and understandable.

*Maxim Gorky*

\*

It is ideas not words that have lasting power over society.

*Vissarion Belinsky*

\*

Sound thought is preferable to brilliant diction. Diction is, as it were, the outer garment, while thought is the body beneath the garment.

*Fyodor Dostoyevsky*

\*

The word is an expression of thought and must, therefore, accord with what it expresses.

*Lev Tolstoy*

The word reflects the thought: if the thought is unintelligible then so is the word.

*Vissarion Belinsky*

\*

What you say is not always important, but how you say it always is.

*Maxim Gorky*

\*

An aptly spoken word is as good as the written word, which (as the Russian saying goes.–*Tr.*) cannot be struck out with an axe.

*Nikolai Gogol*

\*

What is vaguely conceived is vaguely expressed; inexact and muddled speaking is evidence of muddled thinking.

*Nikolai Chernyshevsky*

\*

A person speaks clearly when thoughts possess him, and clearer still when he possesses thoughts.

*Vissarion Belinsky*

\*

Error of thought causes error of expression, and error of expression causes error of deed.

*Dmitry Pisarev*

# LANGUAGE AND WORDS

The best tongue is that which is carefully moderated, and the best speech is that which is carefully considered.

*Lev Tolstoy*

*

A word is apt when it correctly expresses the thought; and it correctly expresses the thought when it is to the thought what the hide is to an animal, not what the glove made of animal hide is to the hand.

*Konstantin Ushinsky*

*

Be sure to follow this rule: let thy words be few and thy thoughts be many.

*Nikolai Nekrasov*

*

Heaviness is overcome by force. The more profound and intricate the thought, the more forceful, vivid, and sculptured must be the word.

*Samuel Marshak*

*

Thoughts radiating force are like a thread on which words are strung like pearls.

*Mikhail Lermontov*

It is not the word that counts, but the tone in which it is spoken.

*Vissarion Belinsky*

\*

You may speak from the platform in muddled terms, but if you are carried away, if the points you raise are significant, if up *on that platform you are settling a point*, the mass of people will be carried away as well.

*Mikhail Kalinin*

\*

A speech will not achieve its purpose unless the speaker's heart is in every word he utters and the power and state of mind that impel him are distinctly felt.

*N. V. Shelgunov*

\*

A word that comes from the heart is certain to reach other hearts.

*Nizami*

\*

To be understood, the orator must be sincere.

*V. O. Kliuchevsky*

## LANGUAGE AND WORDS

Words must be dealt with honestly.

*Nikolai Gogol*

\*

A person who is strict with himself does not enter into double-faced relations; he does not speak at all if by dint of some unfavourable circumstance he cannot speak his mind. Once he does speak, it is in upright and honest terms.

*Nikolai Dobrolyubov*

\*

Do not preach to people what you do not believe.

*Maxim Gorky*

## DISPUTE

Polemics is a fine thing. A clever Greek once said that dispute (struggle) is father to all things.

*G. V. Plekhanov*

\*

Dispute is an exceedingly convenient means of clarifying an idea.

*Fyodor Dostoyevsky*

Not only mistakes, but also the greatest of absurdities are removed in free discussion with the help of polemics.

*M. E. Saltykov-Shchedrin*

\*

Open polemics ... is necessary and desirable.

*V. I. Lenin*

\*

A struggle of *shades* in the Party is *inevitable and essential* as long as it does not lead to anarchy and splits, as long as it is confined within bounds approved by the common consent of all comrades and Party members.

*V. I. Lenin*

\*

We must have more confidence in the independent judgement of the whole body of Party workers.

*V. I. Lenin*

\*

No movement, including the working-class movement, is possible without debates, controversy, and conflict of opinions.

*V. I. Lenin*

## LANGUAGE AND WORDS

Only people who are shallow-minded or who fear the participation of the broad masses in politics can think that open and heated controversies ... are inappropriate or unnecessary. As a matter of fact, it is these heated controversies that help and teach all the workers to discuss their own, labour, policy from every angle, and to evolve a firm, distinct, and definite class line for the movement.

*V. I. Lenin*

\*

In all cases, a dispute ought to begin with a precise definition of the concept or topic which is the object of the argument.

*Maxim Gorky*

\*

The polemic will be of benefit only if it makes clear in what the differences actually consist, *how profound they are*, whether they are differences of substance or differences on partial questions, whether or not these differences interfere with common work.

*V. I. Lenin*

\*

What we want is for people to argue, and this not artificially, but over the essence of things, that is, in a way that would lead if not to a fight in the full sense of the word at least to a serious and heated verbal engagement. Then people will not shirk going to political circles. This is the method best suited for the study of Marxism-Leninism.

*Mikhail Kalinin*

\*

An argument should not be hostile if it is not provoked by personal hostility.

*N. P. Ogarev*

\*

Some people contesting their opponent's idea understand neither the idea itself nor the arguments advanced in its defence. Arguing with these people is worse than a toothache.

*G. V. Plekhanov*

\*

If you want people to argue with you and to understand you, you, too, must be scrupulously attentive to your opponent and accept his words and proofs in the spirit in which they are offered.

*Vissarion Belinsky*

# LANGUAGE AND WORDS

One can argue only against something one does not agree with but still understands.

*Vissarion Belinsky*

\*

He who has outargued a hundred persons and led them astray is infinitely worse than the one who has set one person on the right course.

*Abai Kunanbayev*

\*

When two disputants lose their temper, this means they are both wrong.

*Lev Tolstoy*

\*

*When entering a verbal contest*
*Keep your temper and you'll stay in the*
*saddle.*

*Nasir Khosrow*

\*

Hold your tongue the moment you notice that you or the other party is becoming irritated. The unspoken word is golden.

*Lev Tolstoy*

It is better to say nothing than to speak nothings.

*A. F. Koni*

✧

Smile at your troubles and their sting will vanish. Smile at your adversary and his rage will vanish. Smile at your own rage and it will vanish, too.

*Janis Rainis*

## OF BOOKS AND READING

### IN PRAISE OF BOOKS

Books are, probably, the greatest and the most blessed miracle worked by humanity on its road to happiness and power.

*Maxim Gorky*

\*

The greatest of the man-made marvels, books embody all the knowledge of the world, all the history of human reason, the historical labour and experience of the nations of the world; they are the mightiest of all the tools used for the development of man's spiritual powers.

*Maxim Gorky*

\*

As rubles are composed of kopecks so knowledge is composed of snippets gleaned from books.

*V. I. Dahl*

Art and science are the two forces that contribute the most to the education of a person of culture. Both these forces are compounded in books.

*Maxim Gorky*

\*

What can be more precious than daily association with the wisest of this world.

*Lev Tolstoy*

\*

Books give birth to dreams, call them to life, encourage meditation, and stimulate independent thinking.

*S. G. Strumilin*

\*

Many thousands of years ago, in the hands of the finest books became one of the principal tools of their struggle for truth and justice. Books gave these people tremendous power.

*N. A. Rubakin*

\*

We can no longer live without books—or fight, or suffer, or rejoice, or conquer, or advance to that sensible and beautiful future in which we so firmly believe.

*Konstantin Paustovsky*

## BOOKS AND READING

A book is an implement. But it is more than that. It acquaints people with the life and struggle of other people, helps them understand their feelings, thoughts, and strivings; it enables them to draw comparisons, to understand the surrounding world, and to transform it.

*N. K. Krupskaya*

\*

Books are as much a phenomenon of life as man is; they are also a living and articulate fact, and are less an "object" than all the other objects created or being created by man.

*Maxim Gorky*

\*

The wealth of books is, by and large, a literary mirror of life.

*N. A. Rubakin*

\*

A book is the magic lamp that lights man's way along the most distant and dark paths of life.

*Andrejs Upits*

\*

No gaps in history and hollow spaces in time can destroy the human thought recorded in the hundreds, thousands, and millions of manuscripts and books.

*Konstantin Paustovsky*

\*

Literature is not subject to the laws of decay. It alone defies death.

*M. E. Saltykov-Shchedrin*

\*

Everything pales before books.

*Anton Chekhov*

\*

Books are magic. They have transformed the world. They are the memory of the human race, the vehicle of human thought. A world without books is a world of savages.

*Nikolai Morozov*

\*

Books are the testament that one generation leaves to the next, the advice of the dying old to the rising young, the orders passed on by the sentry going off duty to the sentry relieving him.

*Alexander Herzen*

## BOOKS AND READING

All the life of humankind has been consequently recorded in books; tribes, people, and states vanished, books remained.

*Alexander Herzen*

\*

Public libraries are a feast of ideas to which all are invited.

*Alexander Herzen*

\*

A good library is a literary reflection of the Universe.

*N. A. Rubakin*

\*

A book is not the past alone; it is a deed to the present, to the sum of truths and undertakings discovered through suffering, frequently bathed in blood and sweat; it is the programme of the future.

*Alexander Herzen*

\*

Books are the principal and the most powerful weapon of socialist culture.

*Maxim Gorky*

Lacking books, human life is empty. Books are much more than friends to us. They are our constant and eternal companions.

*Demyan Bedny*

\*

You must know books. You must like and trust them. You must cultivate the skill of working with them.

*N. A. Rubakin*

\*

To raise the level of culture go to the sources of it, to the cultural heritage of humanity, and learn Russian literature, especially belles-lettres.

*Mikhail Kalinin*

\*

Consequent and conscious convictions grow in us either under the influence of society or with the help of books.

*Nikolai Chernyshevsky*

\*

One of my teaching beliefs is boundless confidence in the educational value of books. School means books first and last. Education means mainly words, books, and human relationships. The book is a mighty weapon.

## BOOKS AND READING

Sometimes, an intelligent and inspired book can change a man's life.

*Vassily Sukhomlinsky*

\*

Books are a powerful means of communication, work, and struggle. They impart the experience of living and fighting, they broaden our horizons, and supply the knowledge that helps us enlist the forces of Nature into our service.

*N. K. Krupskaya*

\*

A book is a teacher unpaid and unthanked. Every instant it offers revelations of wisdom. It is an interlocutor with a leather-bound brain that silently imports secret things.

*Alisher Navoi*

\*

Reading is one of the sources of thought and intellectual development.

*Vassily Sukhomlinsky*

\*

Respect books; enter this temple of wisdom with reverence.

*Alexander Herzen*

Associating with books prepares one for associating with people. Both are equally necessary.

*Nikolai Karamzin*

\*

Nothing can more extend the horizon of our concepts of Nature and human life than a close acquaintanceship with the world's greatest minds.

*Dmitry Pisarev*

\*

A good book is like a dialogue with someone clever. The reader gets from it knowledge, a summary of the world, and an understanding of life.

*A. N. Tolstoy*

\*

Reading is the best learning. To follow a great man's thoughts is the most entertaining of sciences.

*Alexander Pushkin*

\*

Forget not that reading is the most effective means to a many-sided education.

*Alexander Herzen*

## BOOKS AND READING

There can be no real education without reading, no taste, no word, and no many-sided range of understanding; Goethe and Shakespeare are worth a whole university course. By reading you encompass many ages.

*Alexander Herzen*

\*

Reading makes your thoughts go deeper and directs your mind to search and analysis.

*Mikhail Kalinin*

\*

Search attentively the books of wisdom and thou wilt find great benefit for thy soul.

*Nestor*

\*

A good book gives knowledge and wakens good thoughts.

*N. K. Krupskaya*

\*

All good books have the quality of stimulating thought about what is just, what is beautiful, and what is useful to people.

*Nikolai Chernyshevsky*

Reading a good book, you feel stronger, wiser, and purer.

*Janis Sudrabkalns*

\*

A timely book is a tremendous stroke of luck. Your best friend and mentor could not change your life more fittingly.

*P. A. Pavlenko*

\*

The first book that smites the heart is like a first love. It is a prism that will in time subconsciously refract your perception of life.

*Olga Forsh*

\*

All the good in me I owe to books.

*Maxim Gorky*

\*

I have read avidly, with delight and wonder, but never have books repelled me from reality; on the contrary, they whetted my interest in it, developed my powers of observation and comparison, and sharpened my thirst for knowing life.

*Maxim Gorky*

# BOOKS AND READING

The more I read, the more did books befriend me with the world, and the more vivid and substantial life became for me.

*Maxim Gorky*

\*

Be fond of books, the source of knowledge; knowledge and nothing but knowledge is redeeming, knowledge alone makes you strong in spirit, honest, and sensible, sincerely fond of people, respectful of their labour, and heartily appreciative of the fruits of their great unremitting endeavours.

*Maxim Gorky*

\*

Be fond of books, they will lighten your life, help you as a friend to understand the motley and turbulent confusion of thoughts, feelings, and events, and teach you to respect people and yourself; they give wings to the mind and fill the heart with love of the world, and of man.

*Maxim Gorky*

\*

A high-minded work of art unavoidably sets the reader thinking about life, assessing not only people, but also the methods of assessment, and ruminating about the essential aspects of life, about its purpose, sense, its truth and untruth, and the like.

*N. A. Rubakin*

A book is collective experience. He who has read a score of great books has lived a score of great lives.

*P. A. Pavlenko*

\*

Books give people wings.

*Fyodor Gladkov*

\*

Books make man master of the Universe.

*P. A. Pavlenko*

\*

Books enlighten and assert man on earth. They discover to man the secrets and laws of Nature, and help him master them to become lord of the world.... Books are bearers of all that is best, dearest, wisest, and wonderful.

*Fyodor Gladkov*

\*

Nothing is more enlightening, nothing more purifies your soul than what you experience perusing a masterpiece.

*M. E. Saltykov-Shchedrin*

## BOOKS AND READING

Academic literature delivers people from ignorance, polite literature from coarseness and vulgarity.

*Nikolai Chernyshevsky*

*

Learn, read, cogitate, and extract all that is the most useful.

*Nikolai Pirogov*

*

What good is a lettered man who reads no books? He is condemned to drift back to illiteracy.

*A. V. Lunacharsky*

*

Learn and read. Read serious books. Leave the rest to life.

*Fyodor Dostoyevsky*

*

A house looks glum and joyless without books.

*Maxim Tank*

*

A family that disdains books is spiritually handicapped.

*P. A. Pavlenko*

Morally sound and hard-working people grow up in families where books are held in respect.

*Vassily Sukhomlinsky*

\*

Absence of good reading that would captivate mind and heart and stimulate speculation about the surrounding world and one's self is one of the reasons for a deficient intellectual life.

*Vassily Sukhomlinsky*

\*

A good book is a real feast.

*Maxim Gorky*

\*

No friend in the world is dearer than a book.

*Alisher Navoi*

\*

The society of books can yield the greatest pleasures.

*K. L. Zelinsky*

\*

Dig into books on every convenient occasion. Try to leaf and scan as many different books as you can.

*N. A. Rubakin*

When I see people indulging in worthless pastimes and amusements, because they do not know what to do with their time, I take a book and say to myself: this occupation is enough for a lifetime.

*Fyodor Dostoyevsky*

\*

When you are no longer young and see that everything you could reach in your unrepeatable life has been reached, you will look for a friend. Be warned that he is hard to find. Old age is often burdensome and boring. You may be shown respect, but that is a tribute to your past. You alone will be fond of yourself to the end of your days, and you will have but one constant friend–the book.

*Konstantin Fedin*

# CHOICE OF BOOKS

A book is the life of our time. Everybody needs it–old and young, busy and indolent, and children too. The thing is to choose the right books for them, and here we will be the first to agree that indiscriminate reading is worse and more harmful for them than not reading at all.

*Vissarion Belinsky*

\*

Choosing books for your own and other people's edification is not only a science, but also an art.

*N. A. Rubakin*

\*

In face of the bountifulness of libraries modern man is like a gold prospector looking for grains of gold in a sand dune.

*S. I. Vavilov*

\*

There are very few capital works on each specific subject. The other works only repeat, diffuse, and mar what is much more exhaustively and clearly presented in these few capital works. It is best to read no other books, for all other reading is a waste of time.

*Nikolai Chernyshevsky*

\*

In all things a little of the good is better than much of the bad. The same is true of books.

*Lev Tolstoy*

## BOOKS AND READING

It is quite needless to read everything. Read only that which answers your questions.

*Lev Tolstoy*

\*

Not only when choosing books, but also in the process of reading you must learn to pick out what elevates the mind most.

*Sergei Taneyev*

\*

In books you must look for and find that which is the real sign of the times.

*Alexander Fadeyev*

\*

Read and revere only those books which help understand the purpose of life, and the wishes and true motives of people.

*Maxim Gorky*

\*

Fortify your mind by reading the greatest thinkers who studied Nature in general and human nature in particular.

*Dmitry Pisarev*

For me the dearest book is that behind which I see a great man.

*K. L. Zelinsky*

＊

Make it a rule to read capital books, original works, the source of great ideas and of noble passions.

*Nikolai Chernyshevsky*

＊

Good books can stand any test and will be remembered as the most earnest teachers. These are the books to choose.

*P. A. Pavlenko*

＊

A book is good if life flows between its covers as blood does under the skin.

*Mikhail Kalinin*

＊

There are astonishing books that open your eyes, and exciting books that you will never forget.

*N. K. Krupskaya*

# BOOKS AND READING

Read not indiscriminately, choose your books deliberately, cultivate your taste and thinking.

*Ivan Turgenev*

\*

If it be permissible to laugh at idle people, it should also be permissible to laugh at idle books. If it be permissible to say, "speak and hear no idle gossip", it should also be permissible to say, "write and read no idle books".

*Nikolai Chernyshevsky*

\*

There are books that organise, and books that disorganise. Choosing the right books is, therefore, exceedingly important.

*N. K. Krupskaya*

\*

Books are like society. Good books, like good society, enlighten and ennoble the senses and morality.

*Nikolai Pirogov*

\*

A bad book imparts false ideas and makes the ignorant still more ignorant.

*Vissarion Belinsky*

We must spare no effort to deliver mankind from reading bad and useless books.

*S. I. Vavilov*

\*

Bad books are worse than useless; they are harmful. Try to read the best writers of all ages and nations first.

*Lev Tolstoy*

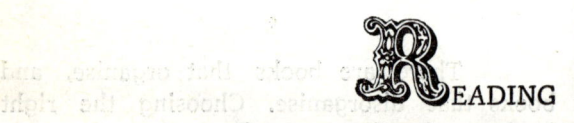

# READING

One of the avenues to knowledge, and a highly fruitful one, is the skill of using books.

*N. K. Krupskaya*

\*

Books are a great thing as long as you know how to use them.

*Alexander Blok*

\*

There's many a good book in the world, but it's good only for those who are skilled readers. And skilled reading is not the same as simply knowing how to read.

*Dmitry Pisarev*

\*

Reading is nothing: the thing is what you read and how you understand what you read.

*Konstantin Ushinsky*

\*

Reading a book is neither here nor there; the book has got to be understood.

*Pyotr Lavrov*

\*

Reading is like shaping one's own thoughts with the help of another's.

*N. A. Rubakin*

\*

Reading is not just learning facts. Reading is also cultivating good taste through association with beauty.

*Konstantin Fedin*

\*

Read books by all means, but remember that a book is a book, and that you must use your own brains.

*Maxim Gorky*

To read a book through and to understand it properly means putting yourself on a par with the writer.

*P. A. Pavlenko*

\*

To leaf through a book is not reading. Read as you would listen to a confession. Go deep. Then, the book will open itself to you, and you will taste its delights.

*Konstantin Fedin*

\*

Books, which are so important for developed people, are like Nature and the experience of life—mute not only for those who cannot read, but also for those who, having mechanically perused a page, fail to extract the living thought from the dead letter.

*Konstantin Ushinsky*

\*

It is better to read little, but to read profoundly. Thumbing through books is the most unproductive of occupations.

*N. K. Krupskaya*

\*

No occupation is more of a waste of time than reading without a system.

*Sergei Taneyev*

Avoid senseless perusal of page after page and docile engrossment in the plot.

*Anton Makarenko*

\*

Bad reading is like a mud-splashed window through which you see nothing.

*Vassily Sukhomlinsky*

\*

It is better to read fewer books, but to give more thought to their content, to the character of the people they portray, and to try and evaluate them on your own—whether or not they are good and why, and to jot down a few lines about it in your notebook.

*Mikhail Kalinin*

\*

Not he is educated who reads avidly, but he who has developed a system of reading—gathering not scraps or crumbs of knowledge, but a connected system of knowledge.

*Mikhail Kalinin*

\*

One-sided reading, though systematic, does more harm than even erratic reading. Nothing warps the brain and narrows the horizon more than reading books on one subject and nothing else.

*A. M. Skabichevsky*

\*

Exercise your habit of reading prolifically and quickly. The mechanics of reading must be automatic and must not distract your thoughts. But that is not all. You must also give an account to yourself of what you have read.

*N. K. Krupskaya*

\*

Reading books is but a start. The goal is to arrange life.

*N. A. Rubakin*

\*

The point is not how one reads, but in one's love of reading and knowledge.

*N. A. Rubakin*

\*

You can read in three ways—first, read and not understand; second, read and understand; third, read and understand even what is between the lines.

*Y. B. Kniazhnin*

\*

Though books are tremendously important, they are not the only means of self-education. Learn not only from books, but also from life.

> *N. K. Krupskaya*

\*

Life always teaches you much more than the best of books. Books are only an instrument. Do not check life against books, that is, against theories, but the other way round.

> *N. A. Rubakin*

\*

Learning is in books and in one's own work of gathering knowledge from books and from life.

> *Nikolai Chernyshevsky*

\*

Woe unto those who think after reading one or two books that they have penetrated to the essence of things and that there is nothing more to it. Those who confine their self-education to mere reading of books and to assimilating their content without relating it to life are also superficial dabblers.

> *N. A. Rubakin*

\*

The advice to read more does not apply to all people by far.

> *N. A. Rubakin*

# OF RELIGION AND SUPERSTITIONS

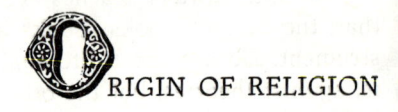

## ORIGIN OF RELIGION

Religion is said to be a human prejudice. This is not quite correct. It is more than a prejudice. In a certain sense, it is the remnant of human weakness in face of the forces of Nature.

*Mikhail Kalinin*

\*

In the light of scientific progress all religious notions about the world appear as a foggy fantasy which flowed naturally from the primitiveness of human culture in its early stages.

*A. V. Lunacharsky*

\*

The belief in God is a belief of savage and barbarian peoples that has survived in modern society.

*I. I. Skvortsov-Stepanov*

## RELIGION AND SUPERSTITIONS

When man gets to know the laws of Nature it becomes clear to him that all natural phenomena come about without the intervention of any divine power.

*Emelyan Yaroslavsky*

\*

People look for the way to heaven simply because they have lost their way on earth.

*G. V. Plekhanov*

\*

The belief in after-life is a burdensome tribute paid by people who know not how to live out their lives and stop living before they die.

*V. O. Kliuchevsky*

\*

Religion is a form of spiritual oppression.

*V. I. Lenin*

\*

The most refined and best-intentioned defence or justification of the idea of God is a justification of reaction.

*V. I. Lenin*

Never has the idea of God "linked the individual with society": it has always tied the oppressed classes hand and foot with faith in the divinity of the oppressors.

*V. I. Lenin*

\*

Impotence of the exploited classes in their struggle against the exploiters just as inevitably gives rise to the belief in a better life after death as impotence of the savage in his battle with Nature gives rise to belief in gods, devils, miracles, and the like.

*V. I. Lenin*

\*

Everywhere, for all nations, religion has been nothing but a halter.

*Nikolai Pirogov*

\*

All religions based morality on submission, that is, on self-imposed slavery.

*Alexander Herzen*

\*

The main aim of all churches was one: to persuade the slave that he cannot expect happiness on earth, that it awaits him in heaven, and that hard labour for the benefit of another is agreeable to God.

*Maxim Gorky*

# SUPERSTITIONS

Idolatrous superstition held the astronomical world in its jaws, and would not let it stir.

*Mikhail Lomonosov*

\*

We Marxists must always remember that there is no essential difference between "faith" and "superstition". If we were to admit a difference, we would also have to recognise that there is "true faith" in contrast to "untrue".

*I. I. Skvortsov-Stepanov*

\*

Superstition is not something independent of faith. It is an element mechanically severed from the once living integral faith in the existence and continuous activity of supernatural forces.

*I. I. Skvortsov-Stepanov*

Drinking is bad. This no one will deny. But superstitions, which preclude a reasonable and sound vision of the world, are no less of an evil.

*Dmitry Pisarev*

\*

Man only fears what he does not know, for knowledge conquers fear.

*Vissarion Belinsky*

\*

Superstition is a belief not based on knowledge. Science fights superstitions as light fights darkness.

*Dmitry Mendeleyev*

\*

Superstitions fade with the advance of civilisation.

*Vissarion Belinsky*

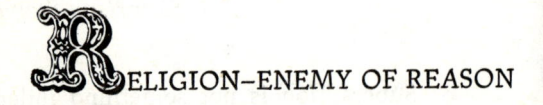

## RELIGION—ENEMY OF REASON

God is an illusion—an extremely harmful one for it fetters reason.

*G. V. Plekhanov*

Consciously, and mainly unconsciously, churchmen try for their own gain to keep people in a state of savage superstitiousness.

*Lev Tolstoy*

\*

Religion is like a blindfold that shuts out the view of the world as it is.

*Emelyan Yaroslavsky*

\*

Like all religious types of community, the church requires the believer to renounce independent thinking before he crosses the threshold of a temple.

*Leonid Leonov*

\*

For the masses religion is nothing more than a halter, a great intimidating of simpletons, a multitude of screens of colossal dimensions that prevent people from seeing what is happening on earth and make them raise their eyes to heaven.

*Alexander Herzen*

\*

Faith is like an anchor that keeps secured to a sand-bank the ship primed for a long voyage to explore the wide world and to study what lies beyond the horizon.

*I. I. Skvortsov-Stepanov*

\*

The fanatical and merciless war of the Christian church on science is the most disgraceful chapter of European history.

*Maxim Gorky*

\*

Religious beliefs halt the flight of the human spirit, limit the regions of thought, and tie up the intellect.

*I. I. Skvortsov-Stepanov*

\*

Churchmen have at all times invariably invented fetters for human reason; they clipped its wings so that it should not direct its flight to greatness and freedom.

*A. N. Radishchev*

\*

Mysticism leads to inactivity; reliance on divine powers is an obstacle to setting right our mundane affairs.

*N. P. Ogarev*

\*

The success of knowledge has undermined all religions. They have become disconnected fragments of a once whole world vision, clear and consummate in its own way. The final break-up of these fragments is only a question of time.

*I. I. Skvortsov-Stepanov*

\*

Human progress is a sentence of death to both religious idea and religious feeling.

*G. V. Plekhanov*

\*

The mathematician who tries to measure the divine will with compasses is no more right than the theologian who thinks astronomy or chemistry can be learned from a psalm-book.

*Mikhail Lomonosov*

\*

I am deeply convinced that the incompatibility of science and religion will fashion us into active fighters for the materialist outlook, because without it we cannot conceive either science or life.

*A. E. Fersman*

\*

He who has learned to think will find it hard to believe.

*Lev Tolstoy*

*Guts and muscles are surer than prayers.
Not for us to beg favours from time!
Each of us hold in the palm of his hand
The transmission belts of fanciful worlds.*

*Vladimir Mayakovsky*

## RELIGION AND MORALITY

Religion is completely out of gear with the consistently socialist outlook.

*G. V. Plekhanov*

\*

Religion has long since become man-hating.

*Maxim Gorky*

\*

Some think that religion brings people together. In fact, it divides people. It has been, and still is, the cause of many wars.

*Emelyan Yaroslavsky*

By and large, religious ethics contradicts the workers' class interests. It is impotent. And it betrayed its impotence most clearly during the world war. Though preached for nearly two thousand years, it proved unable to prevent the horrors of war.

*N. K. Krupskaya*

\*

No lie is more wanton and disgusting than the lie of the Christian religion.

*Maxim Gorky*

\*

Monkhood is nothing but lechery and sodomy clothed in black habits.

*Mikhail Lomonosov*

\*

For me the stubborn priests who forcibly baptise with cold water are executioners, for following birth and baptism they wish an early funeral for their own profit.

*Mikhail Lomonosov*

\*

The brand of love preached by churchmen and Christians contains a tremendous portion of hate.

*Maxim Gorky*

The ultra-religionists are the harshest and most implacable of people, and are inclined towards hatred and persecution.

*Alexander Herzen*

\*

Religion is alien to our thoughts and pursuit of happiness.

*Alexander Pushkin*

\*

The morality that flows from religion is but a sop which the church and theology confers out of its treasures to impoverished humanity. Morality must have an entirely different foundation. Only materialism can be a dependable foundation for it.

*G. V. Plekhanov*

\*

We must combat religion—that is the *ABC* of all materialism, and consequently of Marxism. But Marxism is not a materialism which has stopped at the ABC. Marxism goes further. It says: we must *know how* to combat religion, and in order to do so we must explain the source of faith and religion among the masses *in a materialist way*.

*V. I. Lenin*

Atheism is not prescribed. It is acquired by people through their enlightenment.

*Mikhail Kalinin*

\*

The solution is not in demolishing churches, but in people forgetting about them and not going there. That is what we want to achieve. We must remember that crude measures will get us nowhere in the painful process of removing religious prejudices from our life.

*Maxim Gorky*

\*

Our increasingly effective power over the forces of Nature and society will eliminate the need to seek consolation in the fancied power of fancied gods over Nature and society.

*I. I. Skvortsov-Stepanov*

\*

Those who cannot know, believe.

*A. V. Lunacharsky*

\*

The working man of our time needs no consoling illusions. He has no use for reassuring tales of after-world rewards. Everywhere, he is shaking off the chains of bondage and thereby rewarding himself not in dreams, but in deeds.

*S. G. Strumilin*

\*

What can be stronger than our will and stronger than our reason? Our reason and will—it is they that perform miracles. Who created the gods? We did—our fancy, our imagination. And as we created them so we may depose them. We *must* depose them.

*Maxim Gorky*

\*

The state has always used the church for the spiritual enslavement of the masses, and the church has always been its willing tool. This is why Socialists have always had it in their books to separate the church from the state.

*N. K. Krupskaya*

\*

The building of socialism is clipping the roots of religion. The church is fast losing importance as a centre of attraction and influence as religion is being pushed out by science, slavish humility by the defiance of fighters for the great aim, and dreams of the kingdom of heaven by the building of socialism on earth.

*N. K. Krupskaya*

*

The power of Nature over man is giving place to the power of man over Nature. From the kingdom of necessity man is stepping into the kingdom of freedom. This is why under communism there will be no social grounds for belief in God, and hence no religion.

*Emelyan Yaroslavsky*

## OF CIVILISATION, SCIENCE, AND SCIENTISTS

### PROGRESS AND SCIENCE

The physical, intellectual, and ethical development of the personality and the embodiment of truth and justice in social forms—this, it seems to me, is the brief formula that encompasses everything we can regard as progress.

*Pyotr Lavrov*

\*

There can be no progress in science and education in the absence of political progress.

*O. Y. Schmidt*

\*

To renounce progress is as silly as to renounce the Earth's force of gravitation.

*Nikolai Chernyshevsky*

## CIVILISATION AND SCIENCE

Without the striving for infinity there is no life, no development, and no progress.

*Vissarion Belinsky*

\*

He who does not go forward is bound to slide back: there is no such thing as immobility.

*Vissarion Belinsky*

\*

Everything new always expresses the striving for progress if not progress itself.

*Vissarion Belinsky*

\*

That which does not develop has no future, and which has no future is bound to die.

*Vissarion Belinsky*

\*

Only that perishes in the stream of time which lacks a strong grain of life and is, therefore, unworthy of living.

*Vissarion Belinsky*

\*

Our time is a time of great discoveries and firm scientific convictions.

*Nikolai Chernyshevsky*

Science is humanity's superior reason, the sun which man has created of his own flesh and blood and has lit to illuminate the darkness of his hard life and to show the way to freedom, justice, and beauty.

*Maxim Gorky*

\*

Science is becoming the nervous system of our time.

*Maxim Gorky*

\*

Science is strength; it shows the relations of things, their laws and interactions.

*Alexander Herzen*

\*

Science plays an auxiliary part in our lives, for it is merely a means to the attainment of wellbeing.

*Dmitry Mendeleyev*

\*

Science can make humanity happy.

*F. A. Zander*

\*

I consider it no sin to rebel even against one's own father if it is for the common weal and especially for the welfare of science in the Motherland.

*Mikhail Lomonosov*

\*

Science is the most important, the most magnificent, and the most necessary element of life.

*Anton Chekhov*

\*

Science is the repository of the experience and thinking of the human race. It is mainly through science that the ideas, and then the morals and life of people, are improved.

*Nikolai Chernyshevsky*

\*

For us natural science is the Archimedes' screw that alone can turn the world to face the sun of reason.

*Maxim Gorky*

\*

There is no science for the sake of science, no art for the sake of art—they exist for the sake of society, for the ennoblement and exaltation of man, to enrich his knowledge and provide his material comforts.

*Nikolai Nekrasov*

No matter what its vicissitudes, science is the best, the most dependable, and the brightest pillar of life.

*K. A. Timiryazev*

\*

On entering into a free alliance based on mutual understanding and hallowed by the red banner, the symbol of world peace, science, democracy, knowledge, and labour can overcome everything and refashion everything for the good of mankind.

*K. A. Timiryazev*

\*

Science is a huge treasury of knowledge collected by mankind.

*N. K. Krupskaya*

\*

There is no national science any more than there is a national multiplication table.

*Anton Chekhov*

\*

Science and art are as indispensable to people as food and drink and clothes, and perhaps even more indispensable.

*Lev Tolstoy*

## CIVILISATION AND SCIENCE

Science and art is what propels people and ensures perpetual development.

*Lev Tolstoy*

\*

*Where science stands high,*
*There man stands high, too.*

*A. I. Polezhayev*

\*

Where the spirit of science reigns, great things can be done with modest means.

*Nikolai Pirogov*

\*

Science is a clear knowledge of the truth, enlightenment of the mind, unsullied enjoyment, a paean to youth, a support in old age, builder of cities and armies, citadel of success in adversity, adornment in good times, and always a faithful and constant companion.

*Mikhail Lomonosov*

\*

With the help of science man can remove the imperfections of his nature.

*Ilya Mechnikov*

Humanity has no force more powerful and victorious than science.

*Maxim Gorky*

\*

My faith is that man's happiness will come from scientific progress.

*Ivan Pavlov*

\*

Labour and science—there is nothing on earth to match these two forces.

*Maxim Gorky*

\*

Science with its strict analysis of the facts, its persevering search for new, more consummate truths, and its relentless struggle against discovered mistakes and prejudices—science must saturate all our technics, our culture, and everyday life.

*A. F. Joffe*

\*

We must take all science, technology, knowledge, and art. Without them we shall be unable to build communist society.

*V. I. Lenin*

# CIVILISATION AND SCIENCE

We must see to it that learning shall really become part of our very being, that it shall actually and fully become a constituent element of our social life.

*V. I. Lenin*

\*

Our prime and most important task is to develop the science of the future. Our second most important task is to determine as best we can what this science of the future can give our practice and life, and then draw up recommendations and make proposals for the practical application of scientific achievements.

*M. V. Keldysh*

\*

The specific weight of science is not to be gauged only by budgetary allocation and the number of research institutes, but also and above all by the scientists' scope of vision and the altitude of their scientific flights.

*S. I. Vavilov*

\*

To convert dead treasures into a living and useful force we must have a tremendous amount of controlled will, extensive scientific knowledge, and a host of technically skilled hands.

*Maxim Gorky*

When science scales some new peak, a view opens of the road to other peaks and of new roads that science will follow.

*S. I. Vavilov*

\*

The human mind is so constructed that the unattained entices it, while the achieved becomes pedestrian—a law of life, as it were, or an axiom.

*I. A. Kassirsky*

\*

The grandeur and virtue of science derives exclusively from the good it does to people by raising the productivity of labour and invigorating the natural powers of their intellect.

*Dmitry Pisarev*

\*

We must strive for bonds between people of mental and manual work, for a harmonious blend of the tasks of science and life, for serving scientific truth and ethics.

*K. A. Timiryazev*

\*

As always conceived and as now conceived by most people, science is a knowledge of subjects that are most essential and important for the life of human beings.

*Lev Tolstoy*

\*

Science, which strives to cognise the infinite, has no limits itself; it is world-wide, though in fact it inevitably acquires a national character.

*Dmitry Mendeleyev*

\*

By gradually studying matter, people finally take command of it. Their predictions concerning it, proved by the facts, become ever more accurate. They use it more widely and more frequently to satisfy their needs. There are no grounds to think that knowledge and our mastery over matter have bounds.

*Dmitry Mendeleyev*

\*

The Earth has limits, knowledge has none. This is why industry, too, joining forces with knowledge and science, promises to develop endlessly.

*Dmitry Mendeleyev*

## WORDS OF THE WISE

Knowledge is not consummate, crystallised, and petrified; it is being eternally created and is eternally in motion.

*D. N. Pryanishnikov*

\*

Science moves in fits and starts, depending on the progress in methods of research. Every step forward in method takes us a step higher, affording a broader view of the horizon and of objects that were invisible before.

*Ivan Pavlov*

\*

I anticipate that some day, perhaps even in our lifetime, Russians will put the most enlightened nations to shame with their success in science, their diligence in labour, and their enduring and universal glory.

*Peter I*

\*

The economist must always look forward, towards technological progress, or else be left behind at once; for he who will not look ahead turns his back on history.

*V. I. Lenin*

It has to be learnt that it is impossible to live in modern society without machines, without discipline—one has either to master modern techniques or be crushed.

*V. I. Lenin*

\*

In replacing hand by machine labour... the progressive work of human technique consists precisely in this.

*V. I. Lenin*

\*

In a socialist society science seeks to lighten man's labour and improve man and his conditions of life.

*A. N. Bach*

# IMAGINATION, HYPOTHESIS, AND DARING

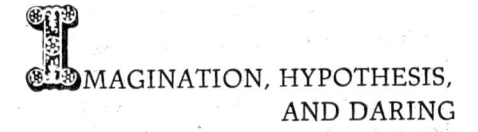

Imagination is a very valuable asset.

*V. I. Lenin*

\*

No active and normally thinking person can manage without an imagination.

*Mikhail Kalinin*

It is only by pursuing its finest dreams that mankind makes progress.

*K. A. Timiryazev*

\*

There is a mountain of poetry in any field of human knowledge.

*Konstantin Paustovsky*

\*

If we were unable to visualise the future in bright and complete pictures, if we were unable to see it in our dreams, nothing could make us build so assiduously, fight so perseveringly, and even stake our lives for the sake of this future.

*Dmitry Pisarev*

\*

First of all, a scientist must be endowed with an imagination, for imagination plays no less important a part in science than it does in art. Imagination is as necessary as is painstaking work on collected material. Without imagination scientific work is just an assortment of facts and conclusions—empty, cachectic, and often barren.

*A. E. Fersman*

\*

One of the mightiest motive forces of culture, art and science, and the desire to fight for the magnificent future would wither away if man were deprived of his ability to dream.

*Konstantin Paustovsky*

\*

A scientist lacking imagination can at best become a splendid walking library and source of information—he absorbs, but does not create.

*F. Y. Levinson-Lessing*

\*

Scientists are in fact imaginers and artists; they are not free with their ideas; they can work well and hard only at what their thinking accepts and what their feelings are drawn to. Ideas alternate; impossible and often mad ones appear; they swarm and whirl, fuse and sparkle. Scientists live among these ideas and work for them.

*V. I. Vernadsky*

\*

Dream as much as you can and as hard as you can if you want to turn the future into the present.

*M. M. Prishvin*

For the architect of human happiness a dream is as effective an instrument as knowledge or ideas.

*Leonid Leonov*

\*

Almost all the lofty and beautiful in our lives, in science and art, is created by the mind with the help of the imagination, and much by the imagination with the help of the mind. It is safe to say that neither Copernicus nor Newton would ever have carved their niche in science without the help of the imagination.

*Nikolai Pirogov*

\*

There is no fantasy that man's will and reason would fail to turn into reality.

*Maxim Gorky*

\*

There are no bounds to fantasy, no limits to the penetration of reason, and none to the technical powers that conquer nature.

*A. E. Fersman*

\*

There is an element of reality in every fairy-tale.

*V. I. Lenin*

Miraculous prophecy is a fairy-tale. But scientific prophecy is a fact.

*V. I. Lenin*

\*

Once the Quixotes become extinct, the Book of History may as well be sealed, for there will be nothing to read in it.

*Ivan Turgenev*

\*

Fear not impudence or madness when it concerns labour and construction.

*Maxim Gorky*

\*

In the realm of scientific thought especially we must not fear audacious conjecture provided we remember that it is conjecture, and provided we do not confuse it with reality and fact.

*A. E. Fersman*

\*

No progress is ever achieved without an element of risk.

*Vikenty Veresayev*

Do not forget to dare the impossible in order to achieve the possible.

*Anton Rubinstein*

\*

All progress would stop in the absence of enterprise.

*Alexander Herzen*

\*

There is no limit to the development of mankind; mankind will never say to itself, "Stop, we've gone far enough, there is nowhere farther to go". If mankind has achieved much, this only means that it must achieve still more, and soon.

*Vissarion Belinsky*

\*

Human reason has discovered many amazing things in Nature and will discover still more, and will thereby increase its power over Nature.

*V. I. Lenin*

\*

Our civilisation is only beginning and we are quite unable to foresee, even with the most lively imagination, the degree of power over Nature it will still give us.

*Nikolai Chernyshevsky*

## CIVILISATION AND SCIENCE

None have ever erred so hopelessly in their predictions as the prophets of a limit to human knowledge.

*K. A. Timiryazev*

\*

The real facts almost always eclipse the imagination of prophets.

*K. E. Tsiolkovsky*

\*

This is a time when the distance between the maddest of fantasies and the most realistic of facts is shrinking at an incredible rate.

*Maxim Gorky*

\*

Science is ascending rung by rung, people's scope of vision is expanding continuously, their needs are increasing, and that which seemed miraculous the day before is commonplace the day after.

*Vladimir Obruchev*

\*

It is impossible to predict the limits to scientific knowledge and anticipation.

*Dmitry Mendeleyev*

Diligence is an inalienable quality of the scientific worker. Experiments usually need repeated verification, which usually involves tremendous strain.

*K. I. Skriabin*

\*

To be able and to foresee—the gift of performing miracles and the gift of prophesying—is what mankind dreamed of from its cradle, attributing these gifts to the heroes of its legends and to its saints. And science has given these two gifts to mankind.

*K. A. Timiryazev*

\*

Scientific discoveries are never ready-made or complete. The process of scientific discovery, illumined by the intellect of great human personalities, is at the same time a slow process of universal human development stretching over the ages.

*V. I. Vernadsky*

\*

Scientific discoveries are rarely made overnight, for usually the heralds do not at once manage to convince the world in the verity of the discovered; but we must not forget that discoveries result from the work of many and from the accumulated aggregate of facts.

*Dmitry Mendeleyev*

First, and inevitably so, come the thought, fancy, and dream. These are followed by scientific calculation, and then, at long last, the thought reaches fulfilment.

*K. E. Tsiolkovsky*

\*

A scientific hypothesis transcends the facts that served as its basis.

*V. I. Vernadsky*

\*

Should hypothesis, that is the guiding thought, be totally renounced, science will become an agglomeration of naked facts.

*K. A. Timiryazev*

\*

However doubtful a hypothesis may be, it is useful if it enables us to compare known phenomena and predict new ones. This is true of the hypotheses of electricity, the structure of the atom, and others.

*K. E. Tsiolkovsky*

\*

Hypotheses help and guide scientific work—the search for the truth—as the tiller's plough helps the cultivation of useful plants.

*Dmitry Mendeleyev*

## WORDS OF THE WISE

It is better to cling to a hypothesis that is ultimately proved incorrect than to cling to none at all.

*Dmitry Mendeleyev*

\*

The chronicler must not be overhasty in rejecting hypotheses. For the greatest of men they have been a means of establishing most important facts.

*Mikhail Lomonosov*

\*

Humanity is going forward, perfecting its powers every step of the way. Everything out of its reach today will one day be near and comprehensible. This calls for hard work. Do your utmost to help those looking for the truth.

*Anton Chekhov*

\*

New ideas must be supported. Not many are daring enough to support them; this daring is a highly precious quality.

*K. E. Tsiolkovsky*

\*

We must carefully study the feeble new shoots, we must devote the greatest attention to them, and do everything to promote their growth.

*V. I. Lenin*

## CIVILISATION AND SCIENCE

In science dogmatism is a hindrance to progress; it petrifies the living thought at its very outset.

*Alexander Herzen*

\*

Dogmatism is uncritical thinking based on unproved propositions.

*N. A. Rubakin*

\*

Dogmatism is the typical result of too little learning.

*N. A. Rubakin*

\*

Intellectual mediocrity is always distinguished by passive conservatism, whose inertness bluntly resists the assault of new ideas.

*Dmitry Pisarev*

\*

Conservatism is fertilised by comfort.

*Maxim Gorky*

\*

To be a Communist means to venture, to think, to want, and to dare.

*Vladimir Mayakovsky*

## WORDS OF THE WISE

In the final analysis, science fiction is the task-setter of science and technology.

*Konstantin Fedin*

\*

The imagination—we have it to complement reality.

*V. O. Kliuchevsky*

\*

Nothing in the world is insurmountable.

*A. V. Suvorov*

\*

Science has taught people to use the energy concealed in the bowels of the Earth. It must lead man to the treasure-chests of heaven, too, and teach him to accumulate the energy of the Sun's rays.

*N. A. Umov*

\*

That which is impossible today will be possible tomorrow.

*K. E. Tsiolkovsky*

\*

So much of what we cannot do today we will learn to do tomorrow. The primitive man knew very little of what we know now.

But only the fools among the primitives thought what they know is all there is to know.

*K. E. Tsiolkovsky*

\*

Should man penetrate the solar system, should he learn to comport himself there as the mistress in her home—would the secrets of the world then open for him? Not in the least. Not any more that inspecting a pebble or shell would reveal to him the secrets of the ocean.

*K. E. Tsiolkovsky*

\*

There is a side to dreaming that transcends reality. And reality has a side that transcends dreaming. A blend of both would lead us to total happiness.

*Lev Tolstoy*

\*

A real imagination requires ultimate knowledge.

*Alexander Pushkin*

\*

I plead for creative fantasy, for accomplishing dreams that repose on precise knowledge.

*I. P. Bardin*

Progress is founded on mental development; indeed, its essential side consists in the success and development of knowledge.

*Nikolai Chernyshevsky*

The power of imagination increases proportionately to the growth of knowledge.

*Konstantin Paustovsky*

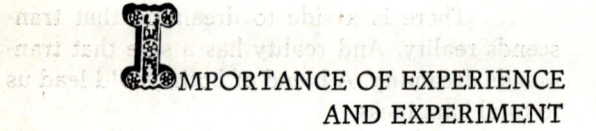

# IMPORTANCE OF EXPERIENCE AND EXPERIMENT

I value one experiment higher than a thousand opinions born of the imagination.

*Mikhail Lomonosov*

\*

Facts not explained by the existing theories are probably the most valuable for science, for their study is most likely to lead to its early advancement.

*A. M. Butlerov*

## CIVILISATION AND SCIENCE

A seemingly trivial fact, singular and insignificant today, may tomorrow become the nucleus of a new, fruitful field of knowledge in connection with some new discovery.

*A. M. Butlerov*

\*

Science breathes but one air—the oxygen of facts. New methods of research are the trees that clear its atmosphere of the carbon dioxide of inaccurate conclusions and saturate it with the oxygen of first discovered, seen and apprehended phenomena.

*V. V. Parin*

\*

Facts are the bricks of human experience, your implement in creation. Search for facts tirelessly, collect them in nature and in books, and read good textbooks from cover to cover.

*Vladimir Obruchev*

\*

In science you must look for ideas. No ideas, no science. Knowledge of the facts is precious, because facts are laden with ideas. Facts without ideas are tripe for the brain and for the memory.

*Vissarion Belinsky*

## WORDS OF THE WISE

One must learn to extract sense from fact.

*Maxim Gorky*

\*

Without a plan one is sure to lose one's way in the labyrinth of known facts.

*Dmitry Mendeleyev*

\*

It is the facts, always the facts, that teach and educate; ideas are but companions of the facts, not their forerunners.

*Maxim Gorky*

\*

Doubt rebounds from facts like a rubber ball from iron.

*Maxim Gorky*

\*

As speech is composed of sets of words and as images are composed of aggregates of shades, so from the mass of apprehended facts connected with one another there arises knowledge in its loftiest and finest sense.

*A. M. Butlerov*

# UNDERSTANDING THE TRUTH

Truth expressed in words is a most powerful force in the life of people.

*Lev Tolstoy*

\*

Man needs the truth as much as the blind needs a sober guide.

*Maxim Gorky*

\*

The truth about any important question cannot be found unless a certain amount of independent work is done, and anyone who is afraid of work cannot possibly arrive at the truth.

*V. I. Lenin*

\*

A theory not verified by experiment loses credence and is not accepted, however attractive the conception may be; practice not backed by a considered theory is the worse off for it.

*Dmitry Mendeleyev*

For one man to discover a fruitful fact a hundred must burn up their lives in unsuccessful search and sad error.

*Dmitry Pisarev*

\*

Respect for the truth is the beginning of wisdom.

*Alexander Herzen*

\*

It is not knowledge that ennobles, but love and striving for the truth. This love and striving awakens when one begins to acquire knowledge. He who escapes the effect of this feeling will not be ennobled by university learning, extensive information, or a diploma.

*Dmitry Pisarev*

\*

The truth is a tool of cognition. To attribute to a passing truth the importance of an "eternal" one is to turn that tool of cognition into chains for critical and creative thought.

*Maxim Gorky*

\*

Nature is the best and most objective teacher for solving the most difficult questions of science.

*V. V. Dokuchayev*

## CIVILISATION AND SCIENCE

Science alone can teach us to extract the truth from its one and only source—the surrounding world.

*K. A. Timiryazev*

\*

To be a materialist is to acknowledge objective truth, which is revealed to us by our sense-organs.

*V. I. Lenin*

\*

From living perception to abstract thought, and *from this to practice*—such is the dialectical path of the cognition of *truth*, of the cognition of objective reality.

*V. I. Lenin*

\*

Truth is a process. From the subjective idea, man advances towards objective truth *through* "practice" (and technique).

*V. I. Lenin*

\*

The scientific vision of the world imbued by natural science and mathematics is the greatest force of the present and future.

*V. I. Vernadsky*

The basic postulate of dialectics is: truth is never abstract, it is always concrete.

*V. I. Lenin*

\*

An abstract truth becomes an empty phrase if it is applied to every concrete situation.

*V. I. Lenin*

\*

The loftier the truth, the more carefully it must be treated: otherwise it may suddenly turn into a commonplace, and commonplaces are never believed.

*Nikolai Gogol*

\*

The greatest truths are the simplest.

*Lev Tolstoy*

\*

The truth speaks a simple tongue.

*G. S. Skovoroda*

\*

The great truths are intelligible to all and within reach of all.

*Dmitry Pisarev*

Not lies but the semblance of truth is the main obstacle to learning the truth.

*Lev Tolstoy*

\*

Truth meets strong resistance only in the beginning. The more obvious and the more of a fact it becomes, the greater is the number of its friends and champions.

*Vissarion Belinsky*

\*

Fear not the truth, look it squarely in the eye. Do not pretend it is not there. Do not take the false, imagined hues for the real thing. Only the timid and weak mind fears doubt and search. Those who believe in reason and truth will not be frightened by negations.

*Vissarion Belinsky*

\*

The truth stands above people and must not fear them.

*Vissarion Belinsky*

\*

A false understanding of the truth does not destroy it.

*Vissarion Belinsky*

The truth has indomitable vital powers.

*Dmitry Pisarev*

\*

The bitterest of truths is better than the sweetest of delusions.

*Vissarion Belinsky*

\*

Truths are old, while delusions are always new; old delusions are invariably replaced by new ones.

*Janis Rainis*

\*

The truth does not become less true for being endlessly repeated.

*Konstantin Fedin*

\*

The purpose of the mind is to discover the truth; it is, therefore, a big and harmful mistake to use the mind for concealing or distorting the truth.

*Lev Tolstoy*

\*

Every man can and must use everything that the aggregate intellect of humanity has worked out, but also can and must verify for himself the truths worked out by people who had lived before him.

*Lev Tolstoy*

\*

Love the truth so ardently as to be ready to renounce everything you had previously held to be truth the minute you learn the supreme truth.

*Lev Tolstoy*

\*

The truth alone contains life and goodness, for the truth never needs the help of a lie.

*Vissarion Belinsky*

\*

Be persistent and persevering, but never stubborn. Do not cling to your judgements. Remember that there are many clever people in the world liable to spot your mistakes. If they are right, be not reluctant to agree with them.

*Vladimir Obruchev*

\*

Hiding the truth is base. Lying from fear is cowardly.

*N. P. Ogarev*

Stick to your principles. We need the truth and nothing but the truth. Do not try to please your friends or humour your teachers, or to avoid offending anyone. By doing so you will find peace of mind, perhaps even prosperity. But you will do no good to anyone or anything.

*Vladimir Obruchev*

\*

The scientist must look for the truth and value it higher than his personal wishes or relationships.

*Nikolai Chernyshevsky*

\*

Scientists must be absolutely honest. The slightest departure from honesty is, in my view, the basest of crimes.

*K. I. Skriabin*

\*

Knowledge without a moral foundation is meaningless.

*Lev Tolstoy*

\*

What can be more harmful than a man knowing the most difficult sciences, but lacking a kind heart? He will use his knowledge for an evil purpose.

*G. S. Skovoroda*

For the corrupt science is a weapon for doing wrong. Education elevates only the virtuous.

*Denis Fonvizin*

✻

Usually, the companion of true science is quiet modesty. There can be no true science where scathing comment and a judge's high-handedness muzzles all dissent.

*Dmitry Mendeleyev*

✻

The true scientist must strictly adhere to principle, must be honest in discussion and well-intentioned in relation to other scientific judgements. The truth is but one, though the search for it may be long and not always smooth.

*V. N. Sukachev*

✻

Science cannot be truly democratic unless there is complete freedom of thought, press, conscience, and speech, and unless its doors are flung open for every gifted personality.

*N. A. Rubakin*

✻

No real Soviet scientist is covetous; intrigue is hostile to him. What he prizes most is the search for the truth, and service to the Fatherland and the people. All personal considerations recede to the background. The main thing for us is not material gain, but the gain a scientific discovery may yield to the whole people, to our country.

*N. F. Gamaleya*

\*

A Soviet scientist must not forget that he works for the people and that the scientific truth is not an aim in itself, but the true road to cultural growth, to mastering the forces of Nature for the good of the people.

*A. F. Joffe*

\*

There are two sides to all things in the world.

*V. I. Lenin*

\*

Any truth, if "overdone" ... if exaggerated or if carried beyond the limits of its actual applicability, can be reduced to an absurdity, and is even bound to become an absurdity under these conditions.

*V. I. Lenin*

## CIVILISATION AND SCIENCE

## THE SCIENTIST'S RESPONSIBILITY

Every individual is in debt to society for his mental development.

*Nikolai Chernyshevsky*

\*

An intellectual's purpose in life is continuous accumulation of scientific knowledge for its selfless distribution in the thick of the masses.

*Maxim Gorky*

\*

The select who engage in science must look upon knowledge as a treasure entrusted to their care, but belonging to the whole people.

*K. A. Timiryazev*

\*

It is no exaggeration to say that popularising science is the most important job facing the modern world.

*Dmitry Pisarev*

Awareness of and identification with the public interest is what makes science really useful, interesting, and necessary for society.

*Nikolai Dobrolyubov*

\*

If a person conscious of the conditions of progress sits on his hands expecting progress to come about by itself, without any effort on his part, he is the worst enemy and obstructionist of progress.

*Pyotr Lavrov*

\*

A one-sided specialist is either a crude empiricist or a common charlatan.

*Nikolai Pirogov*

\*

Science is often identified with knowledge. This is a gross misunderstanding. Science is not merely knowledge, but also consciousness, that is, the skill of properly using knowledge.

*V. O. Kliuchevsky*

\*

Knowledge is a tool, not a goal.

*A. N. Tolstoy*

## CIVILISATION AND SCIENCE

Knowledge must serve man's creative aims. It is not enough to accumulate knowledge; knowledge must be spread as widely as possible and used in life.

*N. A. Rubakin*

\*

One must know not merely for the sake of knowing, but for doing.

*Maxim Gorky*

\*

The most distinctive feature of science is that it demands eager activity.

*Ilya Mechnikov*

\*

Science wants total dedication with readiness to sacrifice and no second thoughts. The reward will be the heavy cross of sober knowledge.

*Alexander Herzen*

\*

Science has its own logic of development, which it is important to bear in mind. It must always have a reserve for future use. Only on these terms will it thrive in conditions which are natural for it.

*S. I. Vavilov*

From a clever and learned man much must be demanded; if he utters trivialities he may be legitimately rebuked, because the condescension one bestows on simpletons is unfit in his case.

*Nikolai Chernyshevsky*

\*

There is a very close and unbreakable bond between science and life. Nor is this bond humiliating for either of them. The more science serves life, the more life enriches science.

*G. V. Plekhanov*

\*

We cannot have science divorced from life: that would be contrary to our nature.

*Alexander Herzen*

\*

The job of science is to serve people.

*Lev Tolstoy*

\*

I value true science very highly—the kind of science that takes an interest in man, in his happiness, and destiny.

*Lev Tolstoy*

# CIVILISATION AND SCIENCE

To work for science and for common ideas is what I call personal happiness.

*Anton Chekhov*

\*

In its true sense, scientific and artistic work can be fruitful only if it ignores privileges and minds its duties.

*Lev Tolstoy*

\*

Science has exceedingly palpable, so to say gastronomic, importance.

*K. E. Tsiolkovsky*

\*

Science plays a subsidiary role—it is a means to attaining prosperity.

*Dmitry Mendeleyev*

\*

Always forward, poised for the next step after every accomplished one, devoting all one's being to what is still undone.

*N. N. Burdenko*

\*

Science is continuous revelation—not only discovery, but also discovering.

*N. A. Rubakin*

Despite all obstacles, the scientist must follow unblazed trails.

*N. I. Lobachevsky*

\*

It is not difficult to put one's foot forward along a trodden path, and far more difficult, but also more deserving, to lay the path oneself.

*Jakub Kolas*

\*

My successors must overtake me, contradict me, even destroy my labours, for that is how they will continue them. It is out of such successively destroyed labour that progress is born.

*Ivan Michurin*

\*

Discoveries come about where the teacher's knowledge ends and the pupil's new knowledge begins.

*Konstantin Fedin*

\*

Nothing comes about by itself, without effort and will, without sacrifice and labour.

*Alexander Herzen*

## CIVILISATION AND SCIENCE

We must be braver and not give up if there are setbacks. Look for their causes and eliminate them.

*K. E. Tsiolkovsky*

\*

There is no other coin in science than the sweat of one's brow—neither zeal, nor fantasy, nor striving can take the place of hard work.

*Alexander Herzen*

\*

Science begins with the intellect, and the intellect with patience.

*Effendi Kapiev*

\*

Not the truths of science are difficult, but clearing the human consciousness of all the inherited tripe, the sediments, the mistaking of the unnatural for the natural and the incomprehensible for the comprehensible.

*Alexander Herzen*

\*

Science imposes great strains and great passions. Be passionate in your work and search.

*Ivan Pavlov*

Recognition is gained and proved only by the sacrifice which the scientist or artist makes of his tranquillity and wellbeing in order to dedicate himself to his vocation.

*Lev Tolstoy*

\*

Ardent faith in science is not merely a good quality, but a precious one, for scientific progress is inconceivable without it.

*Sergei Yudin*

\*

No substantive scientific gain would, probably, have seen the light of day without ardent, committed, and zealous dedication on the part of the researcher.

*K. A. Timiryazev*

\*

Talent is colourless; it acquires colour only with use.

*M. E. Saltykov-Shchedrin*

\*

He who strives not will not achieve, and he who dares not will not receive.

*Vissarion Belinsky*

Those who do not use their spiritual powers are bound to lose them.

*Janis Rainis*

\*

In all philosophical and scientific camps there are vandals and parasites who not only fail to think their own thoughts, but do not even digest the thoughts of others. All they do is memorise them and dilute ready-made ideas in buckets of water, compiling articles and books.

*Dmitry Pisarev*

\*

Look not upon learnedness as a crown in which to strut about or a cow which to milk.

*Lev Tolstoy*

\*

Honesty in science is part of honesty in life. He who sees science merely as a milch cow is not its faithful servant, but a merchant who turns the virtuous name of science into a trading enterprise.

*Fyodor Inozemtsev*

\*

Science does not tolerate pursuit of selfish gain.

*Vassily Williams*

A scientist's labours are the possession of all mankind, and science is a realm of the greatest self-abnegation.

*Maxim Gorky*

\*

Regrettably, very many so-called scientists treat science as a milch cow which they expect to supply their daily needs. This turns scientists into ordinary artisans, sometimes even common charlatans.

*N. N. Miklukho-Maklai*

\*

Blend knowledge with labour, give knowledge to those who will of necessity extract from it all the practical benefits it contains, and you will see that the riches of the country and people will increase at an incredibly rapid rate.

*Dmitry Pisarev*

\*

Uniting broad theoretical vision, general theory and abstraction with sound practicalness is the best and probably the only way that science can help the people.

*S. I. Vavilov*

# CIVILISATION AND SCIENCE

Science has long since stopped snubbing life, and has inscribed on its banner the words, "the seeds of science will yield their harvest to the people".

*Dmitry Mendeleyev*

## OF LAW AND FREEDOM

The laws and instructions of the Soviet Government must be faithfully observed, and care must be taken that they are obeyed by all.

*V. I. Lenin*

\*

The slightest lawlessness, the slightest infraction of Soviet law and order is a *loophole* the foes of the working people take immediate advantage of.

*V. I. Lenin*

\*

Lawlessness cannot be put down as a credit, and cannot merit respect.

*Alexander Kazbegi*

\*

Those write laws best who write them for others to follow and who need not impose them upon themselves.

*G. S. Skovoroda*

## LAW, FREEDOM, AND DISCIPLINE

Woe unto the land where not the law but subordinates, chiefs, and tribunals wield power over citizens and state affairs. They all fancy themselves sagacious and wise, and, as a result, "tended by seven nannies, the infant is bereft of care".*

*M. I. Kutuzov*

## FREEDOM AND DISCIPLINE

The more developed a nation is, the more complete is the independence of the individual, and the safer the individual from encroachments by another.

*Dmitry Pisarev*

\*

The more honoured sensible freedom is in a country, the mightier is the rule of law and the more fully citizens perform their civic duty, because the idea of freedom always blends with

---

* Enclosed in inverted commas is a Russian proverb roughly equivalent to "too many cooks spoil the broth".—*Tr.*

the idea of truth, and because it stimulates the obligation to strive for the common weal.

*Mikhail Kutorga*

\*

In our society discipline is an ethical and at once a political concept.

*Anton Makarenko*

\*

In a group discipline must prevail over the interests of its individual members.

*Anton Makarenko*

\*

Without discipline there can be no collective, and without a collective there can be no organisation.

*Dmitry Furmanov*

\*

Learn to obey the law, to maintain order and discipline, and to follow the rules of behaviour in socialist society. To obey the world's most humane laws is a supreme expression of freedom.

*Vassily Sukhomlinsky*

## LAW, FREEDOM, AND DISCIPLINE

Who are the truly free? It is those who do not indulge their own passions or the whims of others.

*Fyodor Glinka*

*

Pure freedom is not independence, but merely a knack of not assuming fortuitous dependence.

*P. A. Fedotov*

*

The most important thing the Revolution has given us is liberation of creative thought from formal limits and prejudices, and from the narrow horizons that had contained it heretofore.

*Vladimir Nemirovich-Danchenko*

## WRONGDOINGS AND CRIMES

There are three kinds of scoundrels—naive scoundrels are certain their villainy is noble, scoundrels ashamed of their villainy, but, nevertheless, firmly determined to complete it, and finally rank or pure-blooded scoundrels.

*Fyodor Dostoyevsky*

*

You fall into trouble as precipitously as you fall into an abyss; to crime you descend step by step.

*A. A. Bestuzhev-Marlinsky*

*

Horrible crimes entail horrible consequences.

*Alexander Herzen*

*

Not to confess one's wrongdoing means adding to it.

*Lev Tolstoy*

*

If you're a scoundrel, don't humour yourself that you're being original.

*Maxim Gorky*

## OF HUMAN VIRTUES

### COURAGE, GENUINENESS, AND MODESTY

Courage is a great quality of the soul; a nation endowed with it has every reason to be proud.

*Nikolai Karamzin*

\*

Display courage for the glory of your Fatherland.

*Mikhail Lomonosov*

\*

True courage shies from loud talk: it shows itself so naturally that it regards heroism a duty, not an exploit.

*A. A. Bestuzhev-Marlinsky*

\*

Courage is cultivated day after day through dogged resistance to difficulties.

*Nikolai Ostrovsky*

The courage of working day in and day out, year after year is of the toughest variety. Find your ideal of courage and follow it without fail.

*Vassily Sukhomlinsky*

\*

Courage is usually a companion of mild character, and those who have courage are usually more generous.

*N. V. Shelgunov*

\*

Artlessness is the chief element of moral beauty.

*Lev Tolstoy*

\*

Artlessness is a quality I wish to have more than any other.

*Lev Tolstoy*

\*

Strong people are always genuine.

*Lev Tolstoy*

\*

It is best not to think yourself special and to be like all other people.

*M. M. Prishvin*

## HUMAN VIRTUES

The only terms on which it is easy to associate with another is not to think yourself higher or better than he or him higher and better than you.

*Lev Tolstoy*

\*

Modesty is often mistaken for weakness and irresolution, but when experience shows people they are wrong, modesty lends fresh attraction, strength, and respect.

*Lev Tolstoy*

\*

Every person is like a fraction, the numerator being that what he is, and the denominator that what he thinks he is. The greater the denominator the smaller the fraction.

*Lev Tolstoy*

\*

Nearly in all cases modesty is directly proportional to the degree of talent.

*G. V. Plekhanov*

\*

No one has ever regretted having lived too simply.

*Lev Tolstoy*

Modesty from weakness is no virtue.

*Abai Kunanbayev*

\*

Beware of reducing modesty to plain abasement.

*Abbas-Kouli Bahihanov*

\*

People who try to look genuine are least of all genuine. Deliberate artlessness is the greatest and most disagreeable artfulness.

*Lev Tolstoy*

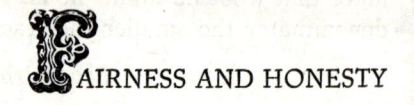

## FAIRNESS AND HONESTY

Justice should be the standard of all human behaviour.

*Nikolai Chernyshevsky*

\*

The finest and most typical trait of our people is its sense and thirst of justice.

*Fyodor Dostoyevsky*

## HUMAN VIRTUES

Justice should be behind all our actions and our very wishes.

*Kondraty Ryleyev*

\*

To be fair in thought is not yet being fair in deed.

*Konstantin Ushinsky*

\*

Once one loses love of honesty one is swiftly drawn into so many wrongdoings that one acquires the habit of dishonesty.

*Nikolai Chernyshevsky*

\*

If you know you have lived honestly, life seems better and easier.

*Mikhail Kalinin*

\*

To be honest means living for the common good and sacrificing your own to the common interest.

*N. P. Ogarev*

\*

Honesty in solely one's personal affairs unaccompanied by any definite notions about general matters of the common weal yields much too little benefit to society.

*Nikolai Chernyshevsky*

What is honesty? Honesty is an open and sincere attitude, dishonesty a secret and concealed attitude.

*Anton Makarenko*

\*

Our honesty must always make us as exigent with ourselves as we are with others.

*Anton Makarenko*

\*

Scoundrels tend to prosper because they treat honest people as scoundrels, while honest people treat scoundrels as honest people.

*Vissarion Belinsky*

\*

Honest people have the bad habit of lowering their eyes in embarrassment before a brazen-faced wrong.

*Vissarion Belinsky*

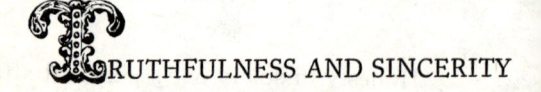

# TRUTHFULNESS AND SINCERITY

A man's degree of veraciousness is the measure of his probity.

*Lev Tolstoy*

## HUMAN VIRTUES

Fidelity to the truth regardless of personal interests or wishes—there you have honesty and integrity.

*N. P. Ogarev*

\*

Truth is the air without which you cannot breathe.

*Ivan Turgenev*

\*

The truth, even though brutal, must not be evaded by anyone.

*Nikolai Pirogov*

\*

The truth is always a bit distressing, but it is also always healthful.

*Maxim Gorky*

\*

The truth is a victory of the conscience.

*M. M. Prishvin*

\*

Be warned against thinking that one must speak and do true only in important things. One must speak and do true at all times, not stoop to lies even in trifles. Who cares whether the evil of your untruth is big or small. The thing is never to be defiled by a lie.

*Lev Tolstoy*

\*

Be truthful even in trifles.

*Maxim Gorky*

\*

Though the truth does not always tell us what we must do, it invariably tells us what we must not do or must stop doing.

*Lev Tolstoy*

\*

In a serious matter, the badly worded truth is preferable to its being hushed up.

*V. I. Lenin*

\*

We must not delude ourselves with lies. That is harmful.

*V. I. Lenin*

\*

The bitterest truth is always better than the sweetest lie.

*Nikolai Ostrovsky*

## HUMAN VIRTUES

The living truth thrives and makes its way forward as all things living, as a green sprig among trash.

*M. M. Prishvin*

\*

No fog can dim the rays of the truth.

*Fyodor Dostoyevsky*

\*

The truth nears a man through his sense of strength. It comes to him the moment he decides to fight—to fight for the truth, to stand up for it. Not all strength stands for the truth, but the truth always announces itself through strength.

*M. M. Prishvin*

\*

The truth lodges in deeds. Not every deed is truth, but truth always lives in deeds.

*M. M. Prishvin*

\*

Truth needs tenacity.

*M. M. Prishvin*

\*

Sincerity is a difficult and delicate thing; it calls for wisdom and genuine tact.

*Vikenty Veresayev*

How narrow are the limits of human frankness and how obstinately are they guarded by vanity.

*Maxim Gorky*

# DIFFIDENCE, CONSCIENCE, AND HONOUR

The most inveterate of rogues understands, too, that something in a diffident person singles him out in the crowd of idlers and fools.

*M. E. Saltykov-Shchedrin*

\*

You experience the greatest shame and the greatest torment when you cannot worthily defend what you love, what you live for.

*Maxim Gorky*

\*

Nothing can more accurately measure a person's moral quality than what he is ashamed of and what he is not ashamed of.

*Lev Tolstoy*

## HUMAN VIRTUES

To be ashamed before people is good, but better still to be ashamed before yourself.

*Lev Tolstoy*

*

A clear or guilty conscience is society's memory as absorbed by individuals.

*Lev Tolstoy*

*

A person is what he becomes face to face with himself. His true human essence surfaces when his behaviour is motivated not by someone, but by his own conscience.

*Vassily Sukhomlinsky*

*

It is not difficult to scorn the judgement of others, and impossible to scorn one's own.

*Alexander Pushkin*

*

It is necessary to cultivate the conscience of people and clear thinking.

*Anton Chekhov*

People are spurred by their conscience to look for better things and are often helped by it to give up the old, cozy, and dear that is *rotting* and *dying* in favour of the new, which is not at first cozy or dear, but holds promise of fresh life.

*Alexander Blok*

\*

He who has no conscience is doomed even though he may be inordinately clever.

*Maxim Gorky*

\*

Conscience is people's most dependable guide.

*Lev Tolstoy*

\*

Beware of all things your conscience disapproves of.

*Lev Tolstoy*

\*

Where else is the greatness of the human spirit put more to the test than in those cases where a person chooses to suffer eternally rather than act contrary to his conscience.

*Vissarion Belinsky*

# HUMAN VIRTUES

Only those who have put on an armour suit of lies, brazenness, and shamelessness fail to flinch before the judgement of their conscience.

*Maxim Gorky*

\*

Guilt is a noble feeling in the case of enlightened people. Only the fool and hardened moral ignoramus never experiences a sense of guilt.

*Vassily Sukhomlinsky*

\*

A sense of guilt is not self-flagellation, but a twinge of conscience, an aspiration to moral purity and probity.

*Vassily Sukhomlinsky*

\*

Often, people pride themselves in their clear conscience merely because they have short memories.

*Lev Tolstoy*

\*

Conscience is truer than memory.

*Mikhail Lermontov*

Conscience is like a beast clawing at the heart.

*Alexander Pushkin*

I know of only two real misfortunes—a guilty conscience and illness.

*Lev Tolstoy*

Honour is the cornerstone of human wisdom.

*Vissarion Belinsky*

## OF FRIENDSHIP

### A GREAT BLESSING

No bonds are more sacred than those of friendship. The father loves his child, the mother loves her child, and the child loves its mother and father. But that isn't the same thing; a wild beast, too, loves its offspring. To be kindred in spirit rather than blood—only man can be so.

*Nikolai Gogol*

\*

A friend is your support in trouble, your doctor in illness, and the one who sacrifices himself in the hour of mortal danger.

*Sulkhan Saba Orbeliani*

\*

A friend is a tall wall, an indestructible stronghold, a fortress well supplied with water.

*Sulkhan Saba Orbeliani*

\*

Friendship is the highest degree of comradeship.

*Maxim Gorky*

It might even please you to be sick if you knew there are people who yearn for your recovery as for redemption.

*Anton Chekhov*

\*

There is no greater joy than to see friends, and no greater sorrow than to part with them.

*Rudaki*

\*

One enemy is much, a thousand friends is little.

*Rudaki*

\*

The most steadfast friendship is that which began in youth. It is the most steadfast and the most pleasant.

*Nikolai Karamzin*

## THE PILLARS OF FRIENDSHIP

Friendship is impossible without mutual respect.

*Anton Makarenko*

# FRIENDSHIP

The most hard-won applause is the applause of one's friends.

*Effendi Kapiev*

*

The prime condition for friendship is sincerity.

*M. M. Prishvin*

*

Friendship wants neither slave nor ruler, it wants equality.

*Ivan Goncharov*

*

Authority and friendship are like fire and water, entirely different and hostile; the basis of friendship is equality.

*Vissarion Belinsky*

*

Equality in love and friendship is a sacred thing.

*Ivan Krylov*

*

Servility and friendship are like parallel lines–they do not meet.

*A. V. Suvorov*

Friendship is not a favour and needs no thanks.

*G. R. Derzhavin*

\*

Sincerity in relations and veracity in speech—this is friendship.

*A. V. Suvorov*

\*

Be honest with your friends, moderate in your needs, and selfless in your conduct.

*A. V. Suvorov*

\*

To be true friends you must be sure in one another.

*Lev Tolstoy*

\*

He is my friend to whom I can say everything.

*Vissarion Belinsky*

\*

Friendship does not and cannot exist where complete sincerity and trust are lacking and even a trifle has been concealed.

*Vissarion Belinsky*

# FRIENDSHIP

Misfortune is the most dependable cement for binding people who may even be diametrically opposite by nature.

*Maxim Gorky*

*

*True friend does not abandon friend in spite of all privations.*

*Shot'ha Rust'hveli*

*

*He who leaves a friend in trouble will himself its victim be.*

*Shot'ha Rust'hveli*

*

*To slight friendship is to quarrel with wisdom.*

*Shot'ha Rust'hveli*

*

Friendship is sincerity first and last, it is criticism of a friend's mistakes. Friends must be the first to criticise and help their comrade mend his ways.

*Nikolai Ostrovsky*

*

If you cannot frankly, sincerely, even harshly tell your friend everything you think of him or his behaviour, or hear him say the truth about you, neither of you really trust one another nor understand and respect one another.

*Ivan Goncharov*

*

A friendship that won't survive the touch of bare truth is not worth lamenting.

*Dmitry Pisarev*

*

Who but a friend will tell me the truth about myself? Yet it is essential to hear the truth about oneself from another.

*Vissarion Belinsky*

*

The rebukes of opponents and enemies, even accusations, can sometimes be ignored, but the rebukes of friends require an explanation or an admission of guilt.

*Alexander Herzen*

## FALSE FRIENDS

An enemy is usually made out of a friend.

*Effendi Kapiev*

# FRIENDSHIP

A dishonest or foolish ally in an intellectual affair, in a clash of principles, will do more harm than an enemy.

*Dmitry Pisarev*

*

A cowardly friend is worse than an enemy, because you are on your guard against enemies, while you depend on friends.

*Lev Tolstoy*

*

Since my friend is friendly with my enemy, I must not nourish friendship for him. Beware of sugar that is mixed with venom, and of the fly that has sat on a dead snake.

*Avicenna*

*

Some are better counted among your enemies than among your friends.

*Fyodor Dostoyevsky*

## OF LOVE

### THE FLOWER OF LIFE

Love is the maker of all that is kind, exalted, strong, warm, and bright.

*Felix Dzerzhinsky*

\*

Love is a summons to action and struggle.

*Felix Dzerzhinsky*

\*

There is no God more magnificent than the Sun, and no fire more magical than the fire of love.

*Maxim Gorky*

\*

Life without love is mere existence. It is impossible to live without love, for man is endowed with a soul in order to love.

*Maxim Gorky*

# LOVE

Love is a life-giving flame in a man's soul, and everything man has created under the influence of love bears the stamp of life and poetry.

*Taras Shevchenko*

\*

Love is a great adornment of life. It makes Nature flower, radiate colours, sing enthralling songs, and dance bewitching dances.

*A. V. Lunacharsky*

\*

Poetic and passionate love is the flower of our life and youth.

*Vissarion Belinsky*

\*

Love is an exalted word, the harmony of creation demands it; without it there is no life, nor can there be any.

*Alexander Herzen*

\*

It is through love that life delights; love is the apotheosis of life.

*Alexander Herzen*

\*

Love is the longing to live.

*Maxim Gorky*

Love must fill people with strength, and it does.

*Anton Makarenko*

\*

True love is purifying, it elevates people whom it happens to visit, and transforms those whom it visits.

*Nikolai Chernyshevsky*

\*

Love is so all-powerful that it transforms us.

*Fyodor Dostoyevsky*

\*

To teach love, to teach to recognise love, to teach to be happy means teaching to respect oneself, and teaching human dignity.

*Anton Makarenko*

\*

In one's young years even a passing infatuation and all the pleasures of love must be aesthetic if they are not to be immoral.

*Vissarion Belinsky*

\*

What good fortune it is for one to love and be loved.

*Anton Chekhov*

# LOVE

When in love you discover such riches in yourself, so much tenderness, so much sweet affection, that it is even hard to believe that you can love so consumingly.

*Anton Chekhov*

\*

What we experience when in love is, perhaps, the normal state. The state of love shows one what one should be like.

*Anton Chekhov*

\*

Only he who is in love has a right to be called human.

*Alexander Blok*

\*

Love is the greatest of all feelings, a feeling that works wonders, that creates new people, and produces the greatest human values.

*Anton Makarenko*

\*

Love is strong as lightning, but it strikes without thunder, and one derives pleasure from even its strongest bolts.

*Mikhail Lomonosov*

Respect has its limits, love has none.

*Mikhail Lermontov*

\*

*As day 'tis bright, though puzzling,*
*All true and real, but like a dream*
*It comes with speech coherent*
*And in its wake comes spring.*

*Alexander Blok*

\*

*He who is never gripped by sinful passion*
*Is like a dried-out brook;*
*All brooks—they ring and hasten seaward,*
*While this one's overblown with sand.*

*Mirza Shafi*

\*

Moral ignorance and wantonness in matters of love do our society tremendous harm. Those for whom love is all pleasure cause grief, tears, and misfortune.

*Vassily Sukhomlinsky*

\*

Love knows no fear. Perfect love banishes fear.

*Alexander Blok*

## LOVE

Love destroys death and turns it into a spectre. It transforms life from an absurdity into something sensible, and unhappiness into happiness.

*Lev Tolstoy*

\*

Love is the most intimate and untouchable of feelings. Cherish the secrets of love.

*Vassily Sukhomlinsky*

## WOMEN AND MEN

All that is beautiful in the world was born of love for woman.

*Maxim Gorky*

\*

For men loving a woman is always fruitful, no matter what it means—even if nothing but torment; for in torment, too, there is always much value.

*Maxim Gorky*

Woman is a great word. It stands for the purity of an innocent, for the devotion of a spouse, and for the exploit of a mother.

*Nikolai Nekrasov*

\*

The measure of culture is one's treatment of women.

*Maxim Gorky*

\*

It should be well understood and remembered that socialism cannot be practised without women.

*Maxim Gorky*

\*

Respect your girl, protect her honour, dignity, and human pride. The girl who attracts you is your future wife, the mother of your children. She is the guarantee of your immortality, she will repeat you in your children.

*Vassily Sukhomlinsky*

\*

The woman's calling is to arouse in men the energy of their soul and the ardour of noble passions, and to sustain their sense of duty and their striving for the lofty and great. This is her purpose in life, and it is great and sacred.

*Vissarion Belinsky*

# LOVE

The woman who tries to be like a man is as warped as an effeminate man.

*Lev Tolstoy*

※

Your treatment of women is a delicate gauge of your honour, conscience, decency, and nobility. It is the high school of considerateness.

*Vassily Sukhomlinsky*

\*

The man she loves is, perhaps, a measure of a woman's worth and virtue.

*Vissarion Belinsky*

\*

A woman is not only capable of appreciating self-sacrifice, but also of sacrificing herself.

*Ivan Turgenev*

\*

Nearly every woman is capable of the loftiest heroism when she is in love.

*Alexander Kuprin*

Before falling in love with the woman in the girl, learn to love the human being in her.

*Vassily Sukhomlinsky*

\*

For any decent man of our time to see and respect the human being in a woman is not only necessary, but also the principal condition of love.

*Vissarion Belinsky*

\*

Girls must be taught to respect themselves more, and their girlish pride, too. They must be taught that even the young men that they like are to be treated with a grain of pepper.

*Anton Makarenko*

\*

Every tear shed in the modern societies by a loving woman is a grave indictment of the man she loves.

*Dmitry Pisarev*

\*

Where the woman or girl is strict and demanding, there the youth grows into a real man.

*Vassily Sukhomlinsky*

## LOVE

Girls, be wise and demanding in love. Love is a passion, but it must be ruled by reason and good sense.

*Vassily Sukhomlinsky*

\*

A woman does not believe the words, "I love you", unless they are spoken quietly and unpretentiously.

*Yaroslav Galan*

\*

We often see men who are neither fish nor fowl, while their women are splendid. This only means that we know not the hidden virtues of the men which their women discerned: their love is selective and this, most probably, is true love.

*M. M. Prishvin*

\*

Nothing is more enchanting than a woman who holds to her principles unflinchingly, incorruptibly, and without affectation, and whose fidelity to her principles is as natural, modest, and feminine as everything else about her.

*Alexander Fadeyev*

## FACETS OF LOVE

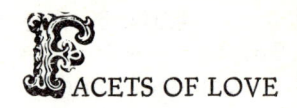

Love has a thousand facets and each of them has its own brightness, its sorrow, happiness, and fragrance.

*Konstantin Paustovsky*

\*

All love is true and beautiful in its own way so long as it is in the heart, not the head.

*Vissarion Belinsky*

\*

The heart has its own laws, though not of the kind easily compiled in a complete and systematic code.

*Vissarion Belinsky*

\*

If in love choice depended on will and reason alone, love would not be a feeling and a passion. There is an element of spontaneity in the most sensible love, because out of several equally worthy people the choice falls on but

# LOVE

one, and this choice is based on the ungovernable attraction of the heart.

*Vissarion Belinsky*

\*

The influence on love of moral qualities is undeniable, but when you love someone, you love all of him not as an idea but as a personality, and especially you love that in him which you can neither define nor name.

*Vissarion Belinsky*

\*

People fall in love quite simply and unquestioningly even before they realise that they have fallen in love. This feeling of love depends not on the head; it is a natural and immediate attraction of heart to heart.

*Vissarion Belinsky*

\*

Love like hate may provoke the most diverse feelings—suffering and pleasure, joy and sorrow, fear and courage, and even anger and hatred.

*Konstantin Ushinsky*

## WORDS OF THE WISE

Love, like human life, has its own laws of development, and its own seasons. It has its own magnificent spring, its own hot summer and, finally, its own autumn, which is warm, bright and fertile for some, and chilly, rank, and barren for others.

*Vissarion Belinsky*

\*

Love is like an unexplored sea, and we sail it each in his own boat; each is his own captain and steers his own course.

*M. M. Prishvin*

\*

It is love's special quality that it does good to those who experience it.

*Lev Tolstoy*

\*

Love flickers out like fire, unless it is fed.

*Mikhail Lermontov*

\*

Love submits only to love.

*Vissarion Belinsky*

# LOVE

Not only those who shout their love from the rooftops are true lovers; clever people express their feelings by deeds as well as words, and some by deeds only; perhaps, the less voluble they are, the stronger they love.

*Nikolai Chernyshevsky*

\*

It is much better to express one's love in useful deeds than melodious praise.

*Dmitry Pisarev*

\*

Everybody knows that ardent love is always tersely, but strongly expressed.

*G. R. Derzhavin*

\*

Love often errs, seeing non-existent virtues in its object ... but betimes love alone discovers the beautiful and great that is invisible to the eye or mind of others.

*Vissarion Belinsky*

\*

The person whom you love in me is certainly better than me: I am different. But love me, do, and I shall try to be better than I am.

*M. M. Prishvin*

# Love and Morality

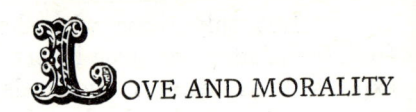

Love should be understood not only as appeasing a healthy sexual instinct. Love, which yields much joy, must be connected with ideological kinship, with a striving for one and the same goal, and with struggle for a common cause.

*N. K. Krupskaya*

\*

Affinity of spirit results in the man seeing the woman and the woman seeing the man first and foremost not as a being of another sex, but as a human being.

*N. K. Krupskaya*

\*

Happiness with a woman is possible only if your spiritual communion with her is entirely sincere.

*Maxim Gorky*

\*

Your relationship with a woman requires you to be completely sincere.

*Maxim Gorky*

# LOVE

The sensation of love can be truly good only if there is inner harmony between the lovers. Then it is the beginning and guarantee of that public wellbeing promised us in the future development of mankind through the triumph of fraternity and personal equality among people.

*Nikolai Dobrolyubov*

\*

Love is a gorgeous and gracious flower crowning and consummating individual life; but like all flowers it must have its one and better side open to the heaven of the universal.

*Alexander Herzen*

\*

Love needs sensible content as fire needs fuel to sustain it.

*Vissarion Belinsky*

\*

A love in which friendship, comradeship, and common interest are lacking is shallow.

*Nikolai Ostrovsky*

\*

What is loving someone? It is rejoicing at what is good for your loved one, and taking pleasure in doing your loved one's needs.

*Nikolai Chernyshevsky*

To love means to live the life of your loved one.

*Lev Tolstoy*

\*

Only he loves truly who helps his beloved rise to independence.

*Nikolai Chernyshevsky*

\*

Deep love and deep intellect are inseparable.

*Ivan Goncharov*

\*

For an enlightened person love is not blind; he knows whom he loves and why.

*N. V. Shelgunov*

\*

Where there is love there must be trust.

*Felix Dzerzhinsky*

\*

Love needs severe trials and, equally, a sharp memory of how it began.

*Alexander Fadeyev*

## LOVE

Deep-felt respect is always more lasting than infatuation.

*Dmitry Pisarev*

※

To love another and not hinder his life, not poison his existence with importunate care and concern is a trick given to only a few.

*Dmitry Pisarev*

※

Man is neither beast nor angel; his love must be neither animal nor platonic love, but human.

*Vissarion Belinsky*

※

Truly human love must repose on mutual respect of one another's human dignity, not on a mere whim of the senses or a caprice of the heart.

*Vissarion Belinsky*

※

Depravity is not anything physical, for physical deformity is not depravity; real depravity is when you shake off all moral restraints towards the woman with whom you enter into a physical relationship.

*Lev Tolstoy*

He who can treat a woman with vulgar and shameless cynicism does not deserve confidence as a citizen; his attitude towards the common cause will be just as cynical; he cannot be wholly trusted.

*Anton Makarenko*

\*

Purity of civic feeling is inconceivable without purity of intimate feeling.

*Vassily Sukhomlinsky*

\*

For us there is no greater misfortune than to assume moral responsibility for a woman's happiness and then break her heart, even if unconsciously.

*Vissarion Belinsky*

\*

Cherish love as a precious thing. Mistreat love once, and your next love will inevitably have a flaw.

*Konstantin Paustovsky*

\*

Love becomes illegitimate when reason disapproves: to suppress the voice of reason is to give free rein to passion and animal instinct.

*Dmitry Pisarev*

# LOVE

Love is the poetry and the sun of life. But woe unto him who sets out to build the edifice of his happiness on love and love alone, and who expects to satisfy all his cravings through the life of his heart. In our time this means shedding one's human dignity and turning from man into beast.

*Vissarion Belinsky*

\*

Depravity of whatever kind emaciates the soul and leaves grains of an eternally active poison.

*Alexander Herzen*

\*

Depravity consists of animal sensuality that is devoid of poetry, because poetry can contain none but elements of reason, while that which reduces man to beast contains no reason.

*Vissarion Belinsky*

# JEALOUSY

All's clear to jealousy, but there's no proof.

*Mikhail Lermontov*

Jealousy is a passion encountered in people who are either egoistic or morally underdeveloped. To consider jealousy a necessary companion of love is an inexcusable mistake.

*Vissarion Belinsky*

\*

Jealousy that lacks sufficient grounds is a malaise of wretches who respect neither themselves nor their right to the affection of their beloved; it is the petty tyranny of a creature that has failed to rise above animal selfishness.

*Vissarion Belinsky*

\*

Neither tears of loss nor tears of jealousy can or should be wiped away. But they can and should be shed humanly; there should be no monastic poison in them, nor the wildness of beasts, nor the howl of a possessor's wounded pride.

*Alexander Herzen*

\*

If you lose the love of a woman, blame none but yourself for failing to preserve it.

*Nikolai Dobrolyubov*

## OF FAMILY, PARENTS, AND CHILDREN

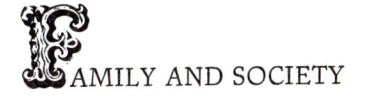

### FAMILY AND SOCIETY

Familial love is the most widespread and the most enduring feeling, and therefore, in the sense of influencing people's lives, it is also the most important and the most benign.

*Nikolai Chernyshevsky*

\*

To live for the family only is animal selfishness, to live for one person only is foul, and to live for oneself only is a disgrace.

*Nikolai Ostrovsky*

\*

He who builds his house with the heart alone builds it atop a fire-breathing mountain.

*Alexander Herzen*

Home life that knows nothing outside its bounds, no matter how well arranged, is sure to be squalid.

*Alexander Herzen*

\*

A love centred upon but one person in whom it concentrates all the joy of life, making everything else a burden and torment—that sort of love is laden with poison for both.

*Felix Dzerzhinsky*

\*

If the aim of our lives consisted solely of our personal happiness, and our personal happiness consisted solely of love, then life would really be a bleak desert.... But praise be unto eternal reason, praise be unto solicitous providence! There is also for every man the great world of life apart from the inner world of the heart—a world of historical contemplation and activity for the social good.

*Vissarion Belinsky*

\*

Love does not provide complete fulfilment, and wretched is he who finds complete fulfilment in love; it follows that no *one* thing can satisfy the *many* needs of man.

*Vissarion Belinsky*

## FAMILY, PARENTS, AND CHILDREN

A woman who is wrapped in love of her husband and children, who lacks understanding of anything else, and who strives for nothing else is as ridiculous, as miserable and unworthy of a man's love as the man whose faculties are confined to just falling in love and loving wife and children.

*Vissarion Belinsky*

## MATRIMONY

Matrimony is the reality of love. None but a wholly mature soul is capable of true love. In that case love sees in matrimony its highest reward and loses none of its lustre in the sparkle of matrimonial crown; on the contrary, it flowers more luxuriantly, as in the rays of the sun.

*Vissarion Belinsky*

\*

Family life can give much happiness if it reposes on reciprocated love.

*N. K. Krupskaya*

Happy is he who is happy at home.

*Lev Tolstoy*

\*

It is interesting to marry, but only for love: marrying a girl just because she is attractive is like buying a useless trinket just because it is appealing.

*Anton Chekhov*

\*

To marry someone you do not love is outrageous.

*Dmitry Pisarev*

\*

Family life is never an endless celebration. Learn to share not only joy, but also sorrow, grief, and misfortune.

*Vassily Sukhomlinsky*

\*

Better not make a family if you are selfish. The sense of happy love is *giving*. He who loves himself only, can give nothing; he only takes, and thereby inevitably poisons the best part of love. Selfishness, like a physical handicap, is an impediment.

*Vassily Sukhomlinsky*

## FAMILY, PARENTS, AND CHILDREN

Take not succour in the phrase that it's paradise in a shack as long as your sweetheart is with you. Matrimony is not only a spiritual, but also a material alliance. Before planning a family, see whether you are independent financially, and whether you can clothe, house, and feed your wife.

*Vassily Sukhomlinsky*

\*

A wife barred from all the interests occupying her husband, alienated from them, and uninvolved, is a mere concubine, housekeeper, and nanny, not a wife in the full, exalted sense of the word.

*Alexander Herzen*

\*

Love is love, but to live with one another there must also be a common viewpoint. Without this there can be no real, happy family.

*N. K. Krupskaya*

\*

He who is old will not catch youthful fire.

*Avicenna*

Old wineskins can't keep young wine, and old hearts can't bear young emotions.

*S. T. Aksakov*

\*

Nothing is more dangerous than binding one's lot with that of a woman merely because she is beautiful and young.

*Vissarion Belinsky*

\*

Honour is the soul of matrimonial concord.

*Denis Fonvizin*

\*

It is my deep-rooted conviction that a matrimonial alliance must avoid public display, for it concerns two and only two people.

*Vissarion Belinsky*

\*

Only those familial and public relations can be strong that flow from an inner conviction and are justified by the free and sensible consent of those who are involved in them.

*Nikolai Dobrolyubov*

# FAMILY, PARENTS, AND CHILDREN

There is the strange, deep-seated prejudice that cooking, sewing, washing, and nursing are exclusively female occupations, and that for a man they are even demeaning. Yet the reverse is demeaning: it is demeaning for a man to spend his time on trifles or doing nothing at all, while the tired, often weak, pregnant woman taxes all her endurance to cook, wash, or look after a sick child.

*Lev Tolstoy*

\*

Many men expect virtues in their wives that they do not deserve.

*Lev Tolstoy*

\*

What the status of a woman is in society, such, too, is the treatment she receives from her husband.

*Nikolai Chernyshevsky*

\*

The chief thing is to get women to take part in socially productive labour, to liberate them from "domestic slavery", to free them from their stupefying and humiliating subjugation to the eternal drudgery of the kitchen and the nursery. This struggle will be a long one, and it demands a radical reconstruction both of social technique and of morals. But it will end in the complete triumph of communism.

*V. I. Lenin*

\*

For an unhappy marriage divorce seems to me more virtuous than inviolability of matrimonial bonds, because it eliminates deceit.

*Anton Rubinstein*

\*

Divorce will not cause the "disintegration" of family ties, but, on the contrary, will strengthen them on a democratic basis, which is the only possible and durable basis in civilised society.

*V. I. Lenin*

\*

In our country woman has been completely emancipated; she has been put on absolutely the same juridical footing as man. But from this entirely correct situation we should on no account draw this other conclusion that you can marry ten times and leave your partner as many times.

*Mikhail Kalinin*

## FAMILY, PARENTS, AND CHILDREN

When someone accepts the idea that he can marry today and unmarry tomorrow, we call it petty-bourgeois individualism. It is a naked personal individualism, and a sign of deficient culture. Because, surely, the more cultivated a person is, the more responsible he is and also the more circumspect in his personal affairs and in his behaviour.

*Mikhail Kalinin*

\*

Love is not a transient thing belonging to the pre-marital period, as some vulgar people would have us believe. It is a feeling that lives and thrives throughout the couple's life.

*Nikolai Chernyshevsky*

\*

A wife is not a mistress, but a friend and companion, and we must grow accustomed to the thought beforehand that she must be loved even when she gets on in years, and even when she is old.

*Vissarion Belinsky*

\*

Idealise love to your heart's content, but you must also see that Nature has gifted us this magnificent state of love for multiplying and maintaining the species, as well as for our happiness.

*Vissarion Belinsky*

The family begins with children.

*Alexander Herzen*

\*

Children are the vital force of society. Without them it is bloodless and cold.

*Anton Makarenko*

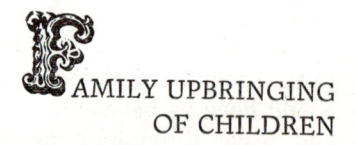

# FAMILY UPBRINGING OF CHILDREN

Bringing up children is the main purpose and aim of family life. The relationship between husband and wife, father and mother, is the children's main school.

*Vassily Sukhomlinsky*

\*

Not petty tyranny or wrath, pleading or persuasion, but quiet and serious instruction—this should be the outward expression of the technique of family discipline. No doubt should arise either in your mind or that of your children that you are entitled to issuing instructions as one of the authorised senior members of the collective.

*Anton Makarenko*

# FAMILY, PARENTS, AND CHILDREN

Many troubles are rooted precisely in the fact that we are not taught from childhood to control our wishes and relate ourselves properly to the notions of "you may", "you must", "you must not".

*Vassily Sukhomlinsky*

\*

It is those parents who bring up their children badly, and in general people who haven't the slightest trace of pedagogical tact—it is they who exaggerate the significance of talks on educational topics.

*Anton Makarenko*

\*

The art of bringing up children has this special distinction of seeming familiar and known to nearly everyone; to some it even seems easy. In fact, it seems more familiar and better known to those least acquainted with it in theory and practice.

*Konstantin Ushinsky*

\*

For parents, bringing up their children amounts most of all to bringing up themselves.

*N. K. Krupskaya*

In education, the whole thing boils down to the personality of the mentor.

*Dmitry Pisarev*

For the upbringing of children to be successful, it is necessary that all the adults concerned should ceaselessly further on their own upbringing.

*Lev Tolstoy*

Everything and everybody is involved in education: people, things, phenomena, but above all and the longest of all it is people. And the first place among them goes to parents and teachers.

*Anton Makarenko*

Nothing has a greater effect on the young souls of children than the general power of example, and yet among all examples none makes a deeper and more lasting impression than that of the parents.

*N. I. Novikov*

The main source of parental authority is the life and work of the parents, their civic identity, and their behaviour.

*Anton Makarenko*

## FAMILY, PARENTS, AND CHILDREN

The faults and merits of children fall mainly on the heads and conscience of their parents.

*Felix Dzerzhinsky*

\*

If people speak badly of your children, it means they are speaking badly of you.

*Vassily Sukhomlinsky*

\*

Don't think you are bringing up your child only when lecturing it or issuing instructions. You are bringing it up every moment of your life. The child senses the slightest change in tone. All the twists and turns of your thinking reach it by invisible paths that you are not even aware of.

*Anton Makarenko*

\*

By bringing up their children the parents of today are bringing up the future history of our country, and hence also the history of the world.

*Anton Makarenko*

\*

Children are our future. They must be well equipped to fight for our ideals.

*N. K. Krupskaya*

Children are our future judges and critics of our views and deeds; they are the people who will enter the wide world and take on the great work of building new forms of life.

*Maxim Gorky*

\*

Our children are our old age. A good upbringing is a happy old age for us, a bad upbringing is our future grief, our tears, our fault before other people, before the country.

*Anton Makarenko*

\*

To bring up children ... is the hardest thing of all. You think: ha, now it is over! Nothing of the sort: it is only beginning.

*Mikhail Lermontov*

\*

Even a hen can be fond of its children. But to bring them up properly is a matter of state importance, requiring a natural talent and a deep knowledge of life.

*Maxim Gorky*

\*

To preach from the pulpit, to captivate from the rostrum, or to lecture from the platform is much easier than to bring up a child.

*Alexander Herzen*

# FAMILY, PARENTS, AND CHILDREN

Nothing is trifling in bringing up children.

*Nikolai Pirogov*

\*

Parents often confuse upbringing with education; they think they have brought up their child by having taught it a certain number of subjects. Hence their frequent disappointment in their children later.

*Anton Rubinstein*

\*

All thinkers, I feel, have arrived at the conclusion that the upbringing of children must begin in the cradle.

*Nikolai Pirogov*

\*

You must teach your children to be fond of people rather than of themselves. For this you, the parents, must also be fond of people.

*Felix Dzerzhinsky*

\*

It is essential for a fuller appreciation of life, that is, for happiness, to teach children the "greater loves"—love of country and nation, and of humanity, and trust in the power of reason, and delight in the beauty of the human soul. This and this alone can instil true respect for people, for the personality.

*Maxim Gorky*

\*

Childhood must not be an endless holiday. If the child is not given work that it can do, it will be deprived of the happiness that work yields.

*Vassily Sukhomlinsky*

\*

Devote your attention less to rooting out faults and defects in children, and more to filling them with fecund love; once there is love there will be no faults. To root out bad without instilling good is futile: it creates a vacuum, and a vacuum is always filled with vacuum. Expel one, the other will come in its stead.

*Vissarion Belinsky*

\*

The early upbringing must see in the child not an official, not a poet, and not a craftsman, but a human being who would later be one or another without ever ceasing to be a human being.

*Vissarion Belinsky*

## FAMILY, PARENTS, AND CHILDREN

A mother must get the requisite education in order that her behaviour towards her child should be proper. With all the good will and love in the world an ignorant mother is a very poor mentor.

*Ilya Mechnikov*

\*

Only a mother who lives a truly full, human, civic life can be a real mother who educates, sets an example, and elicits love, admiration, and a desire to imitate her. A mother who confines her duties to merely servicing her children is rather a slave of her children, not a mother who brings them up.

*Anton Makarenko*

\*

It is much easier to become a father than be a father to one's child.

***V. O. Kliuchevsky***

\*

Not all fathers are able to earn the love of their children.

*Maxim Gorky*

\*

Without good fathers there is no good upbringing regardless of all schooling.

*Nikolai Karamzin*

## WORDS OF THE WISE

Any worker, from watchman to government minister, can be replaced by one just as good or better. A good father cannot be replaced by another who would be just as good.

*Vassily Sukhomlinsky*

*

Parents should be punished for bad children.

*Maxim Gorky*

*

Parental love must not be blind. Pandering to the child's wishes or cramming it with candy and other goodies is tantamount to warping its soul.

*Felix Dzerzhinsky*

*

Pampered children whose every whim is satisfied by their parents grow up degenerate and weak-willed egoists.

*Felix Dzerzhinsky*

*

Anticipating all the child's needs and guiding it in all its acts and thoughts is bound to make it unfit for living; such children do, perhaps, become industrious people, but also, unfortunately, selfish and overly self-confident.

*Pyotr Lesgaft*

## FAMILY, PARENTS, AND CHILDREN

By concentrating all your parental love on one child you are making an appalling mistake.

*Anton Makarenko*

\*

Be truthful even with a child: keep your promises, lest you teach it to lie.

*Lev Tolstoy*

\*

There must be veracity in all things, especially in bringing up children.

*Lev Tolstoy*

\*

Children are not driven off by severity; what drives them off are lies.

*Lev Tolstoy*

\*

Never make a promise you cannot keep to a child, and never deceive it.

*Konstantin Ushinsky*

\*

A person who truly respects the human personality must also respect it in his child from the minute it becomes aware of its "I" and identifies itself in the surrounding world.

*Dmitry Pisarev*

\*

To judge of a child fairly and correctly, we must not transfer it from its own sphere into ours, and must instead transfer ourselves into its spiritual world.

*Nikolai Pirogov*

\*

Let a child be naughty and misbehave, so long as its pranks are harmless and untainted by physical or moral cynicism; let it be mischievous and rash, so long as it is not stupid or dull, for nothing is worse than inertness or indolence.

*Vissarion Belinsky*

\*

For a child play is as important as work is for an adult. What the child is in its games the adult will be in his work. This is why the upbringing of a future individual occurs mainly in play.

*Anton Makarenko*

\*

Play is that huge and bright window through which the child absorbs an exciting stream of ideas and notions about the surrounding world. Play is that spark which lights the flame of curiosity and enterprise.

*Vassily Sukhomlinsky*

\*

From an early age the child must be put in conditions where it lives, plays, works, and shares its joys and sorrows with other children.

*N. K. Krupskaya*

\*

It is only in a group that a child's personality can develop harmoniously and to the fullest extent.

*N. K. Krupskaya*

\*

The collective life of children must be filled with joyous activity; then it instils a strongly developed social instinct.

*N. K. Krupskaya*

\*

Parents are unaware of the harm they do their children when, using their parental authority, they try to impose on them their own convictions and viewpoints.

*Felix Dzerzhinsky*

A child's feelings, as a child's thinking, must be guided without any force.

*Konstantin Ushinsky*

\*

A child that suffers fewer indignities grows up more conscious of its dignity.

*Nikolai Chernyshevsky*

\*

Intimidation will foster in a child nothing but meanness, corruption, hypocrisy, base cowardice, and careerism.

*Felix Dzerzhinsky*

\*

Excessive severity and blind discipline are not fitting teachers for children.

*Felix Dzerzhinsky*

\*

When a child is scolded, beaten, or pained, it feels alone from its littlest age.

*Dmitry Pisarev*

\*

The child hates him who applies the stick.

*Vassily Sukhomlinsky*

Senseless kindness is as foolish as unreasonable severity.

*A. F. Pisemsky*

*

The power of moral influence is greater than any other power.

*Nikolai Gogol*

*

A child loves him who shows it his love—and the only way it can be brought up is on love.

*Felix Dzerzhinsky*

*

He who doesn't get anywhere with kindness won't get anywhere with severity.

*Anton Chekhov*

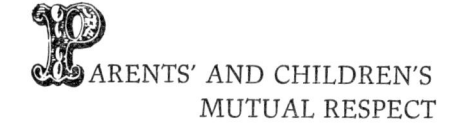

## PARENTS' AND CHILDREN'S MUTUAL RESPECT

Beyond question, love and respect for parents is sacred.

*Vissarion Belinsky*

Mother and Father! All praise is nothing beside these sacred words; all high-sounding tributes are hollow and insignificant beside filial love and gratitude.

*Nikolai Chernyshevsky*

\*

Three great woes hath man—death, old age, and bad children. Nothing can keep his doors closed against old age and death, but his dwelling can be preserved against bad children by the children themselves.

*Vassily Sukhomlinsky*

\*

Mother and Father gave you life, and they live for the sake of your happiness. So, show care for their health and peace of mind. See that you do not cause them any pain.

*Vassily Sukhomlinsky*

\*

Be truthful to Mother and Father. Ask their permission and consent in things you must not do without their approval. The true freedom of daughter and son is to be obedient.

*Vassily Sukhomlinsky*

## FAMILY, PARENTS, AND CHILDREN

For your parents to be happy you must live honestly, and show your application and progress in school and work. Bring joy to your home.

*Vassily Sukhomlinsky*

\*

There is that most splendid of all beings whom we owe everything—our Mother.

*Nikolai Ostrovsky*

\*

Nothing is more sacred and selfless than a mother's love; compared to it all attachments, all loves, and all passions are either weak or selfish.

*Vissarion Belinsky*

\*

It is rare luck if your Mother is also your kin in spirit.

*Maxim Gorky*

\*

All the pride of the world comes from our mothers. Flowers cannot bloom without sunlight, happiness cannot thrive without love,

love cannot exist without woman, and there can be no poet or hero without a mother.

*Maxim Gorky*

\*

Praise be to woman, the Mother, whose love knows no obstacles and whose breast has nurtured the whole world! All that is beautiful in man is from the Sun's rays and the Mother's caress.

*Maxim Gorky*

\*

If you haven't learned as a child to look in your mother's eyes and see her worry or calm, peace or confusion—if you haven't learned this you will be morally ignorant for the rest of your life. And moral ignorance, like wildness in love, brings much grief to people and much harm to society.

*Vassily Sukhomlinsky*

\*

Lack of respect for one's forebears is the main sign of turpitude.

*Alexander Pushkin*

\*

If a growing child hasn't learned to love his parents, brothers and sisters, his school and his country, and if sordid selfishness is instilled in his character, he will hardly be capable of deep love for the woman of his choice.

*Anton Makarenko*

\*

A young man will not love his betrothed or his wife if he does not love his parents, comrades, and friends. The broader the range of his non-sexual love, the more noble will be his sexual love.

*Anton Makarenko*

\*

Our children's future love will be all the more beautiful, the more sparingly and wisely we speak to them about it, but our reserve must go hand in hand with constant supervision of the children's behaviour.

*Anton Makarenko*

\*

First we teach our children, then we learn from them. Those who are reluctant, fall behind the times.

*Janis Rainis*

\*

A loving mother who tries to arrange her children's lives for them often binds them hand and foot by the narrowness of her views, the short-sightedness of her designs, and the unsolicited fervour of her care.

*Dmitry Pisarev*

\*

It is good to be a support for Father and Mother at important junctions in life, but excess attention to their often petty and preposterous demands, inhibits a vital, free, and daring talent.

*Alexander Griboyedov*

## OF CHARACTER

### STRENGTH OF CHARACTER

A strong sense of duty is the crown of character.

*N. V. Shelgunov*

\*

You must have strength of character to speak and do one and the same thing.

*Alexander Herzen*

\*

The theoretical life of the mind develops the mind, but only the practical life of the heart and will develops character.

*Konstantin Ushinsky*

\*

Strength of character is drawn solely from the natural founts of the soul, and a child's upbringing must not impair it, for it is the foundation of human dignity.

*Konstantin Ushinsky*

The greater part of great characters is shaped in struggle, and often this sruggle begins at a very early age.

*Dmitry Pisarev*

\*

Character is steeled in labour. Those who have never worked for their daily bread are mostly doomed to be weak, inert, and spineless.

*Dmitry Pisarev*

\*

Character changes depending on the environment.

*G. V. Plekhanov*

\*

The most paltry of trifles contribute to the making of character.

*Lev Tolstoy*

\*

To develop your character you must participate for a long time in the life of a correctly organised, disciplined, upright, and proud collective.

*Anton Makarenko*

## WILL AND FORTITUDE

Honest and unselfish activity, and no other, is the condition for human dignity, and will power alone is the condition for success in our chosen field.

*Vissarion Belinsky*

\*

Nothing comes about by itself, without effort, will power, sacrifice, and hard work. The human will, the will of just one strong person is immensely great.

*Alexander Herzen*

\*

A man's will can do much, its power is tremendous, it has almost no bounds, provided it is pure and devoted to a good cause, and provided its bearer feels ocean currents coursing through him.

*Alexander Herzen*

\*

What is the will if not a thought translated into action.

*A. A. Bestuzhev-Marlinsky*

Some people take pleasure in being in a state of depression or irritation, and are even proud of it. It is the same as letting go of the reins and belabouring the horse with a stick as it gallops down a steep hill.

*Lev Tolstoy*

*

The will expresses its owner correctly and actively when it blends with his nature.

*A. V. Lunacharsky*

*

In battle victory comes to the strong of spirit.

*K. N. Bestuzhev-Riumin*

*

People lacking will power are cowards, and being cowards they are weak.

*Ivan Pavlov*

*

Strong will is not the mere capacity for wishing and achieving; it is also the ability to deny yourself something when necessary. The will is not simply a wish and its satisfaction, but wish and denial, wish and rejection.

*Anton Makarenko*

## CHARACTER

The most difficult is to be exigent with oneself.

*Anton Makarenko*

\*

Firmness is strength based on an alliance of mind and will. Stubbornness is weakness that only resembles strength; it originates from an imbalance of the alliance of will and mind.

*V. A. Zhukovsky*

\*

Stubbornness is the signboard of fools.

*Y. B. Kniazhnin*

\*

The will, like muscle, grows stronger from increasingly intensive practice; if they are not exercised you will most certainly have weak muscles and a weak will.

*Konstantin Ushinsky*

\*

He who wants to develop his will must learn to overcome obstacles.

*Ivan Pavlov*

\*

You must have faith in yourself and in your powers. This faith is developed by overcoming obstacles, cultivating will power, "exercising" your will. You must learn to overcome the sordid heritage of olden days in yourself and outside you. Even a trifling victory over yourself makes you much stronger.

*Maxim Gorky*

\*

By exercising your body you become healthy, enduring, and agile; you must exercise your mind and will in like manner.

*Maxim Gorky*

\*

More than anyone else we need spiritual health, good cheer, and faith in the creative powers of mind and will.

*Maxim Gorky*

\*

Suppress the slightest signs of weakness—your whims, touchiness and irritability, your snivelling, and your false pride. They are the germs of individualism.

*Vassily Sukhomlinsky*

\*

Learn to control and govern yourself in small things. Make yourself do things that must be done, though you do not want to do them. The imperative mood is the main source of will power.

*Vassily Sukhomlinsky*

A person without a will is a pawn of the first rogue that comes along.

*N. K. Krupskaya*

## TESTS OF CHARACTER

A misfortune is the whetstone of human existence.

*Lev Tolstoy*

The school of misfortune is the best of all schools.

*Vissarion Belinsky*

Disasters best show the strength of character of people and nations.

*Nikolai Karamzin*

Whatever happens, do not lose courage.

*Lev Tolstoy*

\*

There is need for self-assurance.

*V. I. Lenin*

\*

Not the one who has never suffered is an optimist, but the one who has known desperation and has conquered it.

*Alexander Scriabin*

\*

Remember that the harder and the more desperate the circumstances, the more you need firmness, resolve, and action, and the more harmful is apathy.

*Lev Tolstoy*

\*

Though adversity may come to you, never lose heart, because faith in your powers and the wish to live for others is a tremendous force.

*Felix Dzerzhinsky*

\*

In a misfortune take solace in the thought that there were harder times and that they, too, have passed.

*Nikolai Karamzin*

## CHARACTER

Misfortunes are invariably exaggerated. They can always be overcome.

*Anton Makarenko*

\*

Not all resistance to trouble is rewarded by deliverance from adversity, but all adversity begins with loss of the will to resist.

*Leonid Leonov*

\*

Learn to live even when life is unendurable: make it useful.

*Nikolai Ostrovsky*

\*

A wound of the heart, like a physical wound, is mended from within by the exuberant force of life.

*Lev Tolstoy*

\*

What we call good fortune and what we call bad fortune are equally good for us if we take them both as a test.

*Lev Tolstoy*

\*

Misfortune mellows people; their nature becomes more sensitive and able to appreciate things that transcend the understanding of people in ordinary and everyday circumstances.

*Nikolai Gogol*

\*

It is through suffering and pain that we have been ordained to gather grains of wisdom not obtainable from books.

*Nikolai Gogol*

## SELF-CONTROL

All victories begin with victories over yourself.

*Leonid Leonov*

\*

A short temper is not always a bad temper. But the more precipitous and short-tempered one is, the more one must exercise one's self-control.

*N. V. Shelgunov*

## CHARACTER

It is possible to conquer one's nature if one tries; the maturing of the spirit is as difficult as the maturing of the body.

*Alexander Herzen*

\*

Many calm rivers take their source from roaring waterfalls, but no river ever leaps and roars all the way to the sea. Yet, this calm is often the sign of great hidden power: fullness and depth of feeling and thought do not tolerate mad outbursts.

*Mikhail Lermontov*

\*

True power is not in fits of passion, but in inviolate calm.

*Lev Tolstoy*

## OF RULES OF BEHAVIOUR

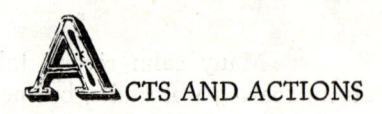

# ACTS AND ACTIONS

Culture is a very wide concept, ranging from face washing to the pinnacles of human thought.

*Mikhail Kalinin*

\*

One must be clear-minded, morally pure, and outwardly neat.

*Anton Chekhov*

\*

Only a person with a good mind and a good heart is entirely good and trustworthy.

*Konstantin Ushinsky*

\*

Every time you very much want to do something, stop and think: is it virtuous?

*Lev Tolstoy*

## RULES OF BEHAVIOUR

Be hesitant as you consider a deed, but act without hesitation once you have considered it.

*Lev Tolstoy*

*

Every one of your deeds reflects on other people; never forget there are others beside you.

*Vassily Sukhomlinsky*

*

Think well and your thoughts will ripen into good deeds.

*Lev Tolstoy*

*

An extreme is sister to dull-mindedness.

*Vissarion Belinsky*

*

All extremes, of course, are bad. All that is good and useful, if carried to extremes, may become—and beyond a certain limit is bound to become—bad and injurious.

*V. I. Lenin*

*

In people everything ought to be beautiful—face, clothes, soul, and thought.

*Anton Chekhov*

A man's faults are, as it were, a continuation of his merits. But if merits persist longer than they are needed or are displayed when and where they are no longer needed, they become faults.

*V. I. Lenin*

\*

In every man and his deeds one can always recognise one's own self.

*Lev Tolstoy*

\*

Discussing deeds of others, remember your own.

*Lev Tolstoy*

\*

A dirty house-fly can besmirch the whole wall, and a dirty trick can besmirch the whole cause.

*Anton Chekhov*

\*

The most common temptation leading to the most sordid consequences of temptation is the temptation to say: "But everybody does it."

*Lev Tolstoy*

For the perpetrator every evil deed is pregnant with the knout.

*V. O. Kliuchevsky*

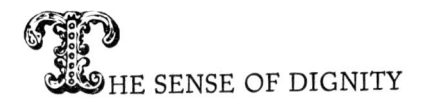

## THE SENSE OF DIGNITY

A man must have self-respect.

*Maxim Gorky*

\*

Richness of spirit is inconceivable without a sense of dignity.

*Vassily Sukhomlinsky*

\*

Lacking self-respect there is no moral purity and richness of spirit. Self-respect, honour, pride, and dignity are the whetstone that sharpens the delicacy of feeling.

*Vassily Sukhomlinsky*

\*

Those who lack self-esteem are nonentities. Self-esteem is like the screw of Archimedes, which can shift the Earth.

*Ivan Turgenev*

Self-love is suicide. An egoist withers like a lone and barren tree, whereas self-respect as an active striving for perfection is a source of greatness.

*Ivan Turgenev*

\*

If the quarrel between the higher world and our inner self is very great, stop and ask yourself: who am I if I am ashamed to confess things even to myself?

*Nikolai Ostrovsky*

\*

It is an insult to humanity if people scorn the human dignity of others, and the insult and injury is doubly great if they do not respect their own dignity.

*Vissarion Belinsky*

\*

Loathsome is the brazen braggart; but no less loathsome is a person with no sense of strength or dignity.

*Vissarion Belinsky*

\*

He who does not respect himself cannot respect others, and in both cases betrays lowliness of thought.

*N. I. Novikov*

## RULES OF BEHAVIOUR

He who lacks respect for himself will never earn the respect of others.

*Nikolai Karamzin*

\*

A worthy man is not one who is devoid of failings, but one who has virtues.

*V. O. Kliuchevsky*

\*

Masculine dignity consists, among other things, in not being a hanger-on and parasite.

*Vassily Sukhomlinsky*

## THE ART OF CONVERSATION

A word is a deed.

*Lev Tolstoy*

\*

The more quickly and precipitously an impression is voiced, the more often it is superficial and transient.

*Nikolai Dobrolyubov*

For your own sake it is no less essential to watch your word than your step.

*N. V. Shelgunov*

\*

Be warned that an unreasonable, chill, or indifferent word can injure, wound, hurt, embarrass, stun, or destroy.

*Vassily Sukhomlinsky*

\*

Be the first to listen and the last to speak.

*Effendi Kapiev*

\*

The person who says little looks cleverer.

*Maxim Gorky*

\*

People learn how to speak, while what they should learn is how and when not to speak.

*Lev Tolstoy*

\*

By keeping silent one can say a lot and also do a lot.

*Effendi Kapiev*

After a long talk try to remember everything said and you will be surprised how hollow, needless, and often shabby, it was.

*Lev Tolstoy*

\*

He who has nothing of his own to say will do better not to speak at all.

*Vissarion Belinsky*

\*

Speak only of what you know, or else say nothing.

*Lev Tolstoy*

\*

I do not consider myself ignorant if I do not know something and keep silent; ignorant is he who holds forth on matters he does not know.

*M. M. Prishvin*

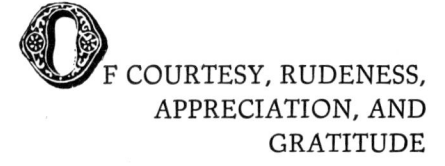

# OF COURTESY, RUDENESS, APPRECIATION, AND GRATITUDE

Good manners do not consist in not spilling gravy on the tablecloth, but in not noticing when someone else spills it.

*Anton Chekhov*

True and good courtesy is founded on sincerity. Real courtesy is a companion of respect for another; without this it is a fiction.

*N. V. Shelgunov*

\*

Those who want to be pleasant are always unpleasant precisely for wanting to be pleasant.

*Yevgeny Vakhtangov*

\*

To be rude is to forget one's dignity.

*Nikolai Chernyshevsky*

\*

Nothing can justify rudeness.

*Taras Shevchenko*

\*

Rudeness is as ugly as a coffin.

*Maxim Gorky*

\*

Harsh words never strong arguments make.

*V. O. Kliuchevsky*

Strength has no need for curses.

*Fyodor Dostoyevsky*

\*

It takes little to curse a man, but the good of it is little, too.

*Dmitry Pisarev*

\*

Gratitude is not the right of the thanked, but the duty of the thanker; to demand gratitude is foolish, to be ungrateful is foul.

*V. O. Kliuchevsky*

\*

Having done someone a service, speak not of it to either friend or foe.

*Aboul Kasim Firdousi*

# MENTORSHIP, ADVICE, AND PRAISE

Chary replies kill legitimate questions and drive the mind off the right course.

*Alexander Herzen*

To fashion people into likenesses of yourself is to commit narrow intellectual despotism.

*Dmitry Pisarev*

\*

Praising him who is unworthy does not elevate the praised, but demeans the praiser.

*P. A. Vyazemsky*

\*

Praise is always chaste.

*Fyodor Dostoyevsky*

\*

Excessive praise I see as poison.

*Ivan Krylov*

\*

Lie and flatter not even in jest. Let them think of you what they wish, and be what you are.

*Vissarion Belinsky*

\*

Never lend ear to those who speak badly of others and well of you.

*Lev Tolstoy*

## OF FAULTS, WEAKNESSES, AND FAILINGS

# IDLENESS

The habit of idleness is the worst of all disasters.

*Lev Tolstoy*

\*

Loafers and never-do-wells injure the people's wellbeing.

*Alexander Blok*

\*

I'd kill myself if I did not work even for a day.

*Lev Tolstoy*

\*

It is a strange and harmful misconception that indolence is a boon and work a punishment.

*Lev Tolstoy*

There is no joy in inactivity.

*Fyodor Dostoyevsky*

\*

Nothing is a greater ordeal than doing nothing.

*Alexander Herzen*

\*

Sloth and senseless bluster have a most degrading effect on people.

*Dmitry Pisarev*

\*

Unless he works a person cannot advance, cannot stand still, and is bound to slide backwards.

*Konstantin Ushinsky*

\*

Those immersed in foul indolence are like the stagnant waters of a marsh that makes nothing but ill smells and loathsome snakes.

*Mikhail Lomonosov*

\*

Apathy and sloth are, in fact, a freezing of soul and body.

*Vissarion Belinsky*

## FAULTS, WEAKNESSES, AND FAILINGS

Indolence is the source of mental and physical flabbiness.

*Dmitry Pisarev*

٭

A slothful life cannot be clean.

*Anton Chekhov*

٭

Idleness is the root of all evil.

*A. V. Suvorov*

٭

Indolence is the mother of all faults.

*Mikhail Doodin*

٭

He who works knows no boredom.

*Maxim Gorky*

٭

Nothing encourages indolence more than idle talk.

*Lev Tolstoy*

٭

He who does nothing always has many helpers.

*Lev Tolstoy*

No leisure is sweeter than the leisure earned through work.

*Anton Chekhov*

\*

Repose is a change of occupation.

*Ivan Pavlov*

# DRUNKENNESS

How many are the splendid undertakings and how many the splendid people destroyed by evil habits.

*Konstantin Ushinsky*

\*

Though consumed for the sake of joy, alcohol is the cause of grief rather than joy to all mankind. How many gifted and strong men have perished or are perishing from it.

*Ivan Pavlov*

\*

Drinking is the greatest of evils for the individual, for society, and for the state.

*Pavel Kovalevsky*

Addiction to alcohol is a social evil that can hardly be exaggerated.

*Vladimir Bekhterev*

\*

Wine destroys people's physical health, mental faculties, and the wellbeing of families; what is worst of all, it destroys the souls of men and their progeny.

*Lev Tolstoy*

\*

The vodka that husbands drink is matched by the tears their wives and children spill.

*Nikolai Semashko*

\*

A drunkard never makes progress either intellectually or in the matter of morals.

*Lev Tolstoy*

\*

Spirits conserve the drunkard's soul and mind as they conserve anatomical preparations.

*Lev Tolstoy*

Drunkenness has neither intelligence nor virtue.

*G. S. Skovoroda*

\*

Vodka is colourless, but it reddens the nose and blackens the reputation.

*Anton Chekhov*

\*

For a drunkard it is dark even in a well-lit street.

*Konstantin Ushinsky*

\*

Wine stupefies, invites oblivion, cheers artificially, but also irritates, and this state of stupefaction and irritation is all the more attractive to people the less developed they are and the more they are reduced to a meagre and narrow existence.

*Alexander Herzen*

\*

Wine turns men into swine, makes them violent, distracts them from bright thoughts, and dulls their minds.

*Fyodor Dostoyevsky*

## FAULTS, WEAKNESSES, AND FAILINGS

From the use of wine men become cruder, duller, and meaner.

*Lev Tolstoy*

*

Alcohol is an entirely reliable means if you want to reduce your mental capacity.

*Vassily Danilevsky*

*

Alcohol paralyses the subtle and lofty movements of the soul, and first of all the sense of shame.

*Ivan Sikorsky*

*

Drunkenness and culture are two concepts that exclude one another like ice and fire, light and darkness.

*Nikolai Semashko*

*

Physical fitness and drunkenness are incompatible.

*Nikolai Semashko*

*

All people eat and drink, but only savages eat and drink too much.

*Vissarion Belinsky*

Excessive drinking bodes no good and only brings disorder to the brain and injury to health, loss of chattels, and premature death.

*I. T. Pososhkov*

\*

Continuous drinking is harmful; it spoils the nature of liver and brain; it weakens the nerves, provokes nervous disorders and brings about sudden death.

*Avicenna*

\*

Alcohol destroys a man's health not only by poisoning his body, but also makes the drinker susceptible to all kinds of other diseases.

*Nikolai Semashko*

\*

Alcohol is a pitiless killer. Figures, which are objective witnesses to fact, show that more human lives are accounted for by alcohol than by murderers, than by poison, or by the winter's cold.

*Ivan Sikorsky*

\*

A little wine is medicine, and much is deadly poison.

*Avicenna*

## FAULTS, WEAKNESSES, AND FAILINGS

An alcoholic with shaking hands, with eyesight dimmed, hearing impaired, and breath laboured, is a poor worker.

*Nikolai Semashko*

\*

Alcoholics are lazy and given to indolence.

*Ivan Sikorsky*

\*

Drinking is a focus from which paths spread like beams to gambling dens, bribery, embezzlement, sexual dissipation, and violence.

*Emelyan Yaroslavsky*

\*

Few thieves and murderers commit their crimes in a sober state.

*Lev Tolstoy*

\*

Most evil deeds are done in a state of inebriety.

*Lev Tolstoy*

\*

Nine-tenths of all the crimes besmirching humanity are committed under the influence of liquor.

*Lev Tolstoy*

Crimes of all varieties, the hoarse yells of the hooligan, and all the tarnish on life in general—there's one way to measure them all today, and that is by the consumed amount of beer and vodka.

*Vladimir Mayakovsky*

\*

Not every drinker is a drunkard. But it is the special trick of alcohol that he who begins drinking can easily become a drunkard.

*Pavel Kovalevsky*

\*

Casual bouts of drinking develop little by little into continuous and habitual drinking, entailing chronic alcoholism.

*Sergei Korsakov*

\*

It would seem that what people need most in life is their reason; yet so many of them do not hesitate, for mere pleasure, to deaden reason through the use of tobacco, wine, and vodka.

*Lev Tolstoy*

\*

It is even hard to imagine what a happy change would come about in our lives

## FAULTS, WEAKNESSES, AND FAILINGS

if people were to stop dulling their minds and poisoning their bodies with vodka.

*Lev Tolstoy*

※

Our mind and conscience demand of us most insistently that we should stop drinking and treating others with liquor.

*Lev Tolstoy*

※

If life were not so irrigated by vodka, it would, perhaps, stop producing all the monstrous trash that blooms so profusely in its loathsome way under the influence of vodka.

*A. V. Lunacharsky*

※

A man is delivered from drink not when he is deprived of access to it, but when he refuses wine that is in the room, where he can smell it and merely reach for it.

*Lev Tolstoy*

※

A man who stops smoking and drinking acquires that mental clarity and calm that lets him see all things in a new and true light.

*Lev Tolstoy*

## WORDS OF THE WISE

Drink no wine and injure not your heart with tobacco, and you will live as long as Titian.

*Ivan Pavlov*

\*

It is a false notion and a hypnotic suggestion that it is hard to break the habit of drinking and smoking, so do not fall prey to it.

*Lev Tolstoy*

\*

It is man who governs habits, not vice versa.

*Nikolai Ostrovsky*

\*

Drinking is an immediate threat to the building of socialism; this is why every worker, every decent citizen must fight it tooth and nail.

*Nikolai Semashko*

\*

The evil known as alcoholism has a bad effect on the state, because, quite certainly, growth of alcoholism is accompanied by a decline of both the physical and mental energy and labour potential of the people, with the result that the country's economic strength declines and there is also a decline in morality, as reflected in a growth of crime.

*Vladimir Bekhterev*

*

A country run by the people themselves must not and cannot tolerate indifference to the lives and health of its citizens; it must combat everything needlessly harmful to people.

*Maxim Gorky*

## SELFISHNESS

To seek happiness in selfishness is unnatural, and the lot of the selfish is not a bit enviable; the selfish are mental cripples, and to be a cripple is unpleasant and distressing.

*Nikolai Chernyshevsky*

*

He who works for himself alone is like a beast that crams its belly. The worthy labour for humanity.

*Abai Kunanbayev*

## WORDS OF THE WISE

To live only for oneself is shameful.

*Nikolai Ostrovsky*

*

To think only of oneself, only of one's own comfort, is to be a swine.

*Vassily Sukhomlinsky*

*

Egoism is the original cause of cancer of the soul.

*Vassily Sukhomlinsky*

*

Selfishness is father to wickedness.

*Maxim Gorky*

*

Selfishness hates the common, it turns its back on humanity, and puts itself in an exclusive state; it is hostile to everything but its own person.

*Alexander Herzen*

*

There are three kinds of egoists—those who live and let live; those who live and do not let live; and those who live not and do not let live.

*Ivan Turgenev*

Selfish people are whimsical and shy away from duty: there is in them an eternal cowardly reluctance to tie themselves down to some duty.

*Fyodor Dostoyevsky*

✻

If the personal takes most space in a man, while the civic takes little, then a failure in his personal life is a near catastrophe.

*Nikolai Ostrovsky*

✻

If all you love is yourself, then bitter trials in your life will make you curse your fate and suffer terrible anguish.

*Felix Dzerzhinsky*

✻

Where there is love, no suffering can break a man. Selfishness is a real misfortune.

*Felix Dzerzhinsky*

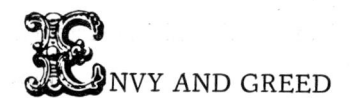

## ENVY AND GREED

The honest envy no one.

*Maxim Gorky*

Ordinarily, people delight less in what they have and rather lament what they have not.

*Vissarion Belinsky*

\*

Envy is an evil. Envy not and rejoice at your neighbour's success. But as you rejoice, strive to overtake him.

*Vassily Sukhomlinsky*

\*

Nonentity cannot stomach greatness.

*V. V. Vorovsky*

\*

Step clear of the envious, for the sting of envy is full of venom.

*Mahtumkuli*

\*

Self-interest is a great evil. The self-interested are neither truthful, nor honest, nor brave, nor true to their duty. From childhood learn to live disinterestedly.

*Vassily Sukhomlinsky*

\*

What you must treasure is not "mine" but "ours", that is, the values belonging to all society and created by society for the happiness and joy of all.

*Vassily Sukhomlinsky*

\*

Improvident is he who lusts for wealth, demeaning himself by his greed.

*Shot'ha Rust'hveli*

\*

The simplest method of not needing money is not to earn more than you need and spend less than you might.

*V. O. Kliuchevsky*

## COWARDICE AND FAINT-HEARTEDNESS

Fear is evidently the most agonising of all psychological conditions occurring in human nature.

*Dmitry Pisarev*

\*

Fear is the most depressing of all the human senses.

*Konstantin Ushinsky*

Fear is the most prolific source of faults and vices.

*Konstantin Ushinsky*

\*

In our country a coward is a despicable creature, ... the next thing to a renegade today, and doubtlessly a traitor in battle.

*Nikolai Ostrovsky*

\*

A man's deeds must all be imbued with manly courage.

*Alexander Kazbegi*

\*

A man of effeminate nature is the most venomous parody of a man.

*Vissarion Belinsky*

\*

Live more bravely. Only for a coward everything is frightening and hard; for the brave even the difficult seems easy.

*Fyodor Gladkov*

## FAULTS, WEAKNESSES, AND FAILINGS

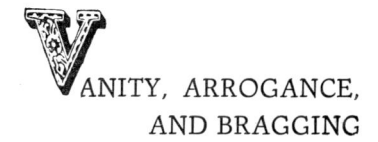

## VANITY, ARROGANCE, AND BRAGGING

Under no circumstances permit yourself to be either arrogant or conceited.

*Anton Chekhov*

\*

A vain man is always base.

*Pyotr Chaikovsky*

\*

When an empty and weak man hears a flattering remark about his dubious virtues he revels in his vanity, is overcome by conceit, and completely loses his meagre capacity of judging his acts and person critically.

*Dmitry Pisarev*

\*

For society, the smug and self-satisfied is like a hardened tumour.

*Maxim Gorky*

\*

One can no more exalt oneself than raise oneself bodily. On the contrary, any attempt to bepraise oneself demeans one in others' eyes.

*Lev Tolstoy*

A man's endeavours to capture everybody's attention are bad for him, because nothing deadens the soul as rapidly as the wish to be admired.

*Maxim Gorky*

*

Inner indecency is often very ingeniously concealed beneath a varnish of outer decency.

*Maxim Gorky*

*

It is cowards who speak most of all of bravery, and scoundrels who speak of decency.

*Lev Tolstoy*

*

Speak not of yourself without need. Never brag of what was, of what is, or of what will be.

*Konstantin Ushinsky*

# PRIDE, HAUGHTINESS, AND MENDACITY

True pride is very shy and fears public judgement.

*N. V. Shelgunov*

## FAULTS, WEAKNESSES, AND FAILINGS

Excessive pride is the signboard of a paltry soul.

*Ivan Turgenev*

\*

The proud seem to grow a coating of ice, and no other sentiment can penetrate this coating.

*Lev Tolstoy*

\*

He who is over-fond of himself is not liked by others, because out of tact they do not wish to be his rivals.

*V. O. Kliuchevsky*

\*

Excessive self-love and self-satisfaction have nothing in common with self-respect.

*Fyodor Dostoyevsky*

\*

Self-confidence has a surprising side to it. No matter what the virtues of a man—his intellect, scholarship, gifts of all kinds, even his good heart they turn into failings if he is over-confident.

*Lev Tolstoy*

The more a person is pleased with himself, the less he has of that which warrants his pleasure.

*Lev Tolstoy*

※

The higher a man rises in his own judgement, the more undependable his position becomes.

*Lev Tolstoy*

※

Only scoundrels lie.

*Fyodor Dostoyevsky*

※

What I am ashamed of most is lying, which always has its roots in cowardice and weakness.

*Alexander Kuprin*

※

Lies cause endless pain to soul and body.

*Shot'ha Rust'hveli*

※

Lying to oneself is the most widespread and lowest form of man's enslavement by life.

*Leonid Andreyev*

## FAULTS, WEAKNESSES, AND FAILINGS

A lie is the concomitant of coercion.

*Konstantin Fedin*

⁂

Lying is like drinking—liars lie even on their deathbed.

*Anton Chekhov*

⁂

The plant louse devours grass, rust devours iron, and lies devour the soul.

*Anton Chekhov*

⁂

A lie is a poor helper in life.

*N. K. Krupskaya*

⁂

He who is in the habit of lying must always keep his memory sharp lest he alter the lie.

*N. I. Novikov*

## HYPOCRISY, SERVILITY, AND TIME-SERVING

Hypocrisy, servility, and time-serving are a great evil. Learn to spot this evil of many faces, and be intolerant and irreconcilable to it.

*Vassily Sukhomlinsky*

\*

Speak your mind of the individual, action, or event. Never try to guess what someone expects you to say, for this could turn you into a hypocrite, toady, and, in the final count, into a scoundrel.

*Vassily Sukhomlinsky*

\*

Toadies are a special breed that has come into being and that has this motto—lie and cast off restraints.

*M. E. Saltykov-Shchedrin*

\*

Avoid people who see your faults and failings, and excuse or even approve them. Such people are either flatterers or cowards, or simply fools. Expect no help from them in trouble or grief.

*G. S. Skovoroda*

\*

Flattery is used to dominate under the guise of submission.

*Nikolai Chernyshevsky*

# FAULTS, WEAKNESSES, AND FAILINGS

*How often has the world been told
That flattery is foul and bad;
                but what's the good.
For in the heart the flatterer will
                always find a spot.*

*Ivan Krylov*

\*

Better an overt enemy than a vile flatterer and hypocrite who is a disgrace to humankind.

*Peter I*

## TALKATIVENESS

He speaks the most who has nothing to say.

*Lev Tolstoy*

\*

Multiloquence is a trait of human dull-wittedness.

*A. P. Sumarokov*

\*

A wise man's tongue is in his heart, a fool's heart is in his tongue.

*N. V. Shelgunov*

The urge to speak is almost always stronger than the urge to learn.

*Dmitry Pisarev*

*

The gift of gab has always aroused the admiration of idle people.

*Nikolai Dobrolyubov*

*

Nothing encourages indolence more than empty talk.

*Lev Tolstoy*

*

Idlers are the most talkative people on earth.

*P. A. Pavlenko*

*

All continence requires effort, but of all such efforts the most difficult is that of containing one's tongue. It also is the most necessary.

*Lev Tolstoy*

*

A sharp tongue is a gift, a long tongue a calamity.

*D. D. Minayev*

# FAULTS, WEAKNESSES, AND FAILINGS

A man always feels a bit guilty and awkward after he has spoken more than his share.

*Ivan Turgenev*

\*

Talkativeness conceals lies, and lies, as we know, are mother to all vices.

*M. E. Saltykov-Shchedrin*

\*

For every time you regret not having said something, you will regret a hundred times that you have spoken.

*Lev Tolstoy*

\*

*A loose tongue is self-inflicted pain,*
*It brings a hundred mishaps and disdain.*

*Alisher Navoi*

\*

The tongue is like a flint, and words are sparks. They may cause fire. Be warned, o Speaker!

*Effendi Kapiev*

Brag not of your knowing, take pride in silence.

*P. A. Pavlenko*

\*

To relate something with no special purpose even to one's friends is the trait of an idle gas-bag.

*Dmitry Pisarev*

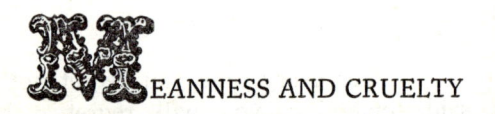

# MEANNESS AND CRUELTY

There are people of all sorts, and passions of all sorts. In some, for example, all the passions and all the fires of their nature consist in icy rage, and they are clever, talented, even healthy only when they sink their teeth into something or someone.

*Vissarion Belinsky*

\*

Nothing pleases the wicked more than to avenge their meanness by flinging the mud of their views and notions at the great and sacred.

*Vissarion Belinsky*

## FAULTS, WEAKNESSES, AND FAILINGS

The vicious is as unreasoning as the unreasoning is vicious. These qualities go in a pair, and the absence of one paralyses the other.

*N. V. Shelgunov*

\*

Bad news to learn is for the bad the greatest of all pleasures!

*Shot'ha Rust'hveli*

\*

People whose hearts lack pity take joy in the misfortunes of others.

*Vazha Pshavela*

\*

Scoundrels are always truculent and heroes always magnanimous.

*I. I. Dmitriev*

\*

Anger is a variety of faint-heartedness.

*Anton Chekhov*

\*

Invariably, evil walks on the crutches of virtue.

*M. M. Prishvin*

Jibes at the suffering of others must never be pardoned.

*Anton Chekhov*

## PETULANCE, UNSOCIABILITY, CONTENTIOUSNESS

Calmness is stronger than fury.

*Mikhail Svetlov*

\*

Unpleasant though anger may be to others, it is harder on the one who experiences it. What is begun in rage ends in shame.

*Lev Tolstoy*

\*

Under the influence of temper we accuse the person who aroused it in us of things that will seem funny to us when our temper abates.

*Konstantin Ushinsky*

\*

I have always tried to control my temper and yield in a quarrel, and thus achieved reconciliation, so that later, when the dust settled, matters arranged themselves by themselves. Almost invariably one comes to regret that the quarrel did not stop when it started.

*Lev Tolstoy*

※

Wrath is always improper, and most of all in a worthy cause, for it obfuscates and confuses matters.

*Nikolai Gogol*

※

A state of obtuse and uncontrollable anger is as disastrous as a state of obtuse kindness or tenderness.

***Konstantin Ushinsky***

## OF GOOD HEALTH

### THE GREATEST BOON

Man is the supreme product of Nature. But to enjoy the treasures of Nature, he must be healthy, strong, and clever.

*Ivan Pavlov*

\*

In a socialist country the health of the workers and peasants is the main concern of the state.

*Mikhail Kalinin*

\*

We want to develop man harmoniously, so that he should be adept in running and swimming, so that he should walk quickly and gracefully, and so that all his bodily organs should be in order. In short, we want him to be normal and healthy, ready to work and ready to defend his country, and his intellect to develop soundly alongside all his physical qualities.

*Mikhail Kalinin*

## GOOD HEALTH

Health, so lightly treated in youth, is a boon in riper years; life is usually appreciated more fully when you are past its quicker half.

*Nikolai Karamzin*

\*

Health never loses value in the eyes of people, because even in prosperity and luxury it is a sad life in bad health.

*Nikolai Chernyshevsky*

\*

Humans can live to a hundred. We are ourselves to blame for reducing this normal term to much less by our incontinence, lack of order, and our atrocious treatment of our own organism.

*Ivan Pavlov*

\*

A good man must take good care of himself.

*Maxim Gorky*

# PHYSICAL TRAINING

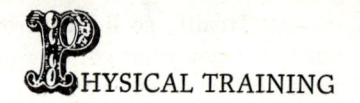

We materialists are people who are fond of life; we are people of health, and, therefore, recognise the gigantic importance of physical training.

*A. V. Lunacharsky*

\*

To keep fit and, more still, to prevent the usual illnesses, there is nothing better than body exercises or movements.

*Matvei Mudrov*

\*

I consider movement the most effective medicine against old age.

*Valentin Gorinevsky*

\*

Movement is life, and any decline of mobility is a clamp on vital processes.

*Valentin Gorinevsky*

## GOOD HEALTH

When you do your work sitting down, without movement and physical effort, you are in for trouble.

*Lev Tolstoy*

\*

Those who are physically fit have a better life.

*Mikhail Kalinin*

\*

Beauty of body is always suggestive of health and strength, and of abundant vital energy.

*Lev Tolstoy*

\*

You must on all accounts shake yourself up physically in order to be healthy in spirit.

*Lev Tolstoy*

\*

Sports generate a culture of optimism and good cheer.

*A. V. Lunacharsky*

\*

Practice has shown that gymnastics, which is a special manner in which free movements are arranged, heals many neglected ailments.

*Konstantin Ushinsky*

\*

Those who do physical exercises in moderation and at the right time have no need for medical treatment.

*Avicenna*

\*

If you do physical exercises, there will be no need for taking drugs prescribed for various diseases provided you also observe all the other rules of normal living.

*Avicenna*

\*

The key condition for improving your memory is a sound nervous system, for which you must do physical exercises.

*Konstantin Ushinsky*

\*

If people shirk physical exercises when they are thirty, forty, or even fifty, this is a prejudice that has come down from a past when indolence was considered the ideal of wellbeing.

*Valentin Gorinevsky*

He who gives up physical exercises often sees himself go to seed, because the strength of his body declines due to lack of movement.

*Avicenna*

Not indolence, but physical labour is the right kind of rest after mental work. It is not only pleasant, but also exceedingly healthy. Mental work must alternate with physical.

*Konstantin Ushinsky*

The best medicines are fresh air, cold water, and a timberer's axe or saw.

*Vassily Polenov*

After walking and swimming I feel younger and, more important still, I feel that my body movements have massaged and refreshed the brain.

*K. E. Tsiolkovsky*

Beauty is inconceivable without the concept of a harmoniously developed and healthy body.

*Nikolai Chernyshevsky*

Those who want to retain their mental faculties for as long as possible and to perform the fullest possible cycle of life must lead a very moderate existence and follow the rules of rational hygiene.

*Ilya Mechnikov*

\*

Nothing is more powerful in the human body than rhythm. Every function, especially vegetative, continuously tends to adopt the regimen imposed on it.

*Ivan Pavlov*

\*

Rhythm is the foundation of life given to each by his nature and his breathing.

*Konstantin Stanislavsky*

\*

The efforts of a sensible person should be directed not to mending and patching his body like a riddled and fragile shell, but to arranging his life so that the body would suffer the least disorder and would, consequently, need the least repairs.

*Dmitry Pisarev*

# THE BENEFITS OF MODERATION

Look after your mouth: it is the gateway for diseases. Make sure you are still hungry when you leave the table.

*Lev Tolstoy*

*

If people were to eat only when they are very hungry, and if they were to eat simple, pure, and healthy food, they would know no ailments and be more successful in controlling their heart and body.

*Lev Tolstoy*

*

Exclusive and excessive indulgence at the table is beastly, and haughty disregard of food, too, is ill-advised, while the truth here, as everywhere, is in the middle: do not overindulge, but accord due attention.

*Ivan Pavlov*

*

Those of us who are accustomed to less are less vulnerable to privation.

*Lev Tolstoy*

Down with oversatiation. Be chary of desire. This will stimulate love, creation, and long life.

*Alexander Bogomolets*

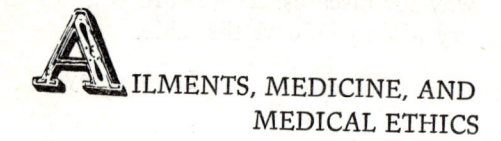

# AILMENTS, MEDICINE, AND MEDICAL ETHICS

Think of your ailments not at all or as little as possible.

*Anton Chekhov*

\*

Joy strengthens the body by making man more sensitive to the pulse of life.

*Ivan Pavlov*

\*

A patient's dejection is the most active ally of his ailment.

*Maxim Gorky*

\*

People like to talk about their ailments, though, in fact, ailments are the most uninteresting thing in their lives.

*Anton Chekhov*

## GOOD HEALTH

Some people are eternally ill, and this only because they are constantly concerned about their health, while others are healthy, and this only because they are not obsessed by any fear of falling ill.

*V. O. Kliuchevsky*

\*

If in childhood and youth you do not allow your nerves to dominate you, they will not learn to become irritated and will obey you.

*Konstantin Ushinsky*

\*

Excessive irritability, leading to contentiousness, tends to shorten life.

*Alexander Bogomolets*

\*

Will power heals more effectively than drugs.

*Maxim Gorky*

\*

*Can you hope of getting well if you keep what ails you from your healer?*

*Shot'ha Rust'hveli*

\*

A doctor's work is truly the most productive: by preventing illness or restoring health he gives society the forces that would perish without his care.

*Nikolai Chernyshevsky*

\*

The doctor's profession is an exploit requiring dedication, a pure heart, and goodwill.

*Anton Chekhov*

\*

All the wonders performed by doctors seem to centre in the power of the attention they show the patient. This is the power whereby poets endow Nature with spirit, and whereby doctors heal their patients.

*M. M. Prishvin*

\*

If a patient doesn't feel better after a talk with his doctor, the doctor isn't worth his salt.

*Vladimir Bekhterev*

\*

Knowing the reciprocal action of soul and body, it is my duty to observe that there are medicines for the soul that also heal the body.

*Matvei Mudrov*

## GOOD HEALTH

Everyone knows the magic effect of a comporting word from a doctor, and conversely, how deadly, sometimes ... a severe and frigid verdict can be for the patient if the doctor does not know, or does not wish to know, the power of suggestion.

*Vladimir Bekhterev*

\*

It is not right to treat an ailment solely by its name, for it is the patient that must be treated—the patient's body, its organs, and vital powers.

*Matvei Mudrov*

\*

The more mature a physician is, the better he appreciates the power of hygiene and the relative weakness of drug therapy.

*Grigory Zakharyin*

\*

The future belongs to preventive medicine. It is a science which, hand in hand with therapy, will, doubtlessly, yield great benefits to mankind.

*Nikolai Pirogov*

## OF YOUTH, OLD AGE, AND IMMORTALITY

# YOUTH

Every man and woman is given this tremendous and priceless gift—youth full of strength, of aspirations, yearnings, lust of knowledge, struggle, hope, and confidence.

*Nikolai Ostrovsky*

\*

Youth is a great magician.

*Alexander Pushkin*

\*

Youth with its noble enthusiasm, its vague yearnings for honesty and justice, and for the social truth is one of the greatest forces working for progress.

*N. V. Shelgunov*

## YOUTH, OLD AGE, AND IMMORTALITY

Human life would freeze to the spot if youth were not to dream; the seeds of many great ideas ripened invisibly in the hopeful atmosphere of youthful utopias.

*Konstantin Ushinsky*

✻

Youth is happy, because it has a future.

*Nikolai Gogol*

✻

Youth is springtime in the lives of people when the seeds of future years are planted.

*Y. B. Kniazhnin*

✻

O youth! O youth! Perhaps, the secret of your splendour is not in the possibility of accomplishing, but in the ability of thinking that you will accomplish.

*Ivan Turgenev*

✻

Youth is the time when noble sentiments are fresh.

*Nikolai Chernyshevsky*

Youth is the poetry of life, and everyone in his youth is better than at other periods of life.

*Vissarion Belinsky*

\*

The brave is more accessible and stronger, and opens up the soul, especially of youth, which still thirsts for nothing but the unusual.

*Nikolai Gogol*

\*

Youth is always selfless.

*Alexander Herzen*

\*

Youth is the most splendid and mobile section of humanity.

*Mikhail Kalinin*

\*

Youth is the main force, the root power of the humanity of tomorrow.

*A. V. Lunacharsky*

\*

The youth of a human being is a resplendent and beautiful spring, a time of action and brimming strength; it occurs once in everyone's life and never returns.

*Vissarion Belinsky*

## YOUTH, OLD AGE, AND IMMORTALITY

Take along with you as you emerge from the soft youthful years into severe and embittering adulthood all human movements; leave them not lying by the wayside for you will never pick them up later.

*Nikolai Gogol*

∗

A definite aim, self-control, honesty with oneself, and untiring labour conscious of time being precious—this is what you must undertake, young people.

*N. P. Ogarev*

∗

Treasure your youth: there is nothing better, nothing more valuable, in the whole world.

*Maxim Gorky*

∗

Life is much too interesting, and engaging occupations much too numerous. Youth must be shown such occupations that are of great value and that help man develop harmoniously.

*Mikhail Kalinin*

∗

Youth occurs only once in lifetime, and in one's youth everyone is more open to all the great and beautiful than at some other age. Blessed is he who retains his youth at an advanced age, not letting his soul grow cold, bitter, and hard.

*Vissarion Belinsky*

\*

Nothing on earth purifies, ennobles, and protects adolescence more than a strongly aroused public interest.

*Alexander Herzen*

\*

He who has in youth failed to establish enduring bonds with some great and splendid cause, or at least with some simple, but honest and useful work, may consider his youth tracelessly lost, no matter how merry it was and how many pleasant memories it has left.

***Dmitry Pisarev***

\*

An empty youth is a calamity.

***Abai Kunanbayev***

\*

Live with your wings spread. This applies not only to artists and poets, but to any young working man or woman.

***Sergei Konenkov***

# YOUTH, OLD AGE, AND IMMORTALITY

Nothing is worse than seeing the limitations of someone.

*Alexander Herzen*

\*

Youthful pessimism is nothing but a malaise of youth.

*Ilya Mechnikov*

\*

I would like every young worker to want to be a heroic fighter, because there is no greater happiness than being a faithful son of the working class and the Communist Party.

*Nikolai Ostrovsky*

\*

In study, labour, science, and dedicated work for the common weal you will find your happiness.

*N. D. Zelinsky*

\*

The purpose of life is in serving the Revolution; in our time there can be no other purpose.

*Maxim Gorky*

\*

Keep ahead of the age if you can, keep in step with it if you cannot, but never fall behind it.

*Valery Briusov*

Our youth must be the youth of Ilyich (of Vladimir Ilyich Lenin.–*Tr.*). It must be imbued not only by his contagious youthfulness, but also by sagacity, circumspection, and the skill to draw conclusions from culture accumulated over the ages.

*A. V. Lunacharsky*

\*

Communism is the youth of the world. It is up to the young to construct it.

*Vladimir Mayakovsky*

\*

It is the youth that will be faced with the actual task of creating a communist society.

*V. I. Lenin*

\*

You must enter life not like a carefree merry-maker entering a pleasure garden, but with awed reverence as you would a sacred forest full of life and mystery.

*Vikenty Veresayev*

\*

Learn to be tolerant of the human weaknesses of old people, and to overlook some of them.

*Vassily Sukhomlinsky*

## YOUTH, OLD AGE, AND IMMORTALITY

May old wisdom direct youthful cheer and strength, and may youthful cheer and strength support old wisdom.

*Konstantin Stanislavsky*

*

Old people have earned the right to teach and advise. Learn to respect this moral right.

*Vassily Sukhomlinsky*

*

The enterprise of youth and wisdom of ripe age–this is the source of the victories that shake the world.

*G. M. Krzhizhanovsky*

## OLD AGE

In old age your eyes shift from the front to the back of your head: you begin looking back and seeing nothing in front, and living by memories, not hopes.

*V. O. Kliuchevsky*

*

The thought of old age adds to your age.

*Effendi Kapiev*

## WORDS OF THE WISE

Old age is an ailment to be treated medically like any other ailment.

*Ilya Mechnikov*

\*

Yes, it is a great art to be a grand old man. It is, probably, true that humanity is never expressed as fully as it is in a wise old man whose heart is open to everything new, who acclaims the rising generation, and who gives it generously of his experience.

*A. V. Lunacharsky*

\*

Old age has its own beauty, radiating not passions, not flashes of desire, but calm and appeasement.

*Alexander Herzen*

\*

Work and creativity hold back senility and wilting.

*Sergei Konenkov*

\*

Old age deceptive is betimes:
It's like a moss-grown cask
That frothing wine contains.

*Mikhail Lermontov*

For a man old age is what dust is for clothes—it reveals all the spots and stains of his character.

*V. O. Kliuchevsky*

\*

Old age cannot be happy. The words "happy old age" come from ignorant people. Old age is either calm or grief. It is calm if respected and grief if neglected.

*Vassily Sukhomlinsky*

# IMMORTALITY

Life is a struggle for immortality.

*M. M. Prishvin*

\*

The wise come to understand at the end that death is frightening only to the onlookers, to the people close by, but that there is no death for oneself, and that for oneself every one is born immortal and departs immortal.

*M. M. Prishvin*

There is no fear of death in the parting with life, and if anything does resist it and tremble, it is just the body, the blood; reason and whatever else comprises man's consciousness remains a passive and unaffected witness.

*Effendi Kapiev*

\*

The better a person is, the less afraid he is of dying.

*Lev Tolstoy*

\*

To look death in the eye, to anticipate its coming, making no effort to deceive oneself and to be true to oneself until the last, not to weaken and not to take fright—this is given only to strong characters.

*Dmitry Pisarev*

\*

Fear of death is inversely proportional to the goodness of life.

*Lev Tolstoy*

\*

The deeper individualism penetrates the human soul, the deeper are the roots of the fear of dying.

*G. V. Plekhanov*

## YOUTH, OLD AGE, AND IMMORTALITY

It is madness for the living to think of death.

*Maxim Gorky*

\*

Death is a serious thing, and a part of life. We must die with dignity.

*A. V. Lunacharsky*

\*

Life is long and death is short. So, why fear it.

*Felix Dzerzhinsky*

\*

Life is eternity, and death a mere instant.

*Mikhail Lermontov*

\*

Isn't it more sensible to live praising life than to curse it and still live?

*Leonid Andreyev*

\*

The death wish is evidence of a false and spectral state of the spirit.

*Vissarion Belinsky*

To hate living one must be in a state of apathy and sloth.

*Lev Tolstoy*

\*

You must live so as not to fear death and not to wish it.

*Lev Tolstoy*

\*

Suicides, I think, take their lives less out of spite against someone and more out of pity for themselves and their impotent and failed lives. Pity for oneself is a terrible feeling.

*Effendi Kapiev*

\*

The purpose of life is to live so as not to die after death.

*Musah Jalil*

\*

An individual does not die if he is inspired by the common ideal and serves the common cause.

*D. N. Mamin-Sibiryak*

\*

*It is not given to man to live in eternity, But happy is he whose name is remembered.*

*Alisher Navoi*

## YOUTH, OLD AGE, AND IMMORTALITY

To have been in the world and to have left nothing that bespeaks one's existence—this seems to me frightening.

*Nikolai Gogol*

\*

It is not good to be ill, still worse to die, but to be ill and to die with the thought that you will leave nothing behind is the worst of all.

*Vissarion Belinsky*

\*

*I fear not death, oh, no;*
*I fear to disappear without a trace.*

*Mikhail Lermontov*

\*

*He who serves the age's bidding,*
*He who dedicates his life*
*To the weal of brother man,*
*Only he outlives his time.*

*Nikolai Nekrasov*

\*

In the totality of what we call mankind there are more of the dead than of the living.

*K. A. Timiryazev*

Human beings are mortal, the people is immortal.

*Maxim Gorky*

\*

People die that mankind should live.

*Vissarion Belinsky*

\*

Machines cannot make humans immortal. But the ethical ideal is not concerned with this. It must work out a general trend of life which, meeting the rules of honour and conscience, would also allow us to meet the inevitable end calmly, with dignity, without fear or reproach.

*N. K. Mikhailovsky*

\*

Approaching the end of your course, you sorrowfully ask yourself if you are fated to see the enticing horizons spreading out ahead. It is a consolation that you are followed by young and strong people, and that old age and youth blend in that endless and interminable search for the truth.

*Nikolai Zhukovsky*

\*

There are different dead. Some continue out of the depth of past millennia imperiously to determine the direction of our better present.

*M. M. Prishvin*

\*

In the literary world there is no death, for the dead interfere in our affairs and act together with us in the same way as the living.

*Nikolai Gogol*

\*

He who leaves behind at least one vivid and new idea, and at least one deed of benefit to mankind, does not die childless.

*A. A. Bestuzhev-Marlinsky*

\*

Immortality, incomplete to be sure, is undoubtedly expressed through one's descendants.

*Lev Tolstoy*

\*

The knowledge that you've fulfilled yourself may destroy your fear of death, and an honest life will assure you a gentle passing.

*Maxim Gorky*

# NAME INDEX

## A

ABAI, IBRAHIM, KUNANBAYEV (1845-1904)—Kazakh poet and educator, founder of the new written Kazakh literature.

ABOVYAN, KHACHATUR (1805-1848)—Armenian writer and educator, pioneer of the new Armenian literary language and modern Armenian literature.

AKHUNDOV, MIRZA-FATALI (1812-1878)—Azerbaijani writer, educator, thinker and public leader, pioneer of the Azerbaijani theatre and dramaturgy.

AKSAKOV, SERGEI TIMOFEYEVICH (1791-1859)—Russian realist writer, connoisseur and bard of Nature.

ANDREYEV, LEONID NIKOLAYEVICH (1871-1919)—Russian writer whose grotesque, contrasts, and subjective vision of the world are akin to impressionism.

ATTAR FARID-AD-DIN MOHAMMED BEN IBRAHIM (c. 1119-?)—Tajik mystical poet, drew extensively on Eastern folklore.

AUEZOV, MUKHTAR (1897-1961)—Soviet Kazakh writer.

AVICENNA—see *ibn-Sina*.

## B

BACH, ALEXEI NIKOLAYEVICH (1857-1946)—Soviet biochemist, a revolutionary.

BAGRATION, PYOTR IVANOVICH (1765-1812)—Russian general, hero of the 1812 Patriotic War against Napoleon.

## NAME INDEX

BAHIHANOV, ABBAS-KOULI, also known as Gudsi (1794-1847)—Azerbaijani writer, scholar, and educator.

BARBARUS, JOHANNES, nom de plume of Johannes Vares (1890-1946)—Soviet Estonian poet.

BARDIN, IVAN PAVLOVICH (1883-1960)—Soviet metallurgist, member of the Academy of Sciences of the USSR.

BATYUSHKOV, KONSTANTIN NIKOLAYEVICH (1787-1855)—Russian poet.

BEKHTEREV, VLADIMIR MIKHAILOVICH (1857-1927)—Soviet neuropathologist, psychiatrist, and physiologist.

BELINSKY, VISSARION GRIGOREVICH (1811-1848)—Russian literary critic, publicist, and revolutionary democrat, pioneer of Russian realistic aesthetics and literary criticism.

BESTUZHEV-MARLINSKY, ALEXANDER ALEXANDROVICH, nom de plume Marlinsky (1799-1837)—member of the nineteenth-century Decembrist plot against tsarist rule, author of critical reviews, stories, and revolutionary songs written jointly with Ryleyev *(q.v.)*, his closest friend.

BESTUZHEV, NIKOLAI ALEXANDROVICH (1791-1855)—member of the nineteenth-century Decembrist plot against tsarist rule, Russian poet, artist, and economist.

BESTUZHEV-RIUMIN, KONSTANTIN NIKOLAYEVICH (1829-1897)—Russian historian.

BLOK, ALEXANDER ALEXANDROVICH (1880-1921)—Russian poet and publicist.

BOGOMOLETS, ALEXANDER ALEXANDROVICH (1881-1946)—Soviet pathophysiologist, scholar, and public leader.

BREZHNEV, LEONID ILYICH (b. 1906)—prominent personality of the Communist Party of the Soviet Union, Soviet state, and the world communist and working-class movement; General Secretary of the CPSU Central Committee, Chairman of the Presidium of the Supreme

Soviet of the USSR, member of the Political Bureau of the CC CPSU.

BRIUSOV, VALERY YAKOVLEVICH (1873-1924)—Russian poet, prose writer, playwright, and translator.

BUNIN, IVAN ALEXEYEVICH (1870-1953)—Russian writer.

BURDENKO, NIKOLAI NILOVICH (1876-1946)—Soviet scientist, neurosurgeon, founding member of the USSR Academy of Medicine (1944).

BUTLEROV, ALEXANDER MIKHAILOVICH (1828-1886)—Russian scientist, chemist, authored the theory of the chemical structure of molecules.

## C

CHAADAYEV, PYOTR YAKOVLEVICH (1794-1856)—Russian idealist philosopher.

CHAIKOVSKY, PYOTR ILYICH (1840-1893)—Russian composer, a classic of Russian music.

CHEKHOV, ANTON PAVLOVICH (1860-1904)—Russian prose writer and playwright.

CHERNYSHEVSKY, NIKOLAI GAVRILOVICH (1828-1889)—Russian revolutionary democrat, literary critic, and writer, a leader of the Russian revolutionary democratic movement of the 1860s and 1870s.

CHISTYAKOV, PAVEL PETROVICH (1832-1919)—Russian artist, painter of historic scenes and portraits, educator.

## D

DAHL, VLADIMIR IVANOVICH (1801-1872)—Russian writer and philologist, compiler of an interpretative dictionary of contemporary Russian.

DANILEVSKY, VASSILY YAKOVLEVICH (1852-1939)—Soviet physiologist.

# NAME INDEX

DAVYDOV, DENIS VASSILEVICH (1784-1839)–Russian poet and military writer.

DEMYAN BEDNY, nom de plume of Yefim Alexeyevich Pridvorov (1883-1945)–Soviet Russian poet.

DERZHAVIN, GAVRILA ROMANOVICH (1743-1816)–Russian poet.

DMITRIEV, IVAN IVANOVICH (1760-1837)–Russian poet.

DOBROLYUBOV, NIKOLAI ALEXANDROVICH (1836-1861)–Russian revolutionary democrat, literary critic, philosopher.

DOKUCHAYEV, VASSILY VASSILEVICH (1846-1903)–Russian soil scientist.

DONSKOI, DMITRY IVANOVICH (1350-1389)–Prince of Vladimir and Moscow from 1359; the first to offer armed resistance to the Tatars.

DOODIN, MIKHAIL ALEXANDROVICH (b. 1916)–Soviet poet, also prose writer and translator.

DOSTOYEVSKY, FYODOR MIKHAILOVICH (1821-1881)–Russian realist writer.

DOVZHENKO, ALEXANDER PETROVICH (1894-1956)–Soviet Ukrainian film director and scriptwriter.

DRAGOMANOV, MIKHAIL PETROVICH (1841-1895)–Ukrainian historian, collector of folklore, literary critic and political figure.

DZERZHINSKY, FELIX EDMUNDOVICH (1877-1926)–prominent personality of the Communist Party of the Soviet Union and Soviet state, professional revolutionary.

# F

FADEYEV, ALEXANDER ALEXANDROVICH (1901-1956)–Soviet writer and public figure.

FEDIN, KONSTANTIN ALEXANDROVICH (1892-1977)–Soviet Russian writer.

FEDOTOV, PAVEL ANDREYEVICH (1815-1852)–Russian painter.

# NAME INDEX

FERSMAN, ALEXANDER YEVGENEVICH (1883-1945)—Russian mineralogist and geochemist.

FET, AFANASY AFANASSEVICH, nom de plume of Shenshin (1820-1892)—Russian poet.

FIRDOUSI, ABOUL KASIM (b. mid-10th century-d. 1026)—a classic of Tajik and Persian poetry.

FONVIZIN, DENIS IVANOVICH (1745-1792)—Russian satirist.

FORSH, OLGA DMITREVNA (1873-1961)—Soviet Russian authoress; contributed to the development of the Soviet historical novel.

FRUNZE, MIKHAIL VASSILEVICH (1885-1925)—conspicuous personality of the Communist Party and Soviet state, an organiser of the Soviet Armed Forces.

FURMANOV, DMITRY ANDREYEVICH (1891-1926)—Soviet Russian writer.

## G

GALAN, YAROSLAV ALEXANDROVICH (1902-1949)—Soviet Ukrainian poet.

GAMALEYA, NIKOLAI FYODOROVICH (1859-1949)—Soviet microbiologist, honorary member of the USSR Academy of Sciences.

GLADKOV, FYODOR VASSILEVICH (1883-1958)—Soviet Russian writer.

GLINKA, FYODOR NIKOLAYEVICH (1786-1880)—Russian poet and publicist.

GLINKA, MIKHAIL IVANOVICH (1804-1857)—Russian composer, first classic of Russian music.

GOGOL, NIKOLAI VASSILEVICH (1809-1852)—Russian writer and playwright.

GONCHAROV, IVAN ALEXANDROVICH (1812-1891)—Russian writer.

GORINEVSKY, VALENTIN VLADISLAVOVICH (1857-1937)—Soviet pediatrician, one of the first Russian specialists in physical education.

## NAME INDEX

GORKY, MAXIM, nom de plume of Alexei Maximovich Peshkov (1868-1936)–Soviet Russian writer, founder of Soviet literature and of the method of socialist realism.

GRANOVSKY, TIMOFEI NIKOLAYEVICH (1813-1855) –Russian historian.

GRIBOYEDOV, ALEXANDER SERGEYEVICH (1795-1829)–Russian writer and diplomat.

GURAMISHVILI, DAVID (1705-1792)–Georgian poet.

### H

HERZEN, ALEXANDER IVANOVICH (1812-1870)–Russian revolutionary, materialist philosopher, writer, publisher of the first free Russian political newspaper *Kolokol* (The Bell) (1857-1867).

### I

IBN-SINA ABU ALI (*Latin* Avicenna) (980-1037)–Tajik philosopher, scholar, and physician.

INOZEMTSEV, FYODOR IVANOVICH (1802-1869)–Russian physician, educator, and public leader.

IVANOV, ALEXANDER ANDREYEVICH ((1806-1858)–Russian painter.

### J

JALIL, MUSAH (1906-1944)–Soviet Tatar poet, Hero of the Soviet Union, laid down his life in the Second World War.

JOFFE, ABRAM FYODOROVICH (1880-1960)–Soviet physicist.

### K

KABALEVSKY, DMITRY BORISOVICH (b. 1904)–Soviet composer, educator; People's Artiste of the USSR.

## NAME INDEX

KACHALOV, VASSILY IVANOVICH (1875-1948)—Soviet Russian actor.

KALININ, MIKHAIL IVANOVICH (1875-1946)—prominent personality of the Communist Party of the Soviet Union and Soviet state, professional revolutionary, chairman of the USSR Supreme Soviet from 1938.

KAPIEV, EFFENDI MANSUROVICH (1909-1944)—Soviet Daghestan writer.

KARAMZIN, NIKOLAI MIKHAILOVICH (1766-1826)—Russian writer and historian.

KARONIN, nom de plume of Nikolai Elpidiforovich Petropavlovsky (1853-1892)—Russian writer.

KASSIRSKY, YOSIF ABRAMOVICH (1898-1971)—Soviet physician and haematologist.

KATAYEV, VALENTIN PETROVICH (b. 1897)—Soviet writer.

KAZBEGI, ALEXANDER (1848-1893)—Georgian writer.

KELDYSH, MSTISLAV VSEVOLODOVICH (1911-1978)—Soviet scientist in mathematics and mechanics; member of the USSR Academy of Sciences.

KHOSROW, NASIR (1003-1088)—Tajik and Persian poet and philosopher.

KHRENNIKOV, TIKHON NIKOLAYEVICH (b. 1913)—Soviet Russian composer, Chairman of the Union of Composers of the USSR.

KIROV, SERGEI MIRONOVICH, real name Kostrikov (1886-1934)—prominent personality of the Communist Party of the Soviet Union and Soviet state, follower of V. I. Lenin.

KLIUCHEVSKY, VASSILY OSIPOVICH (1841-1911)—Russian historian.

KNIAZHNIN, YAKOV BORISOVICH (1742/40?-1791)—Russian playwright, poet, and translator.

KOLAS, YAKUB, nom de plume of Konstantin Mikhailovich Mitskevich (1882-1956)—Byelorussian poet.

KONENKOV, SERGEI TIMOFEYEVICH (1874-1971)—Soviet Russian sculptor.

KONI, ANATOLY FYODOROVICH (1844-1927)—Russian lawyer, public leader, and writer.

## NAME INDEX

KOROLENKO, VLADIMIR GALAKTIONOVICH (1853-1921)—Russian democrat writer.

KORSAKOV, SERGEI SERGEYEVICH (1854-1900)—Russian psychiatrist and public leader.

KOSTYCHEV, SERGEI PAVLOVICH (1877-1931)—Russian biochemist, plant physiologist, and microbiologist.

KOVALEVSKY, PAVEL IVANOVICH (1849-1923)—Russian psychiatrist.

KRAMSKOI, IVAN NIKOLAYEVICH (1837-1887)—Russian artist.

KRAVCHINSKY, SERGEI MIKHAILOVICH, nom de plume S. Stepniak (1851-1895)—Russian writer and revolutionary populist.

KRUPSKAYA, NADEZHDA KONSTANTINOVNA (1869-1939)—Soviet stateswoman and Party leader, eminent educator; wife and companion of V. I. Lenin.

KRYLOV, IVAN ANDREYEVICH (1769-1844)—Russian writer, fabler, pioneer of realistic fables in Russian literature.

KRZHYZHANOVSKY, GLEB MAXIMILIANOVICH (1872-1959)—revolutionary, scientist in power engineering, member of the USSR Academy of Sciences.

KUPRIN, ALEXANDER IVANOVICH (1870-1938)—Russian writer.

KUTORGA, MIKHAIL SEMYONOVICH (1809-1886)—Russian historian, student of the history of Ancient Greece.

KUTUZOV, MIKHAIL ILLARIONOVICH, real name Golenishchev-Kutuzov (1745-1813)—Russian general who defeated Napoleon's army in Russia in 1812.

## L

LAVROV, PYOTR LAVROVICH (1823-1900)—Russian public leader, philosopher, essayist, and literary critic.

LAZHECHNIKOV, IVAN IVANOVICH (1792-1869)—Russian writer.

LENIN, VLADIMIR ILYICH (1870-1924)—founder of

## NAME INDEX

the world's first socialist state; revolutionary and thinker.

LEONOV, LEONID MAXIMOVICH (b. 1899)–Soviet Russian writer who eminently contributed to the development of Soviet literature.

LERMONTOV, MIKHAIL YUREVICH (1814-1841)–Russian poet, prose writer, and playwright.

LESGAFT, PYOTR FRANZEVICH (1837-1909)–Russian physician and educator.

LESKOV, NIKOLAI SEMYONOVICH (1831-1895)–Russian writer.

LEVINSON-LESSING, FRANZ YULEVICH (1861-1939)–Soviet geologist and public figure.

LEVITAN, ISAAK ILYICH (1860-1900)–Russian artist, landscape painter.

LOBACHEVSKI, NIKOLAI IVANOVICH (1792-1856)–Russian mathematician.

LOMONOSOV, MIKHAIL VASSILEVICH (1711-1765)–Russian encyclopaedist, poet, and literary theorist; pioneer of materialist philosophy and natural science in Russia; founder of Moscow University (1755).

LUNACHARSKY, ANATOLY VASSILEVICH (1875-1933)–Soviet Russian political leader, literary and art critic, essayist, playwright, and translator.

## M

MAHTUMKULI (known as Fragi) (c. 1730-d. 1780s)–Turkmen poet and thinker.

MAKARENKO, ANTON SEMYONOVICH (1888-1939)–Soviet writer and educator.

MAMIN-SIBIRYAK, DMITRY NARKISOVICH, real surname Mamin (1852-1912)–Russian writer.

MARSHAK, SAMUIL YAKOVLEVICH (1887-1964)–Soviet poet and translator.

MARTSINOVSKY, YEVGENY IVANOVICH (1874-1934)–Soviet epidemiologist.

MAYAKOVSKY, VLADIMIR VLADIMIROVICH (1893-1930)–Soviet poet.

# NAME INDEX

MECHNIKOV, ILYA ILYICH (1845-1916)–Russian biologist, Nobel Prize laureate (1908); one of the fathers of microbiology.

MENDELEYEV, DMITRY IVANOVICH (1834-1907)–Russian chemist, developed periodic system of classification of chemical elements.

MICHURIN, IVAN VLADIMIROVICH (1855-1935)–Soviet Russian scientist, follower of Darwin, student of plant life and selectionist.

MIKHAILOVSKY, NIKOLAI KONSTANTINOVICH (1842-1904)–Russian sociologist and writer.

MIKLUKHO-MAKLAI, NIKOLAI NIKOLAYEVICH (1846-1888)–Russian traveller, anthropologist, and ethnographer; explorer of New Guinea.

MINAYEV, DMITRY DMITREVICH (1835-1889)–Russian poet.

MIRZA SHAFI (1796-1852)–Azerbaijani poet known by the nom de plume of *Vazekh*, compiler of the first anthology of Azerbaijani poetry.

MOROZOV, NIKOLAI ALEXANDROVICH (1854-1946)–Russian revolutionary, public figure, scholar, and writer.

MUDROV, MATVEI YAKOVLEVICH (1776-1831)–Russian physician, a pioneer of the Russian clinical school.

MUKHINA, VERA IGNATEVNA (1889-1953)–Soviet Russian sculptor.

MUSSORGSKY, MODEST PETROVICH (1839-1881)–Russian composer.

## N

NAKHIMOV, PAVEL STEPANOVICH (1802-1855)–Russian admiral.

NAVOI, NIZADDIN ALISHER (1441-1501)–Uzbek poet and thinker.

NEKRASOV, NIKOLAI ALEXEYEVICH (1821-1878)–Russian poet and revolutionary democrat.

# NAME INDEX

NEMIROVICH-DANCHENKO, VLADIMIR IVANOVICH (1858-1943)—eminent personality of the Soviet Russian theatre; stage director and playwright; friend and associate of Konstantin Stanislavsky (*q.v.*), with whom he jointly founded the Moscow Art Theatre.

NESTOR-LETOPISETS (11th-12th centuries)—ancient Russian writer and chronicler.

NIKITIN, IVAN SAVVICH (1824-1861)—Russian poet.

NIZAMI, full name Abee Muhammad Ilyas ibn Yusuf Sheikh Nizam eddin (c. 1141-1203)—Azerbaijani poet and thinker, eminent twelfth-century Middle East philosopher.

NOVIKOV, NIKOLAI IVANOVICH (1744-1818)—Russian educator, writer of satire, and book publisher.

## O

OBRUCHEV, VLADIMIR AFANASSEVICH (1863-1956)—Russian scientist, geologist, geographer, writer, member of the USSR Academy of Sciences.

ODOYEVSKY, VLADIMIR FYODOROVICH (1803-1869)—Russian writer, philosopher, educator, and music critic.

OGAREV, NIKOLAI PLATONOVICH (1813-1877)—Russian poet and publicist, revolutionary democrat, friend and associate of Alexander Herzen (*q.v.*).

ORBELIANI, SULKHAN SABA (1658-1725)—Georgian writer and political leader.

OSTROGRADSKY, MIKHAIL VASSILEVICH (1801-1862)—Russian mathematician, a pioneer of the St. Petersburg mathematical school, member of the Russian Academy of Sciences.

OSTROVSKY, NIKOLAI ALEXEYEVICH (1904-1936)—Soviet Russian writer.

## P

PARIN, VASSILY VASSILEVICH (1903-1971)—Soviet Russian physiologist.

# NAME INDEX

PAUSTOVSKY, KONSTANTIN GEORGEVICH (1892-1968)—Soviet Russian writer.

PAVLENKO, PYOTR ANDREYEVICH (1899-1951)—Soviet writer.

PAVLOV, IVAN PETROVICH (1849-1936)—Russian scientist, physiologist, surgeon, author of the doctrine on higher nervous activity; Nobel Prize laureate (1904).

PETER I, THE GREAT (1672-1725)—Russian tsar, instituted progressive reforms.

PIROGOV, NIKOLAI IVANOVICH (1810-1881)—Russian surgeon, anatomist, researcher.

PISAREV, DMITRY IVANOVICH (1840-1868)—Russian revolutionary democrat, philosopher, and publicist.

PISEMSKY, ALEXEI FEOFILAKTOVICH (1821-1881)—Russian novelist.

PLEKHANOV, GEORGI VALENTINOVICH (1856-1918)—prominent figure in the socialist movement, revolutionary populist.

POGODIN, MIKHAIL PETROVICH (1800-1875)—Russian historian, writer, and journalist; studied ancient Russian and Slav history.

POLENOV, VASSILY DMITREVICH (1844-1927)—Russian artist, landscapist.

POLEZHAYEV, ALEXANDER IVANOVICH (1804-1838)—Russian poet.

POSOSHKOV, IVAN TIKHONOVICH (1652-1726)—Russian economist and publicist; welcomed the reforms of Peter I (*q.v.*).

PRISHVIN, MIKHAIL MIKHAILOVICH (1873-1954)—Soviet writer.

PROKOFIEV, SERGEI SERGEYEVICH (1891-1953)—Soviet Russian composer, pianist, and conductor.

PRYANISHNIKOV, DMITRY NIKOLAYEVICH (1865-1948)—Soviet scientist, agrochemist, and plant physiologist.

PSHAVELA, VAZHA, nom de plume of Luka Razikashvili (1861-1915)—Georgian poet.

PUSHKIN, ALEXANDER SERGEYEVICH (1799-1837)—Russian poet, founder of Russian classical literature.

## NAME INDEX

### R

RADISHCHEV, ALEXANDER NIKOLAYEVICH (1749-1802)—Russian writer, educator, and philosopher; pioneer of Russian revolutionary literature.

RAINIS, JANIS, nom de plume of Janis Plieksans (1865-1929)—Soviet Latvian poet, playwright, and public figure.

RAKHMANINOV, SERGEI VASSILEVICH (1873-1943)—Russian composer, pianist, and conductor.

REPIN ILYA YEFIMOVICH (1844-1930)—Russian painter, exponent of critical realism in Russian art.

RUBAKIN, NIKOLAI ALEXANDROVICH (1862-1946)—Russian bibliographer and writer; collected two large libraries (c. 200,000 volumes) and gifted them to the people.

RUBINSTEIN, ANTON GRIGOREVICH (1829-1894)—Russian pianist and composer; founded first Russian Conservatoire in St. Petersburg (1862).

RUBINSTEIN, NIKOLAI GRIGOREVICH (1835-1881)—Russian pianist and conductor; founded Moscow Conservatoire (1866).

RUDAKI (b. mid-9th century-d. 941)—Tajik poet.

RUST'HVELI, SHOT'HA (12th century)—Georgian poet, author of *The Knight in the Tiger's Skin*.

RYLEYEV, KONDRATY FYODOROVICH (1795-1826)—Russian poet directly involved in the uprising of 14 December, 1825 (Decembrist uprising).

RYTKHEU, YURI SERGEYEVICH (b. 1930)—Soviet Chukchi writer.

### S

SALTYKOV-SHCHEDRIN, MIKHAIL EVGRAFOVICH (1826-1889)—Russian writer of satire, critical realist.

SCHMIDT, OTTO YULEVICH (1891-1956)—Soviet mathematician, astronomer, and geophysicist; member of the USSR Academy of Sciences; Hero of the Soviet Union; Arctic explorer.

# NAME INDEX

SCRIABIN, ALEXANDER NIKOLAYEVICH (1871-1915) —Russian composer and pianist; he influenced twentieth-century piano and symphony music.

SECHENOV, IVAN MIKHAILOVICH (1829-1905)— Russian scientist, thinker, pioneer of the Russian school of physiology.

SEMASHKO, NIKOLAI ALEXANDROVICH (1874-1949) organiser of the Soviet public health system; member of the USSR Academy of Sciences.

SERGEYEV-TSENSKY, SERGEI NIKOLAYEVICH nom de plume of Sergeyev (1875-1958)—Soviet Russian writer.

SEROV, ALEXANDER NIKOLAYEVICH (1820-1871)— Russian composer.

SHELGUNOV, NIKOLAI VASSILEVICH (1824-1891)— Russian publicist and public figure, revolutionary democrat, an associate of Chernyshevsky *(q.v.)*.

SHEVCHENKO, TARAS GRIGOREVICH (1814-1861)— Ukrainian poet, revolutionary, and thinker; he was a pioneer of the revolutionary-democratic trend in Ukrainian social thinking.

SHOLOKHOV, MIKHAIL ALEXANDROVICH (b. 1905) —Soviet Russian writer, member of the USSR Academy of Sciences; Nobel Prize laureate (1965).

SHOSTAKOVICH, DMITRY DMITREVICH (1906-1975) —Soviet composer.

SIKORSKY, IVAN ALEXEYEVICH (1845-1918)—Russian psychiatrist.

SKABICHEVSKY, ALEXANDER MIKHAILOVICH (1838-1910)—Russian literary critic and historian.

SKOVORODA, GRIGORY SAVVICH (1722-1794)— Ukrainian philosopher, educator, and humanist.

SKRYABIN, KONSTANTIN IVANOVICH (1878-1972)— Soviet helminthologist, member of the USSR Academy of Sciences.

SKVORTSOV-STEPANOV, IVAN IVANOVICH (1870-1928)—Soviet Communist Party functionary, statesman, historian, and economist.

## NAME INDEX

STALSKY, SULEIMAN, nom de plume of Suleiman Khassanbekov (1869-1937)—Soviet Daghestan poet.

STANISLAVSKY, KONSTANTIN SERGEYEVICH, real name Alexeyev (1863-1938)—Soviet Russian stage director, actor, art theorist, and educator; founder and head of the Moscow Art Threatre (jointly with *Nemirovich-Danchenko, q.v.*).

STASOV, VLADIMIR VASSILEVICH (1824-1906) Russian art theorist and historian, art and music critic.

STEPNIAK-KRAVCHINSKY, *see* Kravchinsky.

STOLETOV, ALEXANDER GRIGOREVICH (1839-1896)—Russian scientist, pioneer of the Russian school of physics, researcher in magnetism, and one of the fathers of modern electrotechnics.

STRUMILIN, STANISLAV GUSTAVOVICH, real name Strumillo-Petrashkevich (1877-1974)—Soviet economist and statistician, member of the USSR Academy of Sciences.

SUDRABKALNS, JANIS, nom de plume of Arvids Sudrabkalns (1894-1975)—Soviet Latvian poet and essayist.

SUKACHEV, VLADIMIR NIKOLAYEVICH (1880-1967)—Soviet botanist, sylviculturist and geographer; member of the USSR Academy of Sciences.

SUKHOMLINSKY, VASSILY ALEXANDROVICH (1918-1970)—Soviet educator.

SUMAROKOV, ALEXANDER PETROVICH (1717/8?-1777)—Russian writer, an exponent of the literary school of aristocratic classicism.

SUVOROV, ALEXANDER VASSILEVICH (1729-1800)—Russian general, founder of a school of warfare, Generalissimo of the Russian Army.

SVETLOV, MIKHAIL ARKADEVICH (1903-1964)—Soviet Russian poet and playwright.

### T

TANEYEV, SERGEI IVANOVICH (1856-1915)—Russian composer and educator.

# NAME INDEX

TANK, MAXIM, nom de plume of Evgeny Ivanovich Skurko (b. 1912)—Soviet Byelorussian poet.

TIKHONOV, NIKOLAI SEMYONOVICH (1896-1979)—Soviet writer and prominent public figure.

TIMIRYAZEV, KLIMENT ARKADEVICH (1843-1920)—Russian scientist, plant physiologist.

TOLSTOY, ALEXEI KONSTANTINOVICH (1817-1875)—Russian poet.

TOLSTOY, ALEXEI NIKOLAYEVICH (1883-1945)—Soviet Russian writer.

TOLSTOY, LEV NIKOLAYEVICH (1828-1910)—Russian writer, author of many masterpieces.

TOUMANIAN, HOVANNES (1869-1923)—Armenian poet and public leader.

TSIOLKOVSKY, KONSTANTIN EDUARDOVICH (1857-1935)—Soviet Russian scientist in rocketry and interplanetary travel; predicted and scientifically substantiated space travel.

TURGENEV, IVAN SERGEYEVICH (1818-1883)—Russian writer.

TVARDOVSKY, ALEXANDER TRIFONOVICH (1910-1971)—Soviet poet and public figure.

TYNIANOV, YURI NIKOLAYEVICH (1894-1943)—Soviet Russian writer.

## U

UMOV, NIKOLAI ALEXEYEVICH (1846-1915)—Russian physicist, wrote prolifically on electrodynamics, terrestrial magnetism, and optics.

UPITS, ANDREJS (1877-1977)—Soviet Latvian writer and public figure.

USHAKOV, SIMON (PIMEN) FYODOROVICH (1626-1686)—Russian artist and art theorist; an eminent exponent of the realistic trend in Russian painting of the latter half of the seventeenth century.

USHINSKY, KONSTANTIN DMITREVICH (1824-1871)—Russian educator, founder of the Russian school of pedagogics and public education; author of school primers.

USPENSKY, GLEB IVANOVICH (1843-1902)—Russian writer and revolutionary democrat.

## V

VAKHTANGOV, YEVGENY BAGRATIONOVICH (1883-1922)—Russian actor, stage director and producer, founder of a Moscow theatre (now Vakhtangov Theatre).

VALUYEV, PYOTR ALEXANDROVICH (1815-1890)—Russian statesman, author of several novels.

VAVILOV, SERGEI IVANOVICH (1891-1951)—Soviet scholar and physicist.

VENETSIANOV, ALEXEI GAVRILOVICH (1780-1847)—Russian artist of the realist school.

VENEVITINOV, DMITRY VLADIMIROVICH (1805-1827)—Russian poet and literary critic.

VERESAYEV, VIKENTY VIKENTEVICH, real surname Smidovich (1867-1945)—Soviet Russian writer.

VERESHCHAGIN, VASSILY VASSILEVICH (1842-1904)—Russian artist, painter of battle scenes.

VERNADSKY, VLADIMIR IVANOVICH (1863-1945)—Soviet natural scientist, eminent thinker, founder of several scientific institutions, member of the USSR Academy of Sciences.

VOROVSKY, VACLAV VACLAVOVICH (1871-1923)—Russian revolutionary, literary critic, and Soviet diplomat.

VYAZEMSKY, PYOTR ANDREYEVICH (1792-1878)—Russian poet and literary critic.

## W

WELTMAN, ALEXANDER FOMICH (1800-1870)—Russian writer.

WILLIAMS, VASSILY ROBERTOVICH (1863-1939)—Soviet soil scientist.

# NAME INDEX

## Y

YAROSLAVSKY, EMELYAN MIKHAILOVICH (1878-1943)—prominent functionary of the Communist Party of the Soviet Union, historian, and essayist; member of the USSR Academy of Sciences.

YUDIN, SERGEI SERGEYEVICH (1891-1954)—Soviet Russian scientist, surgeon.

## Z

ZAKHARYIN, GRIGORY ANTONOVICH (1829-1898)—Russian physician, exponent of the functional school in medicine.

ZANDER, FRIDRIKH ARTUROVICH (1887-1933)—Soviet scientist, helped develop Soviet space navigation; he was a founding member of the society for the study of interplanetary communications.

ZARDABI, HASSAN-BEK (1837-1907)—Azerbaijani public leader.

ZELINSKY, KORNELII LUZIANOVICH (1896-1970)—Soviet literary critic and linguist.

ZELINSKY, NIKOLAI DMITREVICH (1861-1953)—Soviet scientist, chemist.

ZHUKOVSKY, NIKOLAI YEGOROVICH (1847-1921)—Soviet Russian scientist in aerodynamics, founder of the Airforce Academy in Moscow.

ZHUKOVSKY, VASSILY ANDREYEVICH (1783-1852)—Russian poet.

REQUEST TO READERS

Progress Publishers would be glad to have your opinion of this book, its translation and design and any suggestions you may have for future publications.

Please send all your comments to 17, Zubovsky Boulevard, Moscow, USSR.

A Book of Russian Quotations